Off The Beaten Track
SCOTLAND

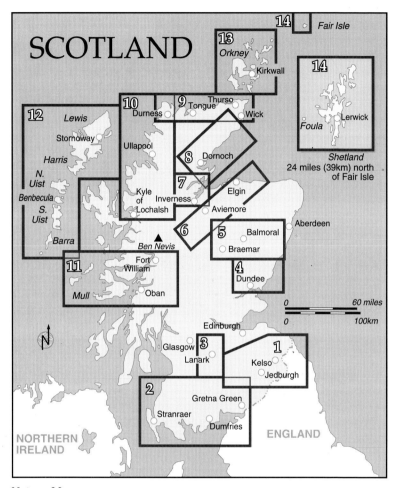

Note on Maps

The maps for each chapter, while comprehensive, are not designed to be used as route maps, but to locate the main towns, villages and places of interest.

Places of Interest

The further Information section at the end of each chapter lists opening times of places of interest. It should be noted that where opening periods are given in months, such as April to October, this rarely means from 1 April to 31 October. More likely the opening date will be on a particular weekend in the middle of the month and likewise the closing date. This date probably changes from year to year. It is therefore particularly worth re-checking opening dates and times if you intend to visit in the first or last month shown. Checking any opening day and time is recommended in any case, especially if a special journey is involved.

While every care has been taken to ensure that the information in this book is as accurate as possible at the time of publication, the publisher and authors accept no responsibility for any loss, injury or inconvenience sustained by anyone using this book.

Off The Beaten Track

SCOTLAND

Patrick Thorne

MOORLAND PUBLISHING

Published by:
Moorland Publishing Co Ltd,
Moor Farm Road West, Ashbourne,
Derbyshire, DE6 1HD England

ISBN 0 86190 502 4 (UK)

The Globe Pequot Press,
6 Business Park Road,
PO Box 833, Old Saybrook,
Connecticut 06475-0833

ISBN 1-56440-478-7 (USA)

© Moorland Publishing Co Ltd 1994

Black and white illustrations have been
supplied as follows:

Dundee Tourist Board; Clyde Valley
Tourist Board; Dumfries and Galloway
Tourist Board; © Landmark Centre;
Michael Emery; © National Trust For
Scotland; Stephen Hopkins; Mull and
West Highland Narrow Gauge Railway
Company Limited; Ron Scholes;
Sutherland Tourist Board; Patrick
Thorne; © Western Isles Tourist Board

Colour illustrations have been supplied
as follows:

Dumfries and Galloway Tourist Board;
© Historic Scotland; Stephen Hopkins;
Ron Scholes; © Sutherland Tourist
Board; Patrick Thorne; © Glamis Castle;
© Paul Buchanan, Dundee Tourist
Board

Origination by:
Forest Graphics (Nottm) Ltd

Printed by:
Wing King Tong Co Ltd, Hong Kong

MPC Production Team:
Editorial: Tonya Monk
Design: Ashley Emery
Cartography: Alastair Morrison
Typesetting & Editorial
Assistant: Christine Haines

British Library Cataloguing in Publication Data:
A catalogue record for this book is available from the British Library.

Library of Congress Cataloging-in-Publication Data
Thorne, Patrick, 1964-
    Scotland/Patrick Thorne.
    'Off The Beaten Track'   p.   cm.
    Includes index.
    ISBN 1-56440-478-1
    1. Scotland—Guidebooks.   I. Title.
DA870. T48   1994
914.1104'859 — dc20

94-29280
CIP

Contents

Acknowledgements

The author would like to thank his mother Catherine for helping with reading, editing and maps prior to delivery to the publisher and his wife Sally for assisting with research and ideas. Thanks to Carolyn Whitaker at London Independent Books and Tonya Monk at Moorland Publishing for constructive comments and practical support.

More than fifty local Tourist Offices helped by supplying up to date information on attractions and their opening times. Additional assistance was provided by Angus MacMillan at Bord Turasachd Nan Eilean, Rachel Gosling and Douglas Ritchie at Dumfries & Galloway Tourist Board, Toni McPherson at Dundee Tourist Board, Anne Burgess at Moray Tourist Board, Josh Gourlay and Elaine Simpson at Orkney Tourist Board, David Richards and Helen Squire at Sutherland Tourist Board, Dee Edwards at the West Highlands & Islands of Argyll Tourist Board, Nicola McShane at Clyde Valley Tourist Board, Judy Aitken and Isla Robertson at the National Trust for Scotland, Joseph White at Historic Scotland, Grant Stenhouse of The Sea Life Centres, Graham Ellis of Mull And West Highland Narrow Gauge Railway Company Limited, Lt. Col. P. J. Cardwell Moore and Joanna Campbell at the Scottish Tourist Board. Thanks also to all those who supplied material which was due to lack of space. Each section of the text was read over prior to delivery to the publisher by people who lived locally and to whom grateful thanks. These include Roger Baker, Joan & Bill Weir, Roz & Brian Bell, Edward and Leah Ley-Wilson and Cecil Smith. Travel assistance for research trips was organised by Walter Bowie at Caledonain MacBrayne Ferries, Jim Davies at the Orkney Islands Shipping Company, Iain Robertson, Dave Edmonston and Pat Campbell at Loganair and Cecil Smith at Star Rent-A-Car. Computer software and hotline support was supplied by Mark Ashton Associates.

Dedication
For Sam

Introduction

Western Europe is a continent of great diversity, well visited by travellers from other parts of the globe and inhabitants of its own member countries. Throughout the year and particularly during the holiday season, there is a great interchange of nationalities as one country's familiar attractions are left behind for those of another.

The sharing of cultures brings us closer in all senses to our neighbours. Yet essential differences do exist, differences which lure us abroad on our annual migrations in search of fresh sights and the discovery of unknown landscapes and people.

Countless resorts have evolved for those who simply crave sun, sea and the reassuring press of humanity. There are, too, established tourist 'sights' with which a country or region has become associated and which the manifestations of mass tourism exploit . This is by no means typical of all well known tourist attractions, but is familiar enough to act as a disincentive for those of more independent spirit who value personal discovery above prescribed experience.

It is for such travellers that this guidebook has been written. In its pages, no more than passing mention is made of the famous and the well documented. Instead, the reader is taken if not to unknown then to relatively unvisited places — literally 'off the beaten track'.

Through the specialist knowledge of the authors, visitors using this guidebook are assured of gaining insights into the country's heartland whose heritage lies untouched by the tourist industry.

From wild, scantily populated countryside whose footpaths and byways are best navigated by careful map reading, to negotiating the side streets of towns and cities, travelling 'off the beaten track' can be rather more demanding than following in the footsteps of countless thousands before you. The way may be less clear, more adventurous and individualistic, but opportunities do emerge for real discovery. With greater emphasis on exploring 'off the beaten track', the essence of Scotland is more likely to be unearthed and its true flavours relished to the full.

Scotland is a wonderful country. Those that have lived all their lives in England and never visited before will be amazed that such a beautiful and spectacular place is part of the same bit of rock as the over populated, highly congested areas they know so well. The introduction gives a quick potted overview of the geography of the land, its history, current culture and environment. Visitors may completely misunderstand the importance of where they are staying or what they are viewing if they do not have some awareness of Scotland's complex and colourful history. There is also an introduction to the different ways of travel available and an advisory note on the weather and the effect this may have on your photographic efforts.

The guide book looks in more detail than most at fourteen areas of Scotland Isles including Orkney Isles and Shetland. Together these count for just over half the total area of the country. In terms of being 'Off The Beaten Track' much of the rest of the country could be considered for inclusion but unfortunately there is only a finite amount of space.

Geography and Environment

Scotland is about two thirds the size of England and the Scottish mainland is nearly as long from north to south as is England. It is a bigger country than many people realise and, having only about a tenth of the population, this clearly means much more open space. There are three main areas, often divided economically and politically as well as geographically. They are the Southern Uplands, the Highlands and, between the two, the industrialised, most heavily populated and fertile Central Belt which contains the two largest cities of Glasgow and Edinburgh.

Geographic characteristics of Scotland today include the fact that most towns and cities still tend to have clearly defined boundaries and will have a definite end. This contrasts with the increasing tendency in the over crowded areas of England for towns and cities to trail in to one another in an endless semi-urban sprawl of housing estates and retail parks. Clear definition of boundaries is often caused by natural restrictions such as mountains, cliffs and rivers. A large proportion of Scottish settlements grew up as a result of fishing or trade routes and many were created between 1700 and 1900 to a plan, for agricultural, herring fishing or forestry reasons or because original settlements in more fertile areas had been brutally 'cleared' by landlords to make way for sheep.

Stac Polly as seen from the shores of Lock Lurgainn

Geologically the rocks below Scottish soil tend to get older the further north you travel. The Isle of Lewis is made up of some of the world's oldest gneiss rock and the Caledonian mountains, once on a par with the Andes for height, are also very ancient. Due partly to Scotland's northerly position, its many upland areas, its often acid soil and its cool climate, over three quarters of its area is still classified as unproductive agriculturally.

Scotland was originally covered by the ancient Caledonian forest, odd pockets of which remain as protected woodland today. Islands, largely treeless now, were also once covered by woodland. The Forestry Commission has used Scotland as a major plantation area for its forests. Until recently their methods of planting trees so close together that not even grass could grow through the carpet of needles, and in regimented rows forming huge rectangular woods on barren hillsides, resulted in a lot of displeasure in the ugly unnatural appearance they gave to areas of outstanding beauty. The policy has now been largely discontinued but many ridiculous looking tracts of forest will remain well in to the twenty-first century.

There are also large areas of peat land, in the north in particular still widely used for fuel. Sheep roam freely around much of the country, as do deer, and both are a common sight by the road side. Fish farms can be seen in many lochs, and oil rigs are visible off shore from the north-east coast.

One of the rocky islets on the east coast of Scotland, Bass Rock on the Firth of Forth

History

The first inhabitants of Scotland probably arrived about 6,000 years ago after the last Ice Age had been over for several millennia and vegetation in the north became adequate for humans. By 2500BC, much of the forest that had grown up was gone and by 700BC Iron Age man had begun to build round houses and brochs. It is believed that the Picts arrived about 600 years BC and that they spoke a Celtic language more akin to Welsh than Gaelic. Their presence was recorded by the Romans who first travelled around Scotland in the first centuries AD. Their battles with the Picts have been recorded in Roman archives, although the battle sites are not known.

The arrival of the 'Scots' or rather a tribe called the 'Scotti' in Scotland began around the second century AD. These were people from Ireland and it is not known whether they needed force to invade or whether there was space for all at that time. Some of the better recorded landings of Christian monks from across the Irish Sea took place around the sixth and seventh centuries AD. At the same time a tribe of Angles was moving up from England to inhabit Lothian and the Central Belt; all too much for the Romans, whose empire was collapsing back home and who had evacuated for good, in the fifth century.

This was all a century or so before the Vikings started to reach Scotland, particularly the north-eastern coast and islands, from

Scandinavia. They brought war and fresh pagan influence, but often settled, became part of the community and converted to Christianity. Many of their names still exist and the Northern Isles still tend to look more towards Scandinavia in the east than Scotland to the south. Orkney and Shetland only became part of Scotland and the United Kingdom when a Danish king could not pay cash for his daughter's dowry in 1471: they have been in hock ever since. Viking influence only waned after defeat by the Scots in the Battle of Largs of 1263.

The period of occupation by Angles, Scotti, Vikings and Picts are the Dark Age of Scottish history. It is known that the first Christian settlements began at Whithorn before the Romans finally left, and that the Vikings defeated the Picts early in the ninth century, but other than that, details are sketchy. It was the Christian influence that would finally unite the different factions, at least in part, later in history.

Following defeat of the Picts the Kingdom of Scotland began to emerge in the south, with Kenneth MacAlpine making Scone the centre of Scottish and Pictish tribes. By the early eleventh century one of MacAlpine's successors, King Malcolm II, had added the Lothians to the territory. Many battles later a northern Pictish tribe leader, Macbeth, was defeated by Malcolm III and much of northern Scotland came under Scottish control.

Even before Scotland became more or less united, and probably for as far back as human history goes, the inhabitants of Scotland had fought with the inhabitants of England, as well as each other, regardless of tribe. King Malcolm III spent much time raiding Northumbria, part of disputed Borders territory throughout history, and eventually died there in 1093. Prior to this he had married Margaret, grand-daughter of English King Edward the Confessor whose death had precipitated the Norman invasion of Britain and Conquest in 1066. She had been on a ship fleeing the Normans that was ship-wrecked in the Firth of Forth and after marrying Malcolm had persuaded him to move the Scottish capital to the rock of Edinburgh, partly because this had an Anglo-Saxon population at the time.

Scotland's and England's fates were further intertwined when Malcolm and Margaret's son, King David I, married a high born English woman. Norman influence pushed northwards, abbeys were built in the Lowlands and the tribal clannish ways of the Gaels began to die out there, surviving only north of the Central Belt.

The 200 year period of relative stability came to an end in 1286 when Scottish King Alexander III fell off his horse, over a cliff and died. This was the opportunity English King Edward I had awaited and he moved to make Scotland part of his own kingdom. By the end of the century a puppet king of Scotland was kneeling at the English throne. This period of English rule was short lived. First William Wallace arose to defend his country and then the great Robert the Bruce, who won back Scottish nationhood in 1314 at the Battle of Bannockburn near Stirling.

Sadly, after King Robert's unifying reign ended the true enemy of the Scottish nation, the varied interests of her inhabitants, led to years of division as lairds and anyone with a tenuous claim to the crown strove for control. The Highland clan chiefs meanwhile rarely owed allegiance to anyone. This was the dawn of the Stewart dynasty (the name was changed to Stuart by Mary, Queen of Scots). It was not a happy time: James I was assassinated, James II was killed by an exploding cannon, James III was murdered following an attempt to quell rebellious subjects and James IV went to support the French at Flodden in 1513, lost badly and died.

James V ruled Scotland about the same period as Henry VIII was King of England and he again made the 'auld alliance' with the French to fight Henry when the latter was excommunicated by the Pope and when the English church broke away. James had married two French wives and the second gave birth to Mary, Queen of Scots, shortly before he was killed in battle with the English. Mary is probably Scotland's most famous monarch, but was rarely more than a political pawn in a complex battle for power in the wake of the Reformation, between Catholicism and Protestantism, English, French and Scottish interests.

Henry VIII, encouraging Scottish Protestants, tried to marry his son to Mary, destroying most of the great Borders abbeys in the attempt. Mary was moved to France and married to the French King's son and heir, the dauphin. This led to her becoming Queen of France as well as Scotland and a complex political situation bordering on farce, as some of the Scots, who had sought French help to eject the English, now sought English help to stop Scotland being absorbed in to France. The religious dimension complicated matters further as the English Queen Elizabeth was not recognised by Scottish Catholics, being the daughter of Anne Boleyn whom Henry had married while his first wife Catherine of Aragon was still alive. They therefore regarded Elizabeth as illegitimate and believed Mary should be Queen of England as well as France and Scotland, due to her descent from Henry VII.

Elizabeth sent troops north and ultimately, in 1560, it was agreed that both French and English troops should leave Scottish soil, this also led to Scotland abolishing papal authority and adopting Protestantism. The celebration of mass was forbidden.

The various claimants to the Scottish throne now pondered on the future, with Mary still Queen of France. They thought about deposing her but were divided as ever and decided it unlikely she would return anyway. After 18 months as the French Queen, Mary's husband died and she decided to return home rather than become a dowager Queen in the French court. The early years of her rule were successful, although she privately celebrated mass she publicly brought forward Protestant legislation and suppressed a Catholic revolt. She travelled widely around the country and attempted to reach an agreement with Elizabeth in England whereby Elizabeth could stay Queen for life. Mary, however, would have right of succession for the English crown. This came to nothing: Mary married a Protestant she had fallen in love with, but the ceremony was a Catholic one and things started to go wrong. Enemies became stronger and, shortly before the birth of the future James VI, Mary's fidelity to her husband came in to doubt and a possible Italian lover as Lord Darney was English born and bred was murdered. Her husband was murdered within a year and Mary soon took another. Rebellion followed and Mary fled to England to appeal, fruitlessly, to Queen Elizabeth. She was imprisoned, though still treated as royalty, and not charged with any crimes due to the further political complications such accusations would bring. From then on Mary was moved from English castle to castle for nearly 20 years. She spent much of the time plotting, and an assassination plan for Elizabeth led to her execution in 1587. Mary had spent a little over a quarter of her life in Scotland.

James VI became king following his mother's forced abdication while he was still a baby and was once again a political pawn during his childhood years. When Elizabeth died in England in 1603, without an heir, he became King of England and Scotland and the Scottish court decamped to England never to return. The major complications now were religious ones and James and his son Charles I carried out religious reforms from south of the border. This eventually led to the Covenanter faction of those opposed to rule from England and the introduction of the new Prayer Book.

In the wars that followed, including the English Civil War, Scotland's history became totally intertwined with England and the people of the British Isles were divided more by religion than nation. Clans took sides according to religious and political beliefs and fought one another as part of British rather than Scottish wars. The national identity was rekindled when Charles I was beheaded and the Scots declared Charles II their king. Cromwell's subsequent invasion, destruction of castles and abbeys, and construction of his own fortress leaves many relics today. The Scots welcomed the crowning of Charles II in 1660, however oppression of the Covenanters became ever more brutal. When Charles died his brother James VII, a strong Catholic, became king. He oppressed the Covenanters still further and was ultimately overthrown by Protestant William of Orange.

It was this move that led ultimately to the genesis of the Jacobite rebellions. Powerful Catholic clans from the Highlands began uprising against the powerful Campbells' supporters of the new king. The gap between Highland and Lowland Scots had grown through the centuries with the Lowlanders now relatively prosperous under William in the south, and the Highlanders still living the harsh clan life and speaking a different language in the mountains to the north.

The massacre of Glencoe took place when the Lowland authorities chose to make an example of the MacDonalds in 1692. William died at the turn of the century and Scotland suffered economic disasters leaving her in a weak position. The Treaty of Union with England came about in 1707 when England refused free trading rights and imposed economic sanctions on Scotland. The Scottish parliament passed the motion by 110 votes to 69 and Scotland as an independent nation ceased to exist.

While infrastructure and agricultural methods raised living standards a little, the Jacobites continued to look to Europe for support, including Spain. Uprisings came and went, before the arrival of Bonnie Prince Charlie in the Western Isles and the great and successful Jacobite crusade, which took him as far as Derby. Then the usual problem of failure of European support and the independence of the clan chiefs led to desertions and retreat. It all ended at Culloden in 1746 with apparently suicidal tactics by the Highland force leading to their defeat. It was not a battle so much of England versus Scotland, a large proportion of Scots fought on the government side. The Bonnie Prince's escape with the aid of Flora MacDonald are the stuff of legend. He lived a further 42 years of luxurious exile in Europe before dying of old age in Italy. Meanwhile the victorious Duke of Cumberland was earning his nickname 'butcher' by slaughtering surviving Highlanders, regardless of allegiance. The cultural heritage of the Highlander was legally banned and more forts built to quell any further uprising, most notably at Fort George.

The Jacobite movement was effectively destroyed and it has since been left to poets and song-writers to attempt to maintain and sometimes create a Scottish identity. The tyranny was not yet over, lands taken from rebel clans were handed over to new landlords — Scottish and English. They saw sheep as more productive tenants than human beings and the often brutal eviction of communities from fertile glens north of Perth began, the notorious 'clearances'. This act of stunning cruelty, combined with the 'voluntary' migration of Scots to a better life in the New World, led to the depopulation of the north of Scotland, still very evident today.

Scottish Culture

The Scots have a well-deserved reputation for hospitality. In the Highlands it was tradition that when your worst enemy called asking for a roof for the night (the common enemy being the weather), you granted it. This was how the famous massacre was organised at Glencoe, as the Campbells, employed by the government, stopped by to take advantage of MacDonald hospitality. The MacDonalds could not refuse and were slaughtered in their beds in recompense (the event was orchestrated as punishment on the MacDonalds for not signing an oath of allegiance to King William quickly enough). The breaking of the code of hospitality had psychological effects, perhaps more significant than the cold blooded murder itself.

Scots generally go out of their way to make you feel welcome and to provide a genuinely personal service. Many who live in remote communities still may not travel widely and are happy to talk and listen for hours on any subject in the world from the price of fuel to the over-population of Japan. It is a very soul-satisfying experience for many people coming from a modern metropolis to be able to talk like this to a complete stranger. Films like *Local Hero* (1983) portray the ironies and realities of this situation well. On the other hand many other Scots are travellers and will have relatives in the four corners of the Globe before they themselves have decided to return and settle in their home village, perhaps having spent many years abroad.

National dress is rarely worn except for formal occasions and tourist areas. Otherwise you are only slightly more likely to see a Scot in a kilt than you are an English man in a bowler hat.

Travel

Opinions on the best way to tour Scotland, and on the quality of the options available, are divided.

A lot of the country is only accessible by foot, pony or mountain bike and ever increasing numbers are enjoying this way of seeing the country. Still others prefer to see it from rather higher up, courtesy of comprehensive and, in many cases, vital air service around Scotland, particularly to many of the islands off the west and north coasts. Those who live in such places regard the planes as the local bus service, and hop on and off eight to sixteen seater planes for a 15 minute flight only a few hundred feet in the air. Where the plane link is a vital connection services are supported by local councils.

For those who prefer to see their islands at ground level, the major ferry operator to the west coast islands is Caledonian MacBrayne or 'Cal Mac' as it is more likely to be referred to. On virtually all routes the standard of service and efficiency is better than one might imagine out to a remote Scottish island, more like a cross Channel ferry, and they have a very flexible approach to ticketing, enabling tourists to link inter-island travel in a wide range of combinations.

Rail services, especially north of the central belt between Glasgow and Edinburgh, have suffered in the past 10 years. The problem is that roads north have improved drastically and many stretches are now regarded as the best in the United Kingdom; with wide firths spanned by causeways and modern highways well on the way to John O'Groats. The drive time is several hours shorter than it was 10 years ago and the new direct roads must have shaved 50 miles (80½km) or more off the road north. Sadly there has been no investment in the railways and they still wander around the firths on ageing tracks. The suburban Sprinter trains seem totally out of place in the rural setting and you can make the journey by road in half the time you can by rail. That being said, for those with time to spare, train travel is still a wonderful way to see parts of Scotland you can not see from the road.

So to the driver. The first point to make is that Scotland is big, by English standards anyway. While folk living in some parts of England might consider a 50 mile (80½km) jaunt a day long trek (and it might take that long), in many parts of Scotland such a distance can be regarded as a 50 minute nip into town for the shopping. No traffic lights, no roundabouts; only the possibility of sheep or deer. Motorists travelling very slowly along single track roads, admiring the views, can be a nuisance to other drivers. Therefore the rules of the road are that if someone approaches from behind you should pull into a passing place as soon as possible and let them pass and always drive with caution. There are many winding stretches, with the possibility of some wildlife around the next bend, and do look in your mirror and be aware of other cars behind you.

1 • The Borders

Visiting the peaceful, gentle rolling landscape of the Borders, it is hard to appreciate how many centuries of war the locality has endured. The picturesque valleys have set the scene throughout history for endless re-runs of the timeless classic story of English kings and lords fighting for lands in Scotland, against the defending population. When the English were not engaged in destroying the ancient abbeys, the feuding clans who ruled the region frequently took the opportunity to have the odd skirmish between themselves or took part in the age-old pastime of raiding and stealing from their opposite members in northern England. For centuries the Border itself was closed, encouraging the Scots to use sea routes to France and trade directly with Europe. The turbulent past is remembered annually when Common Ridings Festivals are held in Borders towns and locals go out to 'ride the marches'.

Today the Borders comprise a tranquil area; green fields and extensive woodland make this one of the most fertile and rural areas in Scotland. It is therefore something of a tragedy that a good proportion of the people who visit the region leave it again within an hour, racing through on the A1 from Newcastle to Edinburgh.

The region is almost a small country in itself, having mountains, hills, lochs and sea coast with the different communities you would expect to find in each. What the Borders do not have are any cities or heavily urbanised areas. Royal and religious connections run deep, partly because of the political toings and froings down through the centuries and partly because of the land's fertility. Four large abbeys at Jedburgh, Melrose, Kelso and Dryburgh lie within a 12 mile (19km) triangle at the centre of the Borders. Three were founded by King David I and all date from the twelfth century. Their richness and power laid them open to repeated English attack and, although all are now in ruins as a result, they remain impressive structures.

The region is crossed almost right through the middle by the Tweed which, at its eastern end, forms the border with England.

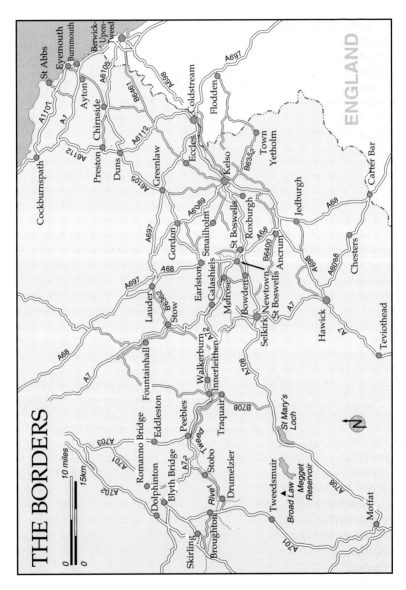

About half of the major Borders towns are located along the river (Coldstream, Kelso, Melrose, Galashiels, Innerleithen and Peebles). There are several themed routes which follow the Tweed for all or part of their length and a 62 mile (100km) Tweed Cycleway running from Berwick to Biggar. Details of both are available from Tourist Offices. The Southern Upland Way, which crosses Scotland from coast to coast, also follows the hills above the Tweed for some of its length.

The A68 offers the most dramatic border crossing in to Scotland. From Darlington to Edinburgh the road is an 'endearing' mix of aged winding roller-coaster, interspersed with long straight wide sections of modern highway, occasionally dual carriageway. It is a far more interesting road than the M6/A74 up the west, or the A1 from Newcastle, which are major arteries of the United Kingdom's road infrastructure. For those in a hurry to reach Edinburgh up the east coast it can also be faster than the A1, being more direct as the crow flies and less congested. It all depends on what you get stuck behind and where. If you are not in a hurry it is a good route too, as there is more to see as you trundle along. The major disadvantage for winter drivers is that you are exposed to the elements, most commonly fog and mist, and occasionally snow.

The last 30 miles (48km) of the road, through England's top county, Northumberland, cruises up in to the Cheviot Hills and culminates in a succession of even tighter bends as the road battles its way up to **Carter Bar**. The large lay-by and viewing area may take you a little by surprise and, if you yourself are not planning to stop, look out for those in front of you, also taken by surprise, who may suddenly swing across the road and in to the lay by. The view across the Borders from this point can be spectacular, but may also be disappointingly gloomy if the weather is bad. The huge rock by the roadside with the name 'Scotland' cut simply in to it perhaps says more than anything about the nature of the land you have just entered. The first choice you must make soon after you commence your descent into the Scottish Borders, is whether to take the left turning off towards Hawick (A6088) or continue on the A68 towards Jedburgh. Those turning towards Hawick (Roxburghshire) skirt through a lot of forestry land, notably Wauchope Forest, as it sweeps down in to the Borders.

Hawick is the largest town in the region and is historically important as a centre for knitwear and hosiery, particularly at the upper-end of the market. The town is therefore a key stop on the Scottish Borders Woollen Trail, actively promoted in the area (further information from the Tourist Office). The major place of interest in this regard is at Trowbridge on the outskirts of the town where visitors can see Border tweeds being manufactured.

There is a local museum dedicated to Hawick's past with displays illustrating textile manufacturing (and rugby football, for those less interested in cloth). This is located in Wilton Lodge Park to the west of the town, and on the banks of the Teviot river which runs through it. The Scott Gallery houses the town's collection of nineteenth and twentieth-century Scottish paintings. The gallery also has a reputation for its lively temporary exhibition program. The horse statue in the main street commemorates the recapture of the town's flag from the English following the Scots' defeat at the Battle of Flodden (1513). As you would expect for an important market town, roads depart in four directions from Hawick, two of them soon to subdivide giving six different options in total. Having come in from the southeast, the next road around the clock is the B6399 heading due south, in a winding sort of way for the Hermitage 'Strength of Liddesdale'. This old stronghold remains an impressive structure today. In fact it is probably more impressive now than it was in the sixteenth century, when it was a stopping off point for Mary Queen of Scots during her Regal 'Progress'. It was first built as a relatively simple tower house in the fourteenth century and was then gifted to the Bothwell family by James IV in 1491. The corbelling parapet, which gives a misleading impression of uniformity in design is an addition from the Victorian era.

Newcastleton, in the most southerly corner of the Borders, is home to the Clan Armstrong Trust and Liddesdale Heritage Association Centre. A vast amount of information on the Armstrong Clan and the area is available here, as well as local leisure walk itineraries. The town is also a major agricultural centre for the Liddesdale District and regular events include sheep-dog trials and a 100-year-old agricultural show in late August.

The main A road out of town is the A7 (south-west) heading back towards England via Langholm, then ultimately Carlisle. Hills on either side of this road become ever more mountainous as the border approaches, with Cauldcleuch Head (1,995ft/608m) to the left and Calfshaw Head to the right. Some 10 miles (16km) along the road is **Teviothead** where there is a Museum of Border Arms and Armour containing original armour from the sixteenth and seventeenth centuries and Scottish silver jewellery.

A side road (right) at Teviothead leads to a perhaps surprisingly significant spot for those interested in the history of the Borders: the old chapel at **Caerlanrig**. It is believed that King James V of Scotland hanged Johnie Armstang (alias Black Jock) of Gilnockie here in the summer of 1530. Although Mr Armstang may not be so well known as the likes of Bonnie Prince Charlie, he is a Borders equivalent of Robin Hood, with a great deal more historical evidence. He was mentioned in Henry VIII's papers as one of 'the gretteste theves upon the Borders.' His popularity north of the border seems to rest on the fact that he preyed only on those living south of the border, unlike many of similar standing. The reason for his execution by the King of Scotland is unclear therefore but was probably due to infighting and manipulation from his court. A plaque erected in the nineteenth century commemorates Black Jock's life and death.

The third main route out of Hawick leaves the A7 south-westerly after a mile or so with a right turning on to the B711. This is a pleasant road leading in to the picturesque Ettrick Valley. For those with time for a tour it is worth taking this road to the Ettrick river before following its course north-easterly on the B7009 up to Selkirk. For people in a hurry, the A7 north out of Hawick makes the trip in about a quarter of the time.

Selkirk differs from most towns in the Borders in being located on the hills, rather than in a sheltered valley. The town looks down upon a wide sweep of the Southern Uplands, stretching across the hills above the Ettrick and Yarrow valleys. Selkirk is closely associated with Sir Walter Scott whose statue stands in the main square. He was once Sheriff of the town and, although there is no specific museum to his memory here, there are some mementos in nearby Bowhill House.

Selkirk once had an abbey but this was removed to Kelso almost 1,000 years ago. It also had walls, but these were burnt down by the English once too often and nothing of them remains. There is a Glass Visitor Centre in the town, and for photography buffs a treat in the shape of R Clapperton's Daylight Photographic Studio. The studio has been in existence since 1867 and has been in the same family's hands throughout that time. The studio is now run by the fourth generation of family owners and is set up as a working museum and photographic archive.

Philiphaugh near Selkirk was the scene of a famous battle in the 1640s. With the English Civil War raging, the religious arguments affecting both sides of the border were causing related fighting within Scotland. Montrose, who on balance supported Charles I's religious stance and who had led successful campaigns in the Highlands, finally suffered defeat at Philiphaugh and went into hiding. Soon afterwards King Charles was executed in England. Neither side in the Scottish conflict agreed with the execution and the country declared Charles II, the executed monarch's heir, as their king. This, of course, was not popular with Cromwell who moved in to stamp down his own authority, right the way up to Lerwick. The resulting ruins and new fortresses are described elsewhere in this and other chapters.

Bowhill House and Country Park (1812) off the A708 a few miles west of Selkirk and just beyond the battle-field is the home of the Duke and Duchess of Buccleuch. The house contains relics of Sir Walter Scott, Queen Victoria and the Duke of Monmouth. There are many works of art in the house, including paintings by Gainsborough, da Vinci and Canaletto. There is also a Victorian kitchen and an audio-visual display. The house has a Visitor Centre, tea room and gift shop.

Heading back to the starting point of Hawick, the A698 (which you will have joined shortly before reaching the town if you entered the region from Carter Bar and taken the A6088), is the most direct route for Jedburgh. The A698 crosses the A68 a few miles north of Jedburgh, on its way to Kelso and Coldstream, before crossing back in to England en route to Berwick-Upon-Tweed. It is possible to reach Jedburgh by taking the earlier right turning 2 miles (3km) past Denholm on to the B6358.

Jedburgh is a major tourist town: people visit it because it is both pleasant and historic. It is impossible to miss the huge ruined abbey as you enter the town, and for those lured off the main road there are many attractions for the visitor to enjoy, with some excellent shops and restaurants thrown in for good measure. Jedburgh also boasts beautiful floral displays in the summer months.

The town is closely associated with Mary Queen of Scots, whose 'house' is a major attraction. Mary based her Queen's Progress on Jedburgh in 1566 but it is not certain that the house where she is traditionally reputed to have stayed was actually built by that year. Regardless of this detail, Mary's house is an excellent example of a fortified home from the period. The Queen was taken seriously ill in Jedburgh, probably suffering from porphyria, a painful hereditary disease. The house was refurbished in the late 1980s in memory of the 400th anniversary of Mary's death. Displays inside tell the story of the tragic Queen. The house itself is set in beautiful gardens and is floodlit at night.

Another visitor attraction in Jedburgh is the Castle Jail on the original site of the medieval castle, towering high above the town. The nineteenth-century jail is the only one in Scotland which remains an example of a Howard Reform Prison. Displays illustrate prison life and there is a picnic site in the grounds.

The abbey was founded around 1118 by King David I for Augustinian canons. It has been destroyed or badly damaged nine times and rebuilt eight. It was finally destroyed in 1545 by the English Earl of Hertford. The architecture that remains is both impressive and, in some parts, beautiful. Huge towers in the nave are linked to Roman-

Mary Queen of Scots' House, Jedburgh

esque arches supporting a high gallery of intricate round arches. The Norman tower used to have a spire on top. There is a visitor centre and viewing route. One of the old entrances to the abbey is through the 1720 arch at Newgate above the market square. It is also the entrance to the county buildings where Sir Walter Scott began his legal career.

Contemporary attractions in the area include the Jedforest Deer and Farm Park near **Camptown**, south of Jedburgh on the A68. This is a working farm which contains rare breeds and offers marked walks, a pets corner and tractor rides.

Heading in the other direction Harestanes Countryside Visitor Centre near **Ancrum** contains walks and displays around the surrounding farmlands and forestry. There is an excellent children's

*The last shop in
Scotland, Jedburgh*

play area here too, as well as café, gift shop and audio visual display.
   It is a few miles further north along the A68 before you will reach
the main artery of the Borders, the River Tweed at St Boswells and
Newtown St Boswells. Just across the river between the two towns
stands the spectacular and remarkably complete twelfth-century
Dryburgh Abbey (on the B6404). It flourished rapidly in early times
but then suffered badly during the wars of independence with the
English a century or two later. In about 1700 the land around the
abbey came into the possession of Sir Walter Scott's great grandfather. His heirs retain the right to be buried here and Sir Walter Scott
does have his grave here, as does Field Marshall Earl Haig. Some of
the monastic buildings and the surviving west portal of the nave are
in a particularly good state of preservation. Near to the abbey is the
most famous viewpoint in the Borders, Scott's View. From here,
weather permitting, there is a wonderful panorama across to the
Eildon Hills and central Borders.
   Two miles (3km) north-east of St Boswells, further on the B6404,
are Mertoun Gardens. These cover 20 acres (8 hectares) with beautiful plants and flowers.

The Eildon Hills are the jewel at the centre of the Borders

Turning on to the A6091 at Newtown St Boswells it is only a few miles drive to **Melrose** which is blessed not only with being a pleasant Borders town in itself, but also in having a wealth of outstanding attractions either in the town or within a 10 mile (16km) radius.

Perhaps the major asset is the ancient abbey, founded by King David in 1136, one of three he founded within a few years in the twelfth century (the others were Jedburgh and Kelso). Together with Dryburgh, also twelfth century, the four abbeys stand in an impressive 12 mile (19km) triangle. The abbey church of St Mary was founded for Cistercian monks and grew rich and powerful under royal patronage. It was continually attacked in the various English invasions however, and, having been restored by Robert the Bruce in 1326 and again after a particularly destructive period in 1385, it was finally abandoned in 1545. The red sandstone ruins show very fine stonework with flying buttresses and splendid pinnacles. There are also some carved figures including a pig playing the bagpipes up on the roof! According to tradition, Robert the Bruce is buried within the abbey.

Next to the abbey are Priorwood Gardens, run by the National

Trust For Scotland and sheltered by high walls. There are display areas and an interesting orchard walk descriptively named 'Apples Through The Ages'. Most of the plants grown in the garden are suitable for drying and there is a dried-flower shop as well as the National Trust shop.

Another major attraction for Melrose is the Roman signal-post and lookout post named *Trimontium*. Roman relics are on display in the Ormiston Institute in the town square. The excavations are ongoing and the display is updated at least annually. *Trimontium* means 'The Three Hills' and the hills now known as Eildon form one of the most distinctive landmarks in the Borders region. Legend has it that the three hills were once one, but were split into three by the devil. The rather boring truth is that they were created by volcanic activity. Another legend, more difficult to disprove, is that the ghosts of King Arthur and his knights, rather a long way from home, live in a cave beneath them.

A waymarked path leads into the hills from Melrose Square, climbing steeply to over 1,365ft (416m), thus offering excellent views of the hills of the Borders (as recommended by the Romans) to the south and Tweedsmuir to the west — always 'weather permitting' of course. More attractions back in Melrose include a Motoring Museum, featuring a 1909 Albion and a 1926 Arrol Johnstone — both made in Scotland. There is also an old Morris bus and some vintage motor-cycles.

The town's newest museum is dedicated to Teddybears. Exhibits record the history of British teds from the early 1900 bruin, right the way up to today's designer bears. Pooh, Rupert, Bully and Paddington are all there, along with informative displays on their creators. The teddybear shop contains contemporary Scottish designers' works and hundreds more from around the world; there is also a tearoom.

Abbotsford House is easily reached from Melrose by taking a left turning on to the B6360 a mile west of the town. This was the home of Sir Walter Scott until his death in 1832. Over the years from 1810 he renovated and reconstructed a former farm, giving it what was then a new, and more romantic name. The house is built in mock baronial style with ideas taken from other famous houses; notable are the porch from Linlithgow Palace and the library ceiling from Rosslyn Chapel. The library itself still contains the 9,000 volumes Scott collected for it. The great writer's collection of artefacts is also displayed, including a lock of Bonnie Prince Charlie's hair. The house remains in the possession of Scott's descendants.

From Melrose it is again just a few miles to **Galashiels** following

Evening time in Galashiels

both the River Tweed and the A6091. This is another town famous for its knitwear industry, the very name being derived from the word 'shielings', the name for summer shelters built by herdsmen to protect their flocks. Since the Industrial Revolution the town has become the centre of the Scottish woollen weaving industry and has won a world-wide reputation for excellent woollens. The Peter Anderson Mill has a small museum with tours twice daily on working days. The Borders Wool Centre offers similar attractions and the Scottish College of Textiles, which attracts students from all over the world, is also located in the town.

As with all of the Tweedside towns, angling is a major activity in and around Galashiels. The School of Casting Salmon and Trout Fishing, the longest established of its kind, is based here. Weekly fly-fishing courses are arranged on the Tweed and neighbouring lochs for both novice and experienced fishers. All necessary equipment may be hired.

The historic Old Gala House is located on what is now Scott Crescent. The building dates from 1583 and was home to the Lairds of Gala. There is a painted ceiling from 1635 and a painted wall (1988). Displays tell the history of the house and early times in Galashiels. There is a small tearoom and shop.

The A72 continues to follow the Tweed, drawing a line about 40 miles (64km) south of Edinburgh. The district of Ettrick and Laudadale now ends and the Borders' most westerly district, Tweedale, begins, an area of some 350sq miles (907sq km). The area was renamed in 1975 as part of local government reorganisation; formerly it was Peeblesshire.

The first town reached is **Walkerburn** which is a popular base for walkers and fishermen. The small town is also an important stop on the Scottish Borders Woollen Trail as it contains the Scottish Museum of Woollen Textiles. Displays chart the history of the industry in the region and include a sample of Prince Albert's Balmoral Pattern which helped to revive Victorian interest in Scottish tartans.

Innerleithen was a prosperous spa town in Victorian times thanks to the mineral wells on Lee Pen, above the town. It was Sir Walter Scott who brought fame to St Ronans Well when he immortalised the spring in his novel of that name. Today St Ronan's Wells Interpretative Centre and Fitness Centre provides both historical displays and the opportunity for visitors to try the waters themselves. There is also a modern gymnasium facility. Innerleithen is another renowned tweed and knitwear centre. Cashmere and lambswool knitwear is supplied to luxury outlets throughout the world from the town. Local firms specialise in intricate intarsia work.

Another major attraction in the town is the sympathetically restored Robert Smail's Printing Works run by the National Trust For Scotland. The buildings contain office, paper store, reconstructed water wheel, composing and press rooms. All machinery has been restored to full working order. There is an adjacent National Trust shop.

South of Innerleithen on the B709 is the village of **Traquair** with its famous ancient house, parts of which are more than 1,000 years old. This is believed to be the oldest continually inhabited house in Scotland. Features include a working eighteenth-century brewery with malt loft gallery, a maze, priest room with hidden staircase, a rich collection of documents, embroideries and books, as well as craft workshops. It has been visited by twenty-seven Scottish monarchs over the years since 1007, including Mary Queen of Scots. The Scottish kings used the house as their hunting lodge, sending their huntsmen to camp across the river in an area known aptly enough as Hornhuntersland. There are gardens open to the public and a popular fair is held in the first weekend of August each year.

Traquair House

Mary Queen of Scots' relics at Traquair House

Traquair also boasts a small art gallery which hosts temporary exhibitions. The village is linked by footpath (past the village hall) to 'dark Minchmoor'. This is located about an hour's walk along the Southern Upland Way. It was along this former drove road that the Marquis of Montrose made his escape from the battle of Philiphaugh in 1645. Today's travellers must ensure they stop at the Cheese Well on Minch Moor and dip their provisions into the well's icy waters to placate the local fairies.

The A72 continues north of the Tweed to Peebles, but it is possible to take the B7062 on the south side which passes **Kailzie Gardens**, 2 miles (3km) east of Peebles. There are 17 acres (7 hectares) of pleasure gardens, greenhouses, formal beds, herbaceous and shrub gardens, woodland and burnside walks, waterfowl pond, children's play corner and a licensed tea room. There is also a small art gallery. The gardens are particularly well known, in season, for their snowdrops, meconopsis, primulas and rhododendrons.

Peebles is Tweedale's county town, situated at the junction of Eddleston Water with the River Tweed. It has long been associated with royalty and has a well documented history thanks to that. The town was a Royal Burgh by the fourteenth century (David II gave it its charter in 1367) and the Crown had considerable interests in lands across the district. The town's name comes from 'pebylls' or 'tents', which were pitched here by the earliest known residents, the wandering Gadeni tribe.

There are plenty of relics from the town's past to be seen. St Andrews Tower is all that remains of an imposing collegiate church founded in 1195. The ruined Cross Kirk, a few minutes walk from the High Street, was once a Trinitarian friary founded by Alexander III in 1261. This was destroyed by local builders who were allowed to use it for building stone from 1783 onwards.

Tweedale Museum on the High Street was originally owned by the Queensberry family but was bought and gifted to the town by famous publisher William Chambers in 1859. It now houses the local museum, library and a gallery which features examples of nineteenth-century plasterwork. A second museum re-creates a plasterer's casting workshop at the turn of the century. The Cornice Museum, also on the High Street, illustrates the main methods of creating ornamental plasterwork used in Scotland at that time. Wellies and aprons are provided for those wanting to try plastering for themselves!

There are many events staged annually in the town, most notably Beltane Week in late June. This links the ancient Celtic festival in honour of the sun god with the old ceremony of riding the marches to protect the common land. A young man on horseback from the village leads celebrations throughout the week. August sees the agricultural show and September the staging of the Borders only Highland Games.

An unlisted road north from Peebles climbs in to the Meldon Hills towards Eddleston village where it joins the main Edinburgh road (A703). The hill on the west is White Meldon and, to the east, Black Meldon. The stream running between is the Meldon burn and there is a picnic site nearby. There are plaques detailing local history and some wonderful views to be had from the area.

Eddleston is located in the midst of some beautiful wooded countryside. The 'current version' of the village was built around 1875 but its history reaches back to the twelfth century. The nearby estate of Blackbarony was once the home of the Murrays, one of whom died with James IV at Flodden. The former family home here is now a hotel.

The A703 continues northwards alongside Eddleston Water towards Edinburgh through some beautiful countryside. Another hotel that was formerly a Murray family home stands 2 miles (3km) from Peebles (and before Eddleston) at Cringletie: in this instance the Wolfe Murray division of the family. The first part of their name was derived from an ancestor who served under General Wolfe at Quebec in 1750.

Just west of Peebles, overlooking the river, is the massive stronghold of **Neidpath Castle**. Modernised in the seventeenth and twentieth centuries the castle still retains its medieval grandeur. Some of the walls are 13ft (4m) thick in places and, unlike many castles in the Borders, it has only been taken by the enemy once, having been besieged in 1650 by Cromwell's army. It can be reached by a walking route from the town centre.

A few miles further on a right turn bridges the Tweed and an unclassified road follows the Manor Water tributary to the south in to Manor Valley. This lonely, peaceful area once contained ten keeps, and Barns Tower at the entrance still survives. The Burnet family home for 500 years, it appeared in John Buchan's tale *John Burnet of Barns*. Further ruins include another Burnet home Castlehill Tower (on the left), then Posso Castle and 1½ miles (1km) further on a large granite runic cross marks the site of St Gordian's Kirk.

The A72 continues to follow the Tweed for a few more miles before finally departing its banks shortly before Kirkton. Those wishing to continue along its banks however can turn left on to the B712 and then on to the A701. This is a rewarding route through continually beautiful countryside.

Having taken the B712 it is a short drive to Stobo and the **Dawyck Botanical Gardens**, a historic arboretum and an off-shoot of the famous Royal Botanic Garden in Edinburgh. There are many flowering shrubs, impressive conifers and some unusual variety of rhododendron. Many of the specimens were brought back by David Douglas, a famous collector who gave his name to the Douglas Fir. The gardens are particularly beautiful in spring and autumn and there are some pleasant riverside walks. Dawyck House is the former home of the Vietches, a well known Borders family.

Stobo Castle may be a familiar name to some, as the current early nineteenth-century building now houses an internationally famous health and beauty spa. This Baronial style building was created by Sir James Montgomery between 1805 and 1811 and is now a listed building. The former manors at Stobo may be traced back at least 1,000 years.

Further along the road is the village of **Drumelzier** which is associated in legend with Merlin the wizard. He is said to be buried near the local kirk at the junction between the Tweed and the Poswail burn. The ruins of Tinnis castle nearby, which once belonged to the Tweedie family, date back to the thirteenth century.

As the A701 skirts Strathclyde before entering Dumfries and Galloway en route to Moffat, the hills on each side of the Tweed becoming increasingly mountainous, the road rising to more than 1,600ft (488m). **Tweedhopefoot**, 5 miles (8km) south of Tweedsmuir is one of the last settlements before the border is crossed and this houses the Tweedhopefoot Sheepdog Centre. The Billingham family's small sheep farm is typical of the area's main business but their attractions have been well developed with refreshments, regular demonstrations, a picnic area and craft shop.

At Tweedsmuir an unclassified road east forms part of a circular route taking in Peebles. This is a spectacular drive through beautiful countryside, passing first the Talla and then the Megget reservoirs beneath the imposing 2,755ft (840m) Broad Law peak to the north. The road then reaches the A708 at St Mary's Loch which goes northeast to Selkirk. However a left turn on to the B709 takes you back up to Innerleithen and the Tweed valley.

Turning right where the B712 meets the A701 leads you quickly to **Broughton** which contains the former church attended by John Buchan during his childhood holidays at his grandparents farm. The building is now the John Buchan Centre. Broughton also has a gallery in another building with historical connections. In this case it is the former home of Mr Evidence Murray, treacherous secretary to Bonnie Prince Charlie. The gallery houses exhibitions of prints, paintings and crafts, changing throughout the summer.

Further north the A701 rejoins the A72 en route west to Biggar. A few miles along that road in that direction is the village of **Skirling** where there has been a church on the hill since at least 1275. Skirling is a conservation village with many reminders of times gone by. There was once a castle here and although this has long been destroyed, one of the stones from its walls has been sculptured into

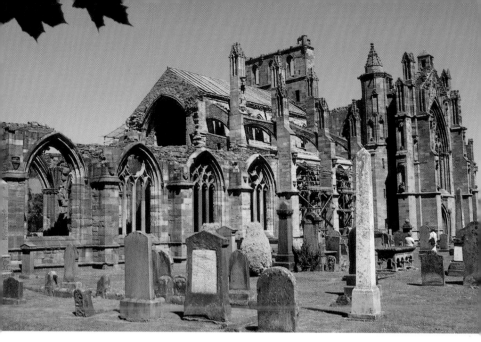

Melrose Abbey (above) and Jedburgh Abbey (below) both founded by King David I in the twelfth century (Chapter 1)

The ancient burgh of Selkirk (Chapter 1)

The River Tweed at Peebles (Chapter 1)

The beautiful scenery surrounding Talla Reservoir

a piper. This stone has been built in to the wall of a farmhouse that stands on the north side of the village green. On the other side of the green is a 'loupin-on-stane' which helped horsemen to climb on to their mounts. The village contains some interesting pieces of iron-work and pottery, with Douglas Davis Pottery giving demonstrations.

After its brief run in with the A72 north-easterly, the A701 resumes its own title when the two roads split by Blyth Bridge. The road now cuts across the north-west corner of the Borders region, marked by 1,752ft (534m) Byrehope Mount. The remains of the Roman fort at this junction can still be seen on the north side of the road. Lyne Kirk is seventeenth century and includes some rare timber furnishings, an original oak pulpit and two canopied pews. At the east end of the churchyard there is an unusual Adam and Eve statue (1712).

Half a mile (1km) before the picturesque little village of **Romanno Bridge** by Lyne Water some of Scotland's best known medieval cultivation terraces can be clearly seen. They are located on the steep hillside near Old Newlands church.

The B7059 crosses the A701 a little further on and the ruins of sixteenth-century **Drochil Castle** stand nearby. The castle has in fact never been completed as its owner, James, Earl of Morton, was executed before he could get the roof on. The B road leads to **West**

Linton where the parish church is famed for its intricate wood carvings. The curious streets and passages make this a popular village and a Visitor Centre which can advise on the best routes has been established. The A702 runs nearly parallel with the A701 and through West Linton. Further along is **Carlops**, the most northerly village in Tweedale, sitting at the foot of the Pentland hills. Another conservation village, Carlops was built in the eighteenth century to house workers in the hand loom weaving industry.

If the traveller is not interested in meandering down by the Tweed and wishes instead to continue past St Boswells and stay on the A68, the only important stop to be made further on would be at **Lauder**, to enable a visit to Thirlestane Castle. This building is very impressive and is undoubtedly one of Scotland's great historic homes. Especially interesting features include seventeenth-century plasterwork ceilings, fine pictures and furnishings and an exhibition of thousands of antique toys. The grounds are also well worth visiting and contain Border Country Life exhibitions.

Lauder itself is a very tidy village with a seventeenth-century church (1673) having an unusual Greek cross design with an octagonal spire at the centre. There is also an attractive tollbooth dating from the same period.

Going back to the starting point of Jedburgh, and leaving north-easterly from the town on the A698, **Kelso** is the next major stop. This is another pleasant town with a lovely central square. It again has some interesting architectural features, including the five-arched bridge, built in 1803 and said to be the model for London's Waterloo Bridge. In fact the lamps at the west end of the bridge originally hung on Waterloo Bridge; they were brought here when the bridge itself was sold to the USA.

Kelso has always been an agricultural centre and was once one of the major religious centres in Scotland. The remaining fragments of the Great Abbey, founded in 1128 by King David I and initially occupied by French monks, are testimony to the former grandeur of the building. They were left standing when the rest of the building was destroyed, along with 100 Scots garrisoned inside, by the English Earl of Hertford in 1545.

Turret House is one of the town's oldest and most attractive buildings, and is owned by the National Trust For Scotland. It opened in the late 1980s as a museum displaying a nineteenth-century market place and Victorian school-room. The local Tourist Information Office is also housed here.

Several other seventeenth and eighteenth-century buildings remain, including Ednam House (1761) which has beautifully carved ceilings and impressive mahogany doors. Just outside the town is the magnificent **Floors Castle**, built by William Adam and later embellished by William Playfair. Furnishings include Louis XV and XVI furniture, Chinese and European porcelain, tapestries and paintings. The house is the largest 'inhabited house' in Scotland, home to the Duke of Roxburgh. There is disabled access, a café and gift shop. If the weather is fine the Teviot Water Gardens with river walks in a beautiful position by the Tweed are well worth a visit. Another short walk from Kelso leads to the site of Roxburgh Castle, where King James II was killed by an exploding canon. Again, the walk is pleasant and the views rewarding.

Further west (6 miles/10km) is Smailholm Tower, a simple rectangular edifice situated on a rocky outcrop and in a good state of preservation. There are good views across the Borders from here and the tower is said to owe its survival in part to Sir Walter Scott's grandfather who once ran nearby Sandyknowe Farm.

The B6352 running south-easterly from the town, nears the English border after traversing some beautiful countryside at **Town Yetholm**. Here there is an interesting old kirk and the Stable Gallery, which in the summer months exhibits all forms of art but with an emphasis on Borders-based artists and crafts people. Half a mile away, and at the northernmost end of the Pennine Way, lies Kirk Yetholm, with a nice village green.

Another 9 miles (14km) along the A698 from Kelso, and 13 miles (21km) from Berwick-Upon-Tweed is the town of **Coldstream**. This is on the border with England, marked by the River Tweed, and crossed by the Tweed Bridge, constructed in 1766. The toll house still stands at the Scottish end of the bridge. Thanks to its location the town was the east coast equivalent of Gretna Green for eloping young lovers.

Coldstream is probably best known for its world-famous Guards, first recruited in the town by General Monck in 1659. The local museum contains information on this and other events in the Guards history, as well as various displays of local history. Further back in the town's military past the battle of **Flodden** was fought 3 miles (5km) south-east of the town in 1513: the Scots were heavily defeated. James IV was slain, together with all 'the flower of Scotland'.

To the north of the town is former Prime Minister Lord Home's home, The Hirsel. The Homestead Museum in the old farm and stables complex contains an exhibition with displays of life in a

Borders estate. Artefacts range from neolithic pottery to modern plastic drainage pipes. There are marked nature walks in the grounds and a craft centre.

Coldstream is the junction between the A697 heading south-easterly and the A698 crossing in to England and following the border on the south side, heading north-easterly. The other option out of the town is the A6112 which runs a winding course up to Duns. A further option from Coldstream is to head for the coast north of Berwick, by leaving the town on the A6112 but taking a right turning 3 miles (5km) along the road, on to the B6437, signposted **Chirnside**. Four miles (6km) south-east of this village is a two-storey tithe barn which was formerly used for storing payments to the parish church, made in grain. This is not open to the public but may be viewed from the road. From Chirnside it is 5 miles (8km) back westerly on the A6105 to Duns, or a little further north-easterly on the B6355 to Ayton and then over the A1 to Eyemouth.

Ayton's main attraction is its restored Victorian castle, now lived in as a family home but open on Sunday afternoons in the summer months to the general public. The magnificent red sandstone castle was constructed in 1846 but seems very much the classic British castle with its wonderful design.

The coastline runs for 28 miles (45km), an appealing mixture of high cliffs with deep clear water below, to sandy coves and quaint fishing villages. Fishing has, not surprisingly, been a vital part of the local economy for centuries and Eyemouth, Burnmouth and St Abbs still land white-fish catches.

Eyemouth is a pleasant old north-eastern fishing community, just 5 miles (8km) north of the English border, which developed its tourism facilities in the early 1980s. The town's museum, new Tourist Information Centre and first Town Trail were opened in 1981 to commemorate the centenary of a local fishing disaster which robbed the town of 129 fishermen, permanently marking the community, to the present day. Fishing has been the mainstay of the community since at least the thirteenth century, when the Benedictine monks, at the nearby priory in Coldingham, were granted rights to the River Eye. The port flourished in the late nineteenth century with haddock fishing. Fishing today is mainly for white fish, prawns, lobsters and crabs.

The restored Auld Kirk in which the museum and Tourist Information Centre are housed was built in 1812 by Alexander Gilkie of Berwick, and could accommodate 450 Church of Scotland worshippers. The museum holds many relics of the town's fishing history, and a beautiful tapestry depicting the 1881 fishing disaster. Those interested in freemasonry or Robbie Burns will want to see the Masonic Lodge beside the Town Square where Mr Burns was made a Royal Arch Mason on 19 May 1787.

The remains of the old parts of the town are still to be seen at the end of Marina Parade. Although much has been demolished for modern buildings, some red pantiled roofs with jutting gable ends can still be seen. The area was once frequented by smugglers with excise men in hot pursuit. Eyemouth also has an old fort, although little remains to be seen now. It was built under orders of the Duke of Somerset in 1547 and was then fought over by French, Scots and English. It was finally destroyed in 1560, only 13 years later.

South of Eyemouth and just across the border from England is **Burnmouth**, originally known as Flemington, having been built by the Flemings in the 1100s as a weaving town. The Flemington Inn and a few local farms still hold the original name. This is the first fishing village in Scotland and pioneered the trade in lobster and crab, sending the catch to London by sea and then rail. The cliffs at Hawkness between Eyemouth and Burnmouth are some of the highest on the British mainland.

The A1107 north from Eyemouth follows the coast for a few miles north-west to **Coldingham**, where the local population will tell you that their first ever 'holiday visitor' was St Cuthbert, 1,300 years ago. He used to drop in on his friends at the monastery here, run by St Ebba, and is said to have liked to do a spot of bathing in the sea. Other past visitors include John of Gaunt, who decided that Coldingham was close enough to his palace of The Savoy in London when Wat Tyler was burning it down in 1381. Mary Queen of Scots was also a visitor, as was famous demolition expert Oliver Cromwell. The young Mary once aroused the indignation of local purists by running barefoot across Coldingham Bay, reached after a mile along 'nuns walk' from the Priory.

The site of Coldingham Priory has been holy ground for certainly 900 years, possibly 1,300 years and potentially 2,000 years. The original monastic house was founded in AD635 and has since been destroyed and rebuilt on numerous occasions. The first 'demolition gang' arrived from Denmark in AD870 and then from England in 1216, sent by King John. It was besieged at least twice by the English in the Border wars between the 1530s and 1560s and although reported destroyed at the end of this period, was still able to accommodate Mary Queen of Scots and her legendary 'train of 1,000' in 1566. Predictably it was Cromwell who finally blasted it to bits in

1648 after besieging the area for 2 days; but parts were rebuilt by 1662, after the Restoration. In the centuries since then the locals finally tired of building it up and instead used some of the rock for their own construction purposes. However from 1850 to 1970 a great deal of rebuilding and renovation work took place and the building continues to be used for Christian worship to this day.

The B6438 runs from Coldingham out to the coast and the famous **St Abbs Head Nature Reserve**. This 192 acre (77 hectare) site, with some 300ft (91m) cliffs and purchased as recently as 1980, is owned by the National Trust For Scotland and managed in co-operation with the Scottish Wildlife Trust. There is a tea room at the centre which also houses an exhibition of the reserve's birdlife, flora and fauna.

There are about 50,000 birds living on the Head itself including colonies of razorbills, kittiwakes, shags, fulmars, puffins and her-ring-gulls. The area is named after St Aebee, the daughter of King Edilfred of Northumbria and ship-wrecked on the Head. She formed, or at least became head of, a monastic order in the locality which was destroyed by Scots or Vikings in the ninth century. Ruined buildings in the area once thought to have been the site of the convent, are now recognised as being probably medieval in origin.

The whole coastal area from Eyemouth to St Abbs is a Voluntary Marine Nature Reserve which means amongst other things that only traditional fishing methods are allowed and all forms of pollution are prohibited. The running costs are paid for by one of the large North Sea oil companies.

The village of **St Abbs** is a traditional fishing community sheltered by the volcanically formed cliffs. The harbour dating from 1832 is still in use. There is also a small gallery here, the Kittiwake, which exhibits local landscapes and wildlife painting. Art and wildlife demonstrations and courses are organised. The Graigholme Studio and Stable Gallery, a few miles in land on the B6438 at **Reston**, has exhibitions of decorative arts, paintings and many forms of craft, with the emphasis on Borders artists and crafts people.

Staying east of the A1 on the coastal A1107, a turning to **Dowlaw**, 2 miles (3km) from Coldingham, leads down to the remote ruins of Fast Castle (1½ miles/2km) coastal footpath, not suitable for the infirm or young children). This location is the 'Wolfs Crag' of Scott's 'Bride of Lammermuir', and in real life was the home of Princess Margaret of England in. She was taken there in 1502 to marry Scotland's King James IV and is said to have been terrified by the place.

The traditional fishing community of St Abbs

The A1107 comes right up to the coast at Pease Bay where there is a sandy beach and nature reserve. Just beyond is the tiny hamlet of **Cove** which is a good example of the east coast phenomenon of a fishing village perched on the cliff top as the harbour below is too small for houses to be built there. The original harbour was started in 1751 but was washed away before the current one was finally completed in 1831. Further on is **Cockburnspath**, which contains a sixteenth-century Mercat Cross in the village centre. This marks the end of the Southern Upland Way.

Another choice from Coldstream is to take the A6112 but this time take the right turning on to the B6461 towards Berwick. This route follows the Tweed to **Paxton** where the Palladian country mansion is open to the public. It was designed by the Adam family and furnished by Chippendale and Trotter. The Regency picture gallery within is an outstation of the National Galleries of Scotland. The house also boasts a particularly good adventure playground for children and lovely riverside and woodland walks. There is a tearoom in some converted stables.

The choice of the A6105 from Chirnside or the A6112 from

Coldstream will take the driver to **Duns**. Travelling via the former route, there is a working farm located some 3 miles (5km) from the town. Crumstane Farm Park opened in the early 1990s for visitors, but farming has gone on in the area for centuries; the lands, in common with much of the more valuable parts of the Borders, have been plundered ceaselessly by all sides throughout history. Plundering is not now permitted at the farm park but there are many different types of sheep, cattle, goats, pigs, horses, ducks, geese and other poultry to view, including many rare breeds. Nearby is Edrom Church which contains a richly carved Norman doorway.

About 1 mile (2km) closer to Duns, but still 2 miles (3km) from the town, it is worth stopping at the impressive Edwardian **Manderston House**, sometimes described as, 'The swan song of the Great Classical House'. Furnishings of particular note include a unique silver staircase and a marble dairy. There are also 56 acres (22 hectares) of very well maintained gardens, a café and a gift shop.

Duns itself will be of particular interest to motor racing buffs, as the town houses the Jim Clark Room, a small museum dedicated to the twice world motor racing champion of the 1960s. Jim Clark was a Berwickshire farmer and died tragically in a motor racing accident in 1968. Nearby is Edin's Hall Broch, one of the few Iron Age brochs to be found in Lowland Scotland and unusually large.

Further Information
— The Borders —

Places to Visit

Ancrum
Harestanes Countryside Visitor Centre
☎ 08353 306
Open: April to October. Daily 10am-5pm.

Ayton
Ayton Castle
Eyemouth, Berwickshire
☎ 08907 81212
Open: Sundays, May to early September, 2-5pm.

Broughton
Broughton Gallery
☎ 08994 234
Open: April to October, 10.30am-6pm, daily except Wednesday.

John Buchan Centre
☎ 0899 21050
Open: May to September, Monday to Saturday, 2-5pm.

Camptown
Jedforest Deer and Farm Park
Mervinslaw
Jedburgh
☎ 08354 364
Open: May to August, 10am-5.30pm; September and October 11am-4.30pm.

Coldstream
The Hirsel
☎ 0890 882834/882965
Open: all reasonable daylight hours
every day of the year.

Cove
Pease Bay Nature Reserve
Open: to public
☎ 0289 330 733 Berwick-on-Tweed
Tourist Information Office for times.

Dawyck House and Botanical Gardens
☎ 07216 254
Open: mid-March to mid-October,
daily, 10am-6pm.

Dryburgh Abbey
☎ 031 244 3101
Open: April to September, Monday to
Saturday 9.30am-7pm, Sunday 2-7pm.
October to March, Monday to Saturday
9.30am-4pm, Sunday 2-4pm.

Duns
Jim Clark Room
44 Newtown Street
☎ 0361 82600
Open: Easter to end October, Monday
to Saturday 10am-1pm and 2pm-5pm.
Sundays 2-5pm.

Crumstane Farm Park
Berwicksshire
Open: 10am-6pm daily (except Tuesday)
from Good Friday to end September.

Edin's Hall Broch
Abbey Street
St Bathans
Open: any reasonable time.

Edrom Church
Edrom
Open: any reasonable time.

Manderston House
☎ 0361 83450
Open: Thursdays and Sundays, early
May to end September, 2-5.30pm.

Eyemouth
Craigholm Studio
Reston
Nr Eyemouth
☎ 08907 61627
Open: all year Monday to Saturday
10am-7pm, Sundays 1-7pm.

Eyemouth Museum
Auld Kirk
Market Place
☎ 08907 50678
Open: April to September, Monday to
Saturday, 10am-5pm. October,
Monday to Saturday, 10am-4pm. Open
Sundays in July and August from 1-
5.30pm and in September from 2-4pm.

Galashiels
Abbotsford House
☎ 0896 2043
Open: late March to end October.
Monday to Saturday 10am-5pm.
Sunday 2-5pm.

Old Gala House
☎ 0750 20096
Open: mid-March to end October.
Monday to Saturday 10am-4pm. For
winter openings telephone to enquire.

Peter Anderson Mill
Hudddersfield St
☎ 0896 2091
Open: all year, Monday to Saturday,
9am-5pm. Open Sundays 12noon-5pm
from June to September. Tours (40
minutes), all year, Monday to Friday,
10.30am, 11.30am, 1.30pm, 2.30pm
(excluding Friday afternoons).

Hawick
Hawick Museum and Scott Gallery
Wilton Lodge Park
☎ 0450 73457
Open: April to September, Monday to
Saturday 10am-12noon and 1-5pm.
Sunday 2-4pm. October to March,
Monday to Friday 1-4pm, Sunday
2-4pm. Closed Saturday. Small
admission charge, locals free.

Wrights of Trowmill Limited
Trowmill
☎ 0450 72555
Mill tours organised all year.

Innerleithen
Robert Smail's Printing Works
7/9 High Street
Tweedale
Borders
☎ 0896 830206
Open: April to October inclusive,
Monday to Saturday 10am-1pm and 2-
5pm. Sundays 2-5pm only. Last tour is
1 hour before closing.

*St Ronan's Wells Interpretative Centre
    and Fitness Centre*
Innerleithen
☎ 0721 20123/0896 830660
Interpretative Centre
Open: Easter to October, daily 2-5pm.
Fitness Centre open daily.

Jedburgh
Mary Queen of Scots' House
Queen Street
☎ 0835 63331
Open: daily from easter to mid-
November, 10am-5pm.

Castle Jail
Castlegate
☎ 0835 63254
Open: Easter to end September.
Monday to Saturday 10am-5pm,
Sunday 1-5pm.

Kelso
Floors Castle
☎ 0573 223333
Open: Easter weekend, late April,
Sunday to Thursday weekly from
10.30am-4.45pm. Open daily July to
August. Opening restricted to Sunday
and Wednesday in October, from
10.30am-4pm.

The Hirsel Homestead Museum
☎ 0890 2834
Open: all year during reasonable
daylight hours.

Kelso Abbey
Open: April to September, Monday to
Saturday 9.30am-7pm, Sunday 2-7pm.
October to March, Monday to Saturday
9.30am-4pm, Sunday 2-4pm.

Kelso Museum
Turret House
Abbey Court
☎ 0573 223464
Open: Easter to end October, Monday
to Saturday 10am-12noon and 1-5pm.
Sunday open 2-5pm.

Kelso Pottery
The Knowes
☎ 0573 224027
Open: all year, Monday to Saturday,
10am-1pm and 2-5pm.

Smailholm Tower
Open: April to September, Monday to
Saturday, 9.30am-6.30pm, Sundays 2-
6.30pm.

Teviot Water Gardens
Teviot Smokery
Kirkbank House
☎ 08355 253
Open: March to October, Monday to
Saturday, 10am-4.30pm mid-April to
mid-September, Sundays, 11am-4pm.

Lauder
Thirlestane Castle
☎ 05782 430
Open: Easter week, May, June,
September, Sunday, Wednesday,
Thursday and July and August daily
except Saturday. Castle 2-5pm (last
admission 4.30pm), grounds open from
12noon.

Melrose
Melrose Abbey
☎ 089682 2562
Open: all year, daily.

Melrose Motor Museum
Annaay Road
☎ 089682 2624
Open: daily, Easter to October.

Priorwood Gardens
☎ 089682 2965
Open: Easter to December, daily, but
closed Sundays in 'low season'.

Teddy Melrose — Scotland's Teddybear Museum
The High Street
☎ 089682 2464
Open: all year Monday to Saturday, 10am-5pm. Open Sundays, 2-5pm, from April to October.

The Trimontium Exhibition
Ormiston Institute
The Square
☎ 089682 2463
Open: April to end October, 10am-12.30pm, 2-4.30pm daily.

Paxton
Paxton House
☎ 0289 86291
Open: Easter to end October, daily, 12noon-5pm. Tearoom opens 10am.

Peebles
The Cornice Museum of Ornamental Plasterwork
31 High Street
☎ 0721 20212
Open: April, June, September, Friday to Monday, 2-4pm. Saturdays only 10.30am-12.30pm. May, Saturday to Monday, 2-4pm. July and August, daily, 2-5pm and Saturday only 10.30am-12.30pm. October, weekends, 2-4pm.

Cross Kirk
Open: April to September, Monday to Saturday 9.30am-7pm, Sunday 2-7pm. October to March, Monday to Saturday, 9.30am-4pm, Sunday 2-4pm.

Kailzie Gardens
☎ 0721 20007
Open: Easter to October, daily, 11am-5.30pm.

Neidpath Castle
☎ 0721 20333
Open: Easter to end September. Monday to Saturday, 11am-5pm, Sunday 1-5pm.

Tweedale Museum
Chambers Institute
High Street
☎ 0721 20123 Open: All year, Monday to Friday, 10am-1pm, 2pm-5pm. Easter to October, weekends, 2pm-5pm.

Reston
Craigholme Studio and Stable Gallery
☎ 08907 61627
Open: all year, Monday to Saturday, 10am-7pm. Sundays 1-7pm.

St Abbs
Kittiwake Gallery
1 The Steading
☎ 08907 71504
Open: February to Easter, Friday to Monday, 12noon-4pm. Easter to October daily, 10am-6pm.

St Abbs Head Nature Reserve
☎ 08907 71443
Open: all year.

Selkirk
Bowhill House and Country Park
Near Selkirk
☎ 0750 207332
Park Open: May to end September daily except Friday from 12noon-5pm. House and Park open in July 1-4.30pm daily.

R Clapperton's Daylight Photographic Studio
The Studio
28 Shotts Place
☎ 0750 20523
Open: April to October, weekends only, 2-4.30pm. Other times by appointment.

Selkirk Glass Visitor Centre
Selkirk TD7 5EF
☎ 0750 20954
Open: Monday to Friday 9am-5pm (glass-making until 4.30pm). Saturday 10am-4.30pm, Sunday 12noon-4pm. No glass making at weekends.

Skirling
Douglas Davis Pottery
☎ 08996 254
Open: Monday to Saturday, 10am-dusk, occasionally closed Tuesdays.

St Boswells
Mertoun Gardens
☎ 0835 23236
Open: April to September, Saturday and Sunday and Monday Public Holidays 2-6pm.

Teviothead
Museum of Border Arms and Armour
Henderson's Knowe
☎ 045085 237
Open: April to September, 9am-7pm
daily. Open most days in March also.

Town Yetholm
Stable Gallery
Back Lane
☎ 057382 742
Open: June to September, Tuesday to
Sunday, 10am-5pm.

Traquair
Traquair Gallery
☎ 0896 830361
Open: 2-6pm during exhibitions, phone
to see if exhibition is on.

Traquair House
☎ 0896 830323
House open: Easter Sunday, May Day;
then Whitsun to end September, daily
1.30-5pm. July and August open daily
10.30am-5.30pm. Gardens open: daily
Easter to end September, 10.30am-
5.30pm.

Tweedhopefoot
Tweedhopefoot Sheepdog Centre
☎ 08997 267
Open: April to October, Sunday to
Friday. Demonstrations at 11am, 2pm
and 3.30pm.

Walkerburn
Scottish Museum of Woollen Textiles
☎ 089 687 281
Open: all year Monday to Saturday,
9am-5.30pm also April to November,
Sunday 11am-5pm.

Tourist Information Offices
The main office of the Scottish Borders
Tourist Board is at:
Selkirk
70 High Street
Selkirk
TD7 4DD
☎ 0750 20555

LOCAL OFFICES
Coldstream
Henderson Park
☎ 0890 882607
Open: April to October.

Eyemouth
Auld Kirk
☎ 08907 50678
Open: April to October.

Galashiels
Bank Street
☎ 0896 55551
Open: April to October.

Hawick
Common Haugh
☎ 0450 72547
Open: April to October.

Jedburgh
Murray's Green
☎ 0835 863435/863688

Kelso
The Square
☎ 0573 223464
Open: April to October.

Melrose
Priorwood Gardens
☎ 089682 2555
Open: April to October.

Peebles
High Street
EH45 8AG
☎ 0721 20138
Open: April to October.

Selkirk
Halliwell's House
☎ 0750 20054
Open: April to October.

HALF DAY CLOSING
Tuesday: Hawick, Innerleithen
Wednesday: Duns, Eyemouth,
Galashiels, Kelso, Peebles
Thursday: Coldstream, Jedburgh,
Lauder, Melrose, Selkirk

2 • The South-West
Dumfries and Galloway

Scotland's Western Border region is largely bypassed by main roads heading to Ayr and the Central Belt in the north, Carlisle in the south. Its geography is the reason for the lack of through traffic, there being no great economic reason for many people suddenly to veer west off the north-south route into Scotland's large south-west corner. Catching the Stranraer ferry is one exception perhaps. But the same geography has blessed this undiscovered country with a south facing coast denied most of the rest of Scotland, with hills and forests in the interior sheltering the region from northerly winds. Instead, southerly breezes blow in off the sea, resulting in a mild, generally frost-free climate and thus some of the best gardens and beaches in Scotland. The climate has clearly been popular through history as there are numerous antiquities to be found, particularly early Christian relics.

The variety of things to see in Dumfries and Galloway is probably unsurpassed. Lovers of the unusual will find, in addition to the local beauties, that Britain's ostrich farming was started here, Western Europe's largest Tibetan temple is here and that there is a large 200-year-old man-made tidal rock pool where the cod like to feed out of your hand. Record watchers will also find plenty to interest them: the world's oldest post office; Britain's shortest village name; Scotland's highest village (surprisingly); Scotland's oldest Christian settlement and the world's oldest savings bank.

As with the Borders, Dumfriesshire is a place much passed through, less frequently visited. The main road through it is the A74 from Carlisle to Glasgow: a dual carriageway currently in the process of being upgraded to motorway, a process which will continue for several years yet.

Most visits to the region will begin with a discreet hop across the border near **Gretna Green**, famous the world over for its marriages of eloping young lovers. This curiosity came about as brides could marry with one witness and without prior notice in Scotland. The

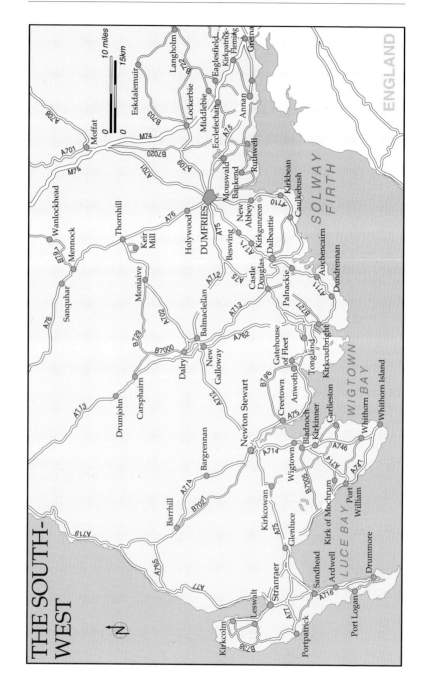

THE SOUTH-WEST

law was changed to stop this in 1940 but elopers aged 16 to 18 still take advantage of Scottish law which does not require the parental permission that is needed in England.

The main attraction of the town is therefore the Old Blacksmith's Shop Visitor Centre which contains an anvil over which marriages were performed and also has a coach museum and large cafeteria. The shop was built around 1712 and the blacksmiths traditionally performed ceremonies at any time of the day or night, upon demand, often with the couple's pursuers hot on their heels. When the latter arrived after the ceremony, the blacksmith would vehemently deny ever having seen the couple he had just married! One of the most famous of the 'Anvil Priests' at Gretna Green was Richard Rennison, who performed over 5,000 wedding ceremonies in the shop. Marriages also used to take place at the old toll bar (more than 10,000), now marketed as Scotland's First House on the road through Gretna, bypassed by the motorway. Gretna's Registry Office is still the second busiest in Scotland, performing 3,500 marriage ceremonies annually.

Gretna and Gretna Green are closely linked neighbours. The former is located on the B721, just south of the A75 running towards Dumfries. There is a museum of childhood here, Alice's Wonderland, containing over 1,000 dolls, dating back to the eighteenth century and up to the present day. Gretna is also the start of a National Tourist Route to Ayr, indicated by a brown thistle symbol on a white background.

Most of the land east of the A/M74 is rural, rising into hill country and quickly entering the Borders district. The B6357 running towards Newcastleton in the Borders passes first through the village of **Canonbie**. Two miles (3km) south of here is the remains of **Scot's Dyke**, a wall made of clods of earth and stones which marked part of the border between England and Scotland. Less well known than the Roman constructions, this dates to the sixteenth century and a time when feuds raged over possession of these 'debatable lands'.

North of Canonbie on the A7 and dating from the same period, is **Gilnockie Tower**, also known as the 'Holehouse'. It has walls 6ft (2m) thick but can only be viewed from outside. It was once home to Johnie Armstrong, hanged without trial by James V of Scotland but regarded by many as a local Robin Hood.

Five miles (8km) further the A7 reaches **Langholm**, a more typically Borders region town than a Dumfriesshire one. The town's most famous son, Hugh McDiarmid 'poet, lover of Scotland and founder of the Scottish National Party', is commemorated by a giant

The Galloway hills

metallic 'open book' on a hillside near the town. Langholm also has strong connections with the sport of rugby and with the famous engineer Thomas Telford. Examples of his work are to be found around Langholm and a memorial to him is located 6 miles (10km) north-west of the town on the B709 at **Westerkirk** in the tiny hamlet of Bentpath. He was born in the valley of Meggat Water in 1757. In and around Langholm there are walks by the Esk river and hill walks by Wauchope and Ewes Water. Deans Bank was a particular favourite of Benjamin Disraeli.

The B709 follows the River Esk to **Eskdalemuir** itself, a pleasant village with two interesting connections. Firstly, a century ago in the neighbouring Castle O'er forest, Richard Bell became Britain's first ostrich farmer. Secondly, just north of the village, the Tibetan Buddhist Centre of Samye Ling is located! It is the largest in Western Europe, opened in 1988. Visitors are welcome and may be pleasantly surprised by the oriental building in this district of sheep farms and woodland. Samye Ling was visited by the Dalai Lama in 1993.

The A75 is the main road west from Gretna, but the more interesting route runs south to Annan, following the line of the Solway Firth; this is the B724 and you can stay on it all the way to Dumfries if you are not in a great hurry.

Annan, at the mouth of the Annan river and Annandale that reaches up beyond Moffat, is the third largest town in the region. It

Smailholm Tower, set on a rocky knoll, near Kelso (Chapter 1)

A winter scene on the Lowther Hills (Chapter 2)

A beam engine at Wanlockhead, the highest village in Scotland (Chapter 2)

owes its prosperity to the ship-building industry under John Nicholson & Co whose clippers once sailed the world. Sandstone from the local quarry has gone to Canada, Sweden and even a Sheikh's desert palace. It was also a smugglers haven, inspiring Robbie Burns to write *The De'ils awa wi' the Excisemen* when he was working in that capacity in the town. The town also marks the start of the Solway Coast Heritage Trail (details from Tourist Information Offices).

The B722 north-east from Annan heads back towards the A/M74. A mile (2km) from the town at **Kirtlebridge** is the Clydesdale Horse Centre, home of the Bandirran Clydesdales, famous in equine circles. The road continues to **Ecclefechan**, hometown of Thomas Carlyle, the famous Victorian historian, essayist, social reformer and visionary, born in 1795. He held strong if conservative views on the impact of industrialisation and secularisation in society and wrote famous works on Chartism, Oliver Cromwell (1845) and Frederick The Great (1861). His work on the French Revolution (1837) had its publication delayed when his friend John Stuart Mill accidentally burnt the first volume of the manuscript. The Arched House where he was born, son of a local mason, is now a museum dedicated to his memory.

Three miles (5km) north of Ecclefechan is **Burnswark**, an earthwork constructed by the local people in the sixth century (as opposed to the usual story of invaders throwing up their own defences). Two Roman camps from the second century AD are also located in the vicinity. There is a pleasant walk to the top, from where there is an excellent view over to the Cumbrian hills (no doubt why it was constructed!). **Eaglesfield** to the south of Ecclefechan contains Kirkconnel Church where two lovers are buried, their tale immortalised in the Border ballad, *Helen of Kirkconnel.*

Moffat sits close to the border with the Borders region (see Chapter 1). Important for the wool trade and once a popular spa town it has remained a pleasant place to visit, winning numerous 'best kept village' awards and the like in recent years. The town's floral displays, boating lake and immaculately cared for greenery of the Station Park bear testimony to these achievements.

The woollens industry is commemorated by the Moffat Ram monument which overlooks the high street, gifted to the town in 1875 by William Colvin as a watering place for travellers and their animals. The wool trade connections are maintained with the annual installation of the Shepherd and His Lass in Gala week. Shepherds crooks are still made locally and those just wanting to buy the finished product will be spoilt for choice with the mill and tweed shops. Toffee lovers will enjoy the famous Moffat Toffee made here.

There is also a local museum which traces the area's history.

There are several famous beauty spots in the area including the Devil's Beef Tub (or Punch Bowl), a great hollow carved out of the local hills (beware of steep sides) which were used by cattle thieves to hide their stolen herds. The waterfall known as the Grey Mare's Tail and St Mary's Loch are close by. North of the town the hill of Hartfell climbs to 2,651ft (808m). It is claimed to have been the seat of Merlin.

North-west of Annan the B723 follows the River Annan to **Lockerbie**, a town with sad notoriety after the Pan Am 747 jet crashed down on it following a terrorist bomb in the late 1980s. Although the impression from the resulting news reports may have been of a small village, Lockerbie is in fact a mid-sized town which has been the Annandale district's leading agricultural centre since the eighteenth century, and a regular livestock market is held here weekly. Once a Border stronghold of the Johnstone clan, the town lost its frontier feel to some extent only in the 1960s when it was thankfully bypassed by the A74.

Lochmaben, east of Lockerbie, contains the ruins of a fourteenth-century castle said to be built on the site of an earlier castle home of the de Brus family. These were ancestors of the great Robert the Bruce, said to have been born here. Situated on an island in a lonely loch the castle was captured and re-captured twelve times and then withstood a further six attacks and sieges. James IV was a frequent visitor and Mary Queen of Scots came here in 1565 during a rare period of good fortune, after her second marriage. There are four other lochs in the area, castle loch to the north is famous for its coarse fishing and both it and neighbouring Hightae are wildfowl nature reserves. The village of **Hightae** is one of the local 'Royal Four Towns' (along with neighbouring Heck, Greenhill and Smallholm) whose 'kindly tenants' hold land direct from the Crown and have free fishing rights. **Mossburn** Animal Centre is also located in the area containing a wide variety of animals from ponies to pot bellied pigs.

Continuing west from Annan on the B724, **Ruthwell** appears after a few miles. The church here contains the Ruthwell Cross, a spectacular monument from the Dark Ages standing 18ft (5m) high and carved with runic characters. It dates back to the eighth century. The village also contains the oldest savings bank, founded by the good Rev Dr Henry Duncan in 1810. A museum dedicated to the savings bank movement is now located therein.

A mile (2km) west of Ruthwell is **Brow Well**, an ancient mineral well which has had a new lease of life ever since Robert Burns visited

Grey Mare's Tail waterfall near the town of Moffat

it in 1796 on his doctor's orders although, sadly for Burns, his illness soon proved fatal. On the coast the seaside village of **Powfoot** contains red brick homes and is popular with visitors. The local 18 hole golf course and bird watching opportunities are principal attractions.

As the road bends northwards for Dumfries it passes the 1,400 acre (560 hectare) **Caerlaverock Wildfowl and Wetlands Trust,** winter home to over 12,000 barnacle geese flying in from Spitsbergen and hundreds of other wildfowl. There are four viewing towers and a heated observatory. Caerlaverock Castle is most people's idea of a medieval castle and has been featured in television advertisements for Historic Scotland. Further north the village of **Collin** is worth a visit if only to sample the home made ice-cream created at Drummuir Farm at a purpose built facility using the milk from their own herd of dairy cattle.

Dumfries on the Nith river is an ancient burgh and now the region's 'county town' It is an important commercial centre with good shopping facilities and provides a pleasant mix of old and new for the visitor.

The town is bursting with museums, mostly with Robert Burns connections. Robert Burns spent his last years here and his home is

The medieval Caerlaverock Castle

now a Burns Museum. This is not to be confused with the Robert Burns Centre and Film Theatre located in the town's attractive old mill house on the river. The Burns Centre shows relevant videos, and has a pleasant bookstall (with much Burns and other local material). The small, comfortable cinema has a year-round programme of current films interspersed with classics. The Burns family mausoleum is located in the churchyard of St Michael's. Dumfries Museum is the largest in the region and houses a fascinating camera obscura, situated in the windmill tower overlooking the town. On the table top screen you will see a panoramic view of Dumfries.

The Old Bridge House Museum is in the town's oldest house (1660), set in to Devorgilla's Bridge (Scotland's oldest surviving multiple arch bridge). The Crichton Royal Museum situated in the hospital has an interesting display of hospital enterprise, including patients' artistic work, over the past two centuries. Finally the Dumfries and Galloway Aviation Museum is the only one of its kind in Scotland. There is even the opportunity here to squeeze into a jet fighter! In addition to the museums there is a gallery containing over 400 Scottish paintings and regular exhibitions of contemporary art in the Gracefield Arts Centre.

Routes depart in all directions from Dumfries. The A701 northeast towards Moffat passes The Barony 8 miles (13km) from town.

This is a farm estate containing prepared walks, nature reserve, bird hide and a well stocked trout lake.

Between the A701 and the A76, north of Dumfries, is the 17,500 acre (7,000 hectare) **Ae Forest**; this is a working forest consisting mainly of spruce trees planted in the 1950s and now ripe for timber production. Spruce trees planted on this 'quality' of land tend to reach maximum height 65ft (20m) by the time they are 40 and are frequently blown over by the wind soon afterwards. In common with many Forestry Commission properties however, there is now a welcome opening up of the forest to visitors, with waymarked trails and mountain bike routes. The new attitude extends beyond receiving visitors: tree-planting is now organised to encourage the return of wildlife and improve the forest environment, another welcome change from the old method of putting trees so close together that not even grass could grow in the narrow needle-covered area between them.

As it is however, there is already a wide variety of birds around the Ae Forest area, everything from siskins and cross-bills to birds of prey such as kestrels, buzzards, sparrowhawks, goshawks and merlins. The unclassified road to the forest car park from which the walks depart starts from the village of **Ae**. The origin of the name Ae is not known, but it has made it into the *Guinness Book of Records* as the shortest village name in Britain! Further northwards on the A76 the road soon passes the remains of **Lincluden Collegiate Church** 1½ miles (2km) from Dumfries. This dates from the early fifteenth century and was built by the Duke of Tourain.

Ellisland Farm, 5 miles (8km) further on the A76, is another place of pilgrimage for Burns lovers. The poet took over the farm in June 1788, built the farmhouse and tried to introduce new farming methods. Fifteen months later he admitted defeat and became an Exciseman, moving to Dumfries in 1791. However, some of his most famous works were written here, including *Auld Lang Syne* of 'New Years Eve' fame around the Western world, and *Tam o'Shanter*. The Granary houses a display showing Burns as a farmer. There is also a walk alongside the Nith River.

The A702, which reaches the sea as a major trunk road in Edinburgh, is a lesser kind of A road when it crosses the A76 between Thornhill and Carronbridge. The left turning at Thornhill on to the A702 should be taken to reach Maxwelton House near **Moniaive** (also accessed more directly on the B729 from Dumfries which in turn crosses the 702). Originally the stronghold of the Earls of Glencairn the house dates back to the fourteenth and fifteenth centuries. In 1682 it saw the birth of Annie Laurie who appears in a famous Scottish ballad. The house has been totally renovated (to award winning standard) by Hugh Stenhouse, who died in 1970. There is a museum and a chapel. The gardens are famed for their daffodils in spring and for their vegetable garden and greenhouses filled with fuchsias and begonias in summer.

The A702 turning also takes you past **Keir Mill**, where, at Couthill Smithy, the world's first pedal bike was constructed by Kirkpatrick MacMillan in 1840. He is buried in the local church yard. One hundred and fifty years later, in 1990, to commemorate this important invention, a 93 mile (150km) cycle trail was established from Keir Mill to Dumfries.

Three miles (5km) north of Thornhill is spectacular **Drumlanrig Castle**, the 300-year-old home of the Dukes of Buccleuch and Queensberry. This is a unique and magnificent example of late seventeenth-century Renaissance architecture, built in pink sandstone on the site of earlier Douglas strongholds. The building is perfectly set in wooded parkland framed by the barren Dumfriesshire hills rising behind. The house contains beautiful furnishings and an impressive art collection, which includes work by Leonardo da Vinci, Holbein and Rembrandt. Other features include two Louis XIV cabinets given by Charles II to his son the Duke of Monmouth and wife the Duchess of Buccleuch on their wedding. There is also a silver chandelier weighing 9 stone hanging above the great oak staircase. The grounds include a falconry centre, an adventure play area, working craft centre, visitor centre, tearoom, and gift shop. There are woodland walks by lochs, rare trees (including the UK's first Douglas Fir), a recently discovered Roman camp and the Nith river.

Nearby (1 mile/2km) from the A76) are the well preserved ruins of fourteenth-century **Morton Castle**, closed to the public but which may be viewed from outside. It was once occupied by Randolph, first Earl of Moray, as Regent for Scotland's king David II, but later passed to the Douglases.

The Dumfriesshire hills now begin to rise dramatically to decisively separate the Solway Firth from Scotland's Central Belt. The A702 to Edinburgh departs north-easterly, passing **Durisdeermill** before leaving Dumfries and Galloway shortly afterwards. The church here dates from 1699 and includes the elaborate Queensberry Aisle, commemorating the second Duke. The Well Path was part of a medieval pilgrimage route to Whithorn.

Back on the A76 and getting well into the hills we reach another right turning, this time the B797 to the Mennock Pass and to **Wanlockhead** in the picturesque Lowther Hills, on the border with the huge region of Strathclyde. This is the highest village in Scotland, surprising perhaps with the Scottish Highlands beginning a good 100 miles (161km) north of here. The village has a history of leadmining and the Museum Of The Scottish Lead Mining Industry is now located here, although the industry itself ceased in the 1950s after 250 years. Mine tours are organised and there is an early nineteenth-century beam engine. Wanlockhead hosted the World Goldpanning Championships in 1992. The gold in the Scottish Crown Jewels came from the Lowther Hills and goldpanning still takes place — nobody gets very rich though!

The A76 leaves the region near here too, although it is going north-west to Kilmarnock. At the Royal Burgh of **Sanquhar** you will find both the world's oldest Post Office, in use since 1738 (and still going strong). It pre-dates the mail coach service by 20 years. There is also a Tolbooth Museum here which examines the history of Upper Nithdale, the mining industry and Sanquhar knitting. Sanquhar and Wanlockhead are linked most directly by the Southern Upland Way which passes through both villages.

Just west of Dumfries, via Terregles, is the **Glenkiln Reservoir**, an area of splendid open views. But the unique surprise is created by large dramatic sculptures by Henry Moore, Jacob Epstein and Rodin, dotted about around the water and on the hillsides. Glenkiln may also be reached by taking the A75 and turning off for Shawhead.

The A75 trunk road continues west from Dumfries and on towards Castle Douglas. The A711 south-westerly to Dalbeattie would be the preferred option for those with rather more time to spare, as it skirts the north side of the forested hills of Solway. The most direct route is in fact the Old Military Road running through Lochfoot and Milton, between the two A roads. It is quiet and very scenic, and avoids the container lorries thundering to and from the Stranraer ferry.

The road now takes us into the historical region of the Stewartry of Kirkudbright (dating from when Kirkudbrightshire was a county), which follows the modern Dumfries and Galloway border in the north and ends before Newton Stewart in the west. Local history here is especially rich, with association with Robert the Bruce and Mary Queen of Scots; as well as numerous artistic residents and visitors including Sir Walter Scott, Robert Louis Stevenson, Dorothy L Sayers and Robert Burns.

Seven miles (11km) before Dalbeattie and 1 mile (2km) north of

Kirkgunzeon is the fortified sixteenth-century towerhouse of Drumcoltran with an adjacent eighteenth-century farmhouse. The A710 is one of the more interesting roads out of Dumfries, heading due south along the side of the River Nith estuary. **Mabie Forest**, a few miles along the road, contains five waymarked trails ranging from 1 to 4 miles (2 to 6km) in length. There is also an adventure trail for children (no dogs) and several more routes for mountain bikes. As with most Forestry Commission forests in Scotland it was planted quickly in 1943 with little regard to the natural environment. With the trees now mature the Commission is felling them, but replanting with a 50 year strategy to improve the environment, encouraging wildlife and leisure opportunities.

After 6 miles (10km) **New Abbey** appears where one of Scotland's National Museums is located. This one is in Shambellie House, a small Victorian country house designed by David Bryce and contains displays from the National Costume Collection, renewed annually.

Sweetheart Abbey nearby was founded in 1273 by local celebrity Devorgilla in memory of her husband John Balliol (she also founded Balliol College, Oxford). It was the last of Galloway's trio of Cistercian monasteries to be built, the others being Dundrennan and Glenluce. Although ruined, it is the most complete, the corn mill is worth a visit and there is an excellent tea shop.

Another 6 miles (10km) along the road, by **Kirkbean**, are the famous Arbigland Gardens where the even more famous Admiral John Paul Jones worked as a boy in the eighteenth century (his father was a gardener here). Built around a secluded sandy bay that is ideal for children, it is made up of part woodland, part formal and water gardens. A project costing a quarter of a million pounds has resulted in John Paul Jone's Cottage being opened as a visitor attraction.

As the road rounds the headland it reaches Colvend coast, one of the most attractive sections of coast in the region, including the lively harbour of **Kippford**. Nearby, there is the 20 acre (8 hectare) Rough Island bird sanctuary, only accessible at low tide, and an oak woodland at Southwick. The popular south facing Sandyhills Bay begins here and there are several golf courses close by. A path from the bay passes through **Portling** and **Port O' Warren** where former smugglers' caves can be seen at low tide. At **Rockcliffe** there is a hill fort, the Mote of Mark, which dates from the fifth century.

The road now bends northwards once more to Dalbeattie, where it meets the A711. The **Dalbeattie Forest** follows the right side of the road and there are prepared walks from a carpark just outside the town.

The A745 goes west to Castle Douglas, while the A711 now goes south and hugs the coast round to Kirkcudbright. Along this road is the fifteenth-century **Orchardton Towerhouse**, sited 1½ miles (2km) south of Palnackie. This is the only Scottish towerhouse built in the typical Irish cylindrical style. Seven miles (11km) from Kirkcudbright is **Dundrennan Abbey**. This is a Cistercian house, founded in 1142, where Mary Queen of Scots, stayed before departing for exile and imprisonment in England.

Castle Douglas is a pleasant market town that received its charter in 1791 when Sir William Douglas developed industries which ensured employment for the growing community. Settlement here goes back at least to Iron Age times however, mostly centred on the 100 acre (40 hectare) island-dotted Carlingwark Loch to the south of the town. Relics found on islands include a Roman cauldron, made of bronze and filled with swords and other blades, and a gold plated Roman dagger. A forge reputed to have been used by Edward 1 when he camped in the area around 1300 has also been found.

The present-day streets were laid out to a regular plan when the township charter was awarded, prior to that it had been known as 'Causewayend' and later 'Carlingwark'. Legend has it that part of the old settlement, including two churches, was swallowed up by a flood and never re-emerged from beneath the Carlingwark. This is rather unlikely of course but, in 1825 in a period of drought, it was reported that the tops of houses were visible in the loch. Even more unlikely is the claim that ghostly peels from the submerged church bells may be heard coming from beneath the waves on stormy nights!

Castle Douglas has modern sports facilities and many of the shops are still, family owned. There is a 3 mile (5km) town trail to follow and an art gallery to visit. The 1930s Palace Cinema is designed in Art Deco style, and is still operational, mainly showing popular films during the holiday season.

Threave Gardens, just west of the town (A75), are operated by the National Trust For Scotland and the private house in their midst is the training college for National Trust gardeners. The result is that the 60 acre (24 hectare) gardens often have unusual and interesting displays created by the enthusiastic trainees. Probably the garden's greatest claim to horticultural fame is the springtime daffodil display, containing more than 200 varieties. There is an adjacent wild-fowl refuge as well as an exhibition, shop, restaurant selling home baking, and plant sales.

Threave Castle, a little further on and located on an island in the River Dee, is a bleak square tower house dating back to the four-

Relaxing on the banks of Loch Ken

teenth century. Traditionally a stronghold of the Black Douglases, who counted 'Archibald the Grim' amongst their number, it was the last Douglas stronghold to surrender to James II in 1455. The tower house was built between 1639 and 1690. Ring the bell to summon the ferry man.

The main route north-west from Castle Douglas is the A713 running relatively straight to Ayr, following Loch Ken for some distance before climbing up into the part barren, part forested, Genkens high hill country.

Nine mile (14km) long **Loch Ken** is actually artificial, having been created through the Galloway Hydro Electric Scheme. It is nonetheless popular with water-sports lovers, fishermen and bird watchers, particularly as it includes an RSPB Reserve for wildfowl and waders. Beyond here there are occasional small villages dotted along the roadside. At **Carsphairn**, 25 miles (40km) north of Castle Douglas, there is a small rural Heritage Centre tracing local history.

On the far side of Loch Ken the huge **Galloway Forest Park** begins, one of Britain's largest forested areas covering nearly 300sq miles (778sq km) and extending well into Ayrshire. The A712 leads west into the heart of the forest. A second left turn takes the driver back south on the westerly side of Loch Ken on the A762 towards Kirkcudbright. A 'Raiders Road' goes for 10 miles (16km) through the forest from Bennan near the Clatteringshaws Dam. This old drove road featured in a nineteenth-century novel *The Raiders* by Samuel Rutherford Crockett. Open in the summer, with an entry fee per car, this is a delightful run between forest and water, with ample provision for parking, picnics and walks. A favourite spot, the Otter Pool, has a bronze otter sculpture. Further on, where the A762 crosses the B795 at **Laurieston**, is the Weather Watchers Network building, where the unique visitor centre gives you the opportunity to find out more about the weather.

Staying on the A712, or 'The Queens Road' as it is known in the area, there is a Forest Wildlife Centre at **Clatteringshaws**. The forest park contains many waymarked trails for all standards and there are opportunities for camping, fishing and cycling. Indigenous species include golden eagles, otters and pine martins. There is also a red deer range, with tours in the forest, and feral goats, which will often obligingly pose for photographers! Robert the Bruce began his attempt to preserve Scotland's independence from the armies of Edward I here and Bruce's Stone, 6 miles (10km) west of **New Galloway** records a victory over the English here in March 1307.

Taking the A712 easterly you will pass signposts for Blowplain Open Farm, where guided tours are arranged round the working farm. A mile (2km) before reaching Kircudbright, on the B727, there is a Wildlife Centre containing Scottish wild cats, fallow deer, arctic foxes, racoons, pigmy goats and others. There is also a pets corner.

Kirkcudbright is one of the major attractions in the region. It is a quietly charming Galloway town, ideally positioned for leisure in the centre of the Stewartry's Solway Coast, with pleasant seventeenth- and eighteenth-century streets. The colourful harbour is overlooked by the ruined MacLellan's Castle (built 1582 by the Provost, Thomas MacLellan, ruined 1752). This was a castellated mansion, elaborately planned, with fine architectural details. There is an adjoining ruined monastery.

The Stewartry Museum contains a fascinating collection of local artefacts and has an extensive natural history collection. The Tolbooth is one of the earliest surviving in Scotland. Dating from 1629 it includes a prison and 'Jougs' where offenders were publicly humiliated. The Tolbooth has been thoroughly restored and the Arts Centre

was opened by Her Majesty the Queen in July 1993: this comple-
ments the Harbour Cottage Art Gallery in a restored building by the
harbour. Kirkudbright's artistic associations go back a long way, and
there is a famed artists' colony. Broughton House, the home of E.A
Homel, one of the 'Glasgow Boys', renowned in artistic circles, is
open to visitors and includes examples of his own work and that of
Jessie M King and Charles Oppenheimer. There is also a Japanese
styled garden.

Three miles (5km) west along the coast is **Dhoon Bay**, sheltered
and safe, with a sandy beach and large grassed area for parking and
picnics. At **Tongland**, a tour of the hydro-power station demon-
strates how modern technology can blend with the local environment. In the neighbouring Barhill Forest there are three waymarked
walks of varying lengths, each giving good views of Kirkcudbright.
Beyond the power station, going towards the A75, is a good place for
spotting 'Belties', the local name for Belted Black Galloway cattle,
peculiar to this area. They resemble the more familiar black Galloways,
but have a broad white stripe round the middle of their bodies. There
is a herd at Park of Tongland, and they also frequently pop up on
postcards, mugs and other holiday souvenirs.

The A755 and the more southerly B727 both join the A75 to follow
the east shore of Wigtown Bay up to Gatehouse of Fleet. To the south
of the town are the **Fleet Oak** woods which contain forest trails. The
Fleet Oakwoods Interpretative Trail is of 2 miles (3km) long and the
Murray Forest Information Centre provides information on this and
forest wildlife.

Gatehouse of Fleet itself is a pleasant town with many buildings
dating from the eighteenth century when it was a planned town.
Fortunately there are few if any unsightly modern developments to
spoil it. Ten thousand acres (4,000 hectares) of land around the town
are protected from development by National Trust Conservation
agreements. The town's origins lie in the cotton trade which once
flourished in the area, but tourism and agriculture are the main local
industries now; most of the old mills and factories are gone. Robbie
Burns is credited with writing *Scots Wha Hae* in the Murray Arms
Hotel in the town in July 1773. Much of the town's local history is
recorded within the Mill on the Fleet, a restored eighteenth-century
cotton mill complex on the river banks, now used as a museum. A
model of the town in its heyday is also on display in the Wee Toon
exhibition.

A mile (2km) south-west of Gatehouse of Fleet, on the A75 is
Cardoness Castle, a severe fifteenth-century towerhouse built by
the McCulloch family overlooking the River Fleet. It is four storeys

high with a vaulted basement. The original stairway, stone benches and fireplaces remain in place.

A little way further along the A75 a sign points off to the Skyreburn Aquarium where more than fifty species of underwater life are on display from sea, river and loch environments. There are then two ancient monuments in the few miles before Creetown. First is a sixteenth-century four-storeyed tower house at **Carsluith**; second, east of Carsluith is the **Cairnholy**, two impressive chambered cairns dating from about 2000BC. These have a slightly eerie appearance as the gaunt standing stones used to support the walls are still upright, while the wall material has disappeared to a large extent over the years. The smaller of the two tombs is known as the tomb of Galdus, a mythical Scottish king.

Creetown is a pleasant village at the top of Wigtown Bay, with several visitor attractions and a nice riverside park. The Gem Rock Museum, based on the private collection of the Stephenson and Dore families, contains a vast array of virtually every known gemstone and mineral, including large and impressive quartz and fluorite crystal displays. There are also many examples of the lapidaries art of working gemstone. Just outside Creetown is Barholm Mains Open Farm where children can feed and touch a wide variety of animals.

Palnure, 4 miles (6km) before Newton Stewart, contains the seventeenth-century Bargaly Gardens, where both plant lovers and salmon fishermen are welcome. There is a water garden, a walled garden and particularly good displays of daffodils and rhododendrons in season.

Newton Stewart is a bustling market town located at the westerly end of the A712 Queens Drive through the Galloway Forest Park. There is a local museum in the town tracing 200 years of local history. The A714 crosses the A75 in the town, the former running north-south and, starting at the coast in Luce Bay, runs alongside the Cree river on the westerly side of the Forest Park. Four miles (6km) north of Newton Stewart is the famous Wood of Cree, maintained by the RSPB. This is one of the finest areas of surviving native oak and birch woodland in Scotland.

The A714 continues to climb towards the border with Ayrshire and passes the last high hills before the west coast. **Glen Trool** is one of Scotland's most scenic spots containing a large part of the Galloway Forest Park and another 'Bruce's Stone' — this one more spectacular, commemorating Robert the Bruce's first victory over the English. There is a 4½ mile (7km) walk around Loch Trool and a hill climb up the Merrick (2,764ft/843m), southern Scotland's highest hill. Forest Enterprise operates a visitors centre and a cycle track

Bruce's Stone at Glen Trool, one of Scotland's most scenic spots

in the area. Nearby is Palgowan Open Farm, a working farm of 7,000 acres (2,800 hectares), where there are demonstrations of dry-stone walling and 'stick making'.

South of Newton Stewart the A714 enters The Machars, the peninsula between the bays of Wigtown and Luce, an area of largely flat farmland. This area, in common with much of southern Scotland, is associated with the seventeenth-century Covenanters. These were people who, among other convictions, refused to accept the new Prayer Book and rule by bishops. They feared that the Restoration of the Monarchy might even lead to the reintroduction of Roman Catholicism. The suppression of the various uprisings were characteristically harsh. On a hill above Wigtown Bay, a monument commemorates the martyrdom of two women in 1685, drowned for their religious beliefs, during this period of persecution known as 'The Killing Times'.

A mile south of Wigtown at **Bladnoch** is Scotland's most southerly distillery. Built in 1814, the original buildings are around a central courtyard. The B733 heads inland from here, and passes the Torhouse Stone Circle, a circle of nineteen boulders standing on the edge of a low mound. The central stones were also known locally as 'King Galdus' Tomb' in the seventeenth century.

South of Bladnoch the B7004 follows the Wigtown Bay coast to **Garlieston**. Galloway House Gardens are situated here, covering some 30 acres (12 hectares) and going down to the sea and sandy beach. There are many fine old trees, and in season displays of snowdrops, traditional daffodils and a collection of rhododendrons and azaleas. You will also find a camellia house and walled garden. Galloway House was built in 1740 by Lord Garlies, eldest son of the seventh Earl of Galloway, but is not open to the public.

South of this, at **Whithorn**, is the world famous Whithorn Dig and visitor centre. Here archaeologists work throughout the summer season at the site of Scotland's first recorded Christian community. Remains of a Norse settlement and early Christian buildings, dating as far back as the fifth century, are being excavated. The visitors centre contains a display on the life of St Ninian. It was he who founded Scotland's first Christian church, in the late fifth century, at the site of nearby Whithorn Priory. The current priory ruins date from the twelfth century and has strong associations with the Scottish Royal Family. Mary Queen of Scots stayed here on 10 August, 1563. There is a museum which contains early Christian crosses, some carved in the rock. Three miles (5km) south of Whithorn is St Ninian's Cave which contains some eighth-century carvings.

The peninsular rounded, the road (A747) now runs relatively straight and direct for Stranraer up the east coast of Luce Bay. Eight miles (13km) from Whithorn the remains of an Iron Age fort can be seen on a beach area 70ft (21m) above the shore. It is enclosed by a ditch some 12ft (4m) deep and 35ft (11m) wide. Five miles (8km) past Port William, further along the road, is the remains of Chapel Finian, probably named after St Finian who studied at Whithorn. Some low walls remain on a long raised beach.

At the top of Luce Bay we once more meet the A75 trunk road and arrive at historic **Glenluce**. The ruined abbey, 2 miles (3km) north of the town, was founded in 1192 by Roland, Earl of Galloway, for the Cistercian order. A fine vaulted chapter house remains impressive today. Glenluce also has a Motor Museum featuring vintage and classic motor cars and bikes, as well as general motoring memorabilia. The imposing castellated mansion by the town is the Castle of Park, built by Thomas Hay in 1590 and still intact.

The choice for the driver now is whether to reach Scotland's south-westerly corner or take the A77 coast road north in to Ayrshire. There are three different gardens to visit in the area, all off the A75, at Castle Kennedy, Glenwhan and Soulseat. The **Castle Kennedy Gardens** are famous in Scotland, beautifully landscaped across 75 acres (30 hectares) and set on a peninsular between two lochs. There is an old and magnificent 'Monkey Puzzle avenue', one of the longest in

Scotland. The ruined Castle Kennedy, which was known to have been standing in 1482, was burned down in 1716 while home to the second Earl of Stair. The present Earl and family live in Lochinch Castle, built in 1867.

By contrast **Glenwhan Gardens** is a unique hilltop garden begun unusually recently in 1979. It takes advantage of the Gulf Stream to grow Mediterranean plants and there are excellent views from the gardens over Luce Bay. The Meadowsweet Herb Garden is located on the site of an old abbey on a tongue of land in Soulseat loch. Over a hundred herbs are grown here for medicinal and culinary uses.

The A75 reaches its end at Stranraer. The hammer-head peninsula of which the town is the main centre is known as the Rinns of Galloway. Much of the local scenery is agricultural, but there are some wonderful beaches, notably Maryport Bay in the far south, as well as cliffs teeming with sea birds.

Stranraer is a busy agricultural and commercial centre with good shopping facilities. This is a familiar town for many who have made the short ferry trip from there across to Larne in Ireland. There is now an even shorter crossing on a giant catamaran. In the town centre the castle, a complete tower house, dates from 1500. It is now a heritage centre (Castle of St John Visitor Centre) devoted to law and order through the centuries. It was once the town jail, so the displays are appropriate enough. A second museum on George Street details local history and has an information point from which details of the local town trail may be obtained.

The A77 then A716 running south from Stranraer reaches the coast at the wonderful beach of **Sandhead**. Two miles (3km) south-west are the fifth-century Kirkmadrine Stones, the second earliest Christian memorials in Scotland after those at Whithorn. Further south is **Ardwell** where there are popular gardens famous for daffodils, rhododendrons or fruit picking according to the season.

Staying on the A77 westerly the road reaches the coast at **Portpatrick**, a cliff-sheltered seaside village. The 'Little Wheels' exhibition here has appeared on television travel shows — a display of toys, dolls and miniature transport, including an excellent model railway. Half a mile (1km) south of the village is Dunskey Castle, dating from the sixteenth century, now ruined but still looking rather impressive perched on the cliff top.

In common with much of Dumfries and Galloway the area benefits from the mild south-westerly influence of the Gulf Stream. Evidence of this is provided at Logan Botanic Garden, an off-shoot of the Edinburgh Royal Garden, near **Port Logan** on the B7065, 16

Castle Kennedy

miles (26km) south of Stranraer. Many species indigenous to the southern hemisphere flourish here including ferns and exotic cabbage plants.

Nearby, a tidal pool in the rocks, 30ft (9m) deep and 53ft (16m) round, was completed in 1800 as a fresh fish larder for Logan House. It was damaged by a war-time mine in the early 1940s but was reopened in 1955. It can hold around thirty sea fish, mostly cod, tame enough to be hand fed!

The village of **Kirkmaiden** of the A716 south has a visitor centre with information on the local area open in the summer. Local attractions include the Mull of Galloway with cliffs and beaches, Scotland's most southerly point less than 25 miles (40km) from both Ireland and the Isle of Man. There are the remains of a prehistoric fortification, a bird sanctuary, lighthouse (1830) and magnificent views of Ireland, Cumbria and the Isle of Man on a clear day!

Further Information
— The South-West —

Places to Visit

A good source of information is *The Galloway News*, published Thursdays.

Ardwell
Ardwell House Gardens
Open: March to October, daily 10am-6pm.

Bladnoch
Bladnoch Distillery
☎ 09884 2235
Open: March to October, Monday to Friday, 10am-4pm.

Caerlaverock
Caerlaverock Wildfowl & Wetlands Trust
☎ 038777 200
Open: all year, except Xmas & Xmas Eve, daily 10am-5pm.

Carsphairn
Carsphairn Heritage Centre
Open: April to October.

Castle Douglas
Threave Castle
☎ 031 244 3101
Open April to September inclusive.
Monday to Saturday, 9.30am-6.30pm, Sunday 2-4.30pm.

Threave Gardens
☎ 0556 2575
Open: all year, daily 9am-sunset. Other facilities open April to October inclusive, 9am-5.30pm (restaurant 10am-5pm).

Clatteringshaws
Clatteringshaws Forest Wildlife Centre
☎ 06442 285
Open: April to September, daily 10am-5pm.

Collin
Drummuir Farm
☎ 038775 599
Open: Easter to September, Tuesday to Sunday 11am-6pm. October to Easter, Friday 12noon-5pm, weekends 11am-5pm.

Creetown
Barholm Mains Open Farm
☎ 067182 346
Open: May to September, daily 10.30am-4pm.

Gem Rock Museum
☎ 067182 337
Open: March to Easter, daily 10am-4pm. Easter to October, daily 9.30am-6pm, November to December, weekends only 10am-4pm.

Skyreburn Aquarium
☎ 067182 204
Open: April to June and September to October, Sunday to Friday 10am-5pm. July and August, daily 10am-5.30pm.

Dumfries
Burns House
Burns Street
☎ 0387 55297
Open: all year, Monday to Saturday, 10am-1pm, 2-5pm; Sundays (April to September), 2-5pm. Closed Sunday and Monday from October to March.

The Barony
College hours: 9-4.30pm all year
☎ 0387 86251

Crichton Royal Museum
Easterbrook Hall
Crichton Hospital
☎ 0387 55301 ext. 2360
Open: all year, Thursday and Friday 1.30-4.30pm. Also open Saturdays Easter to October, or by appointment.

Dumfries and Galloway Aviation Museum
☎ 0387 710491 (office hours)
☎ 0387 59546 (evenings)
Open: Easter to end October, weekends 10am-5pm or by arrangement.

Dumfries Museum and Camera Obscura
The Observatory
☎ 0387 53374
Open: all year, Monday to Saturday 10am-1pm and 2-5pm. Sunday 2-5pm (except October to March when closed Sunday and Monday).

Ellisland Farm
☎ 0387 74426
Open: all year at 'all reasonable times'
but intending visitors are asked to
phone in advance.

Gracefield Arts Centre
☎ 0387 62084
Open: all year.

Lincluden Collegiate Church
☎ 031 244 3101
Open: all year. Summer: Monday to
Saturday 9.30am-6.30pm, Sundays 2-
6.30pm. Winter: Monday to Saturday
9.30am-4.30pm (except Thursday pm
and Fridays when closed). Sunday 2-
4.30pm.

The Old Bridge House Museum
Mill Road
☎ 0387 65904
Open: April to September, Monday to
Saturday 10am-1pm and 2-5pm.
Sundays 2-5pm.

The Robert Burns Centre and Film Theatre
Mill Road
☎ 0387 64808
Open: all year. April to September,
Monday to Saturday 10am-8pm,
Sundays 2-5pm. October to March,
Tuesday to Sunday 2-5pm.

Dundrennan
Dundrennan Abbey
☎ 031 244 3101
Open: summer only, Monday to Saturday 9.30am-6.30pm, Sundays 2-6.30pm.

Ecclefechan
Carlyle's Birthplace
☎ 05763 666
Open: April to October inclusive,
12noon-5pm daily.

Galloway Forest Park
☎ 0556 3626 or 0671 2420 or 06557 637

Garlieston
Galloway House Gardens
☎ 09886 680
Open: daily, March to October, 9am-5pm.

Gatehouse of Fleet
Cardoness Castle
☎ 031 244 3101
Open: summer, Monday to Saturday
9.30am-6.30pm; Sundays 2-6.30pm.
Winter closes 2 hours earlier, all days.

Mill On The Fleet
☎ 0557 814099
Open: April to October, daily 10am-5.30pm.

The Wee Toon
☎ 0557 814442
Open: daily 10am-6pm.

Glenluce
Glenluce Motor Museum
☎ 05813 534
Open: March to October daily 10am-
7pm. November to February, Wednesday to Sunday 11am-4pm.

Gretna
Alice's Wonderland
New House Farm
Annan Road
☎ 0461 37711
Open: all year, every day except
Tuesday 10am to 5pm. Opens an hour
later (11am) on Sundays.

Gretna Green
Old Blacksmith's Shop Visitor Centre
☎ 0461 38363 or 38224
Open: all year.

Kippford
Rough Island Bird Sanctuary
Dawn to dusk
☎ 0556 26111

Kirkbean
Arbigland Gardens
☎ 038788 283
Open: May to end September. Tuesday, Thursday, Sunday 2-6pm. House
opens Whit Week.

John Paul Jones Cottage
Open: April to September. Tuesday to
Saturday 10-5pm, Sunday 2-5pm. Also
Mondays July and August. Closed
daily 1-2pm.
☎ 038788 613

Kirkcudbright
Kirkcudbright Wildlife Centre
☎ 0557 31645
Open: April to October.

MacLellan's Castle
☎ 031 244 3101
Open: all year, weekends only from
October to March.

Stewartry Museum
St Mary Street
☎ 0557 31643
Open: Easter to October, Monday to
Saturday 11am-4pm. July and August
until 5pm.

Tolbooth Art Centre
☎ 0557 31643
Open: June to October.

Tongland Tour
☎ 0557 30114
Open: May to September.

Kirkmaiden
Information Centre
Open end May to end September,
Monday to Saturday 10am-4pm.

Kirtlebridge
The Clydesdale Horse Centre
☎ 046 15 459
Open: Easter to September inclusive,
daily 9.30am-5pm.

Langholm
Tibetan Buddhist Centre of Samye Ling
Open: most days — best time 1.30-
3.30pm.
☎ 03873 73232

Moffat
Museum
Open: Easter, Whitsun to September.
Monday to Saturday 10.30-1pm, 2.30-5pm
☎ 0683 20868

Moniaive
Maxwelton House
☎ 084 82 285
Open: garden, Chapel and Museum
Easter to September, 10.30am-5.30pm.
House open July and August.

Mossburn
Mossburn Animal Centre
☎ 0387 811288
Open: all year, daily 11am-4.30pm.

New Abbey
Shambellie House Museum of Costume
☎ 031 225 7534
Open May to September; Monday,
Thursday, Saturday 10am-5.30pm;
Sunday 12noon-5.30pm.

Sweetheart Abbey
☎ 031 244 3101

New Galloway
Blowplain Forest Park
☎ 06442 206
Open: Easter to October, Sunday to
Friday, Guided tour at 2pm.

Newton Stewart
Glen Trool Visitors Centre
☎ 0671 2420
Open: April to October, daily 10.30am-
5pm.

Kirroughtree Visitor Centre
☎ 067184 231
Open: April to September, daily
10.30am-5pm.

Museum
☎ 0671 2106
Open: April to October, Monday to
Saturday 2-5pm. In July and August
also open 10am-12.30pm and from July
to September open Sundays 2-5pm.

Palgowan Open Farm
☎ 067184 231
Open: Easter week and end May to
October, Tuesday to Thursday;
August, Monday to Friday. Tour at
2pm only.

Palnure
Bargaly Gardens
☎ 0671 2392
Open: Easter to end September,
Sundays 2-5pm.

Port Logan
Logan Botanic Gardens
☎ 077686 231
Open: mid-March to end October daily
10am-6pm.

Logan Fish Pond
☎ 0292 268181
Open: Easter to September, daily
12noon-8pm.

Port Patrick
Little Wheels
☎ 077681 536
Open: Easter to October, daily 11am-4pm. Extended in the summer, phone for latest details.

Ruthwell
Savings Bank Museum
☎ 038787 640
Open: all year, every day except Sunday and Monday in the winter. 10am-1pm and 2-5pm.

Sanquhar
Sanquhar Tolbooth Museum
☎ 0659 50186
Open: April to September, Tuesday to Saturday, 10am-1pm and 2-5pm. Sunday 2-5pm.

Stranraer
Castle Kennedy Gardens
☎ 0776 2024
Open: Easter to September, daily 10am-5pm.

Castle of St John
Castle Street
☎ 0776 5088
Open: April to September, Monday to Saturday 10am-1pm and 2-5pm.

Glenwhan Gardens and Nursery
☎ 05814 222
Open: April to September, daily 10am-5pm.

Meadowsweet Herb Garden
☎ 077682 288
Open: Thursday to Tuesday, May to August, 12 noon-5.30pm.

Stranraer Museum
Old Town Hall
George Street
☎ 0776 5088
Open: all year, Monday to Friday 10am-5pm, Saturdays 10am-1pm and 2-5pm.

Thornhill
Drumlanrig Castle
☎ 0848 30248
Open Monday to Saturday, May to August, 11am-5pm and Sundays 1-5pm. Closed Thursdays.

Wanlockhead
Museum Of The Scottish Lead Mining Industry
☎ 0659 74387
Open: Easter to November, daily 11am-4.30pm (Other dates by appointment).

Whithorn
Whithorn Dig and Visitor Centre
☎ 09885 508
Open: April to October, daily 10.30am-5pm.

Tourist Information Offices
ALL YEAR
Dumfries
Dumfries and Galloway Tourist Board
Whitesands
DG1 2SB
☎ 0387 53862

Southwaite
M6 Service Area (Northbound)
Cumbria
☎ 06974 73445 or 73446
Seasonal - Easter to October.

Castle Douglas
Markethill ☎ 0556 26111

Dalbeattie
Town Hall ☎ 0556 610117

Gatehouse of Fleet
Car Park ☎ 05574 212

Gretna Green
Harbour Square ☎ 0461 37834

Kirkcudbright ☎ 0557 30494

Langholm
High Street ☎ 03873 80976

Moffat
Churchgate ☎ 0683 20620

Newton Stewart
Dashwood Square ☎ 0671 2431

Sanquhar
Tolbooth
High St ☎ 0659 50185

Stranraer
Port Rodie ☎ 0776 2595

3 • The Clyde Valley

The Clyde Valley has always attracted visitors, impressed by both the natural beauty of the area and the power generated by this great river. Further downstream Glasgow was built on its banks, while the giant region of Strathclyde and the famous sea loch, the Firth of Clyde also owe their names to it. Early inhabitants called the area 'Y-strad-cluyd' or 'The Warm Valley'.

In the twentieth century the attractions of the area have been overlooked by many who bye-pass the Clyde as they race north or south on the main routes up and down Britain. But the source of the Clyde is in fact not far north of the English border, in a special little area of Strathclyde that cuts into the northern border of Dumfries and Galloway, west of the A74. It is very much an area that deserves to be visited as it always has been by those who live in the big cities of Glasgow and Edinburgh.

This route begins at **Crawford**, which has been a popular spot for Clyde Valley tourists for at least 2,000 years. The Romans liked the area so much that they set up camp there and used it as a base for their push up the Clyde Valley. They were the first to recognise the area's micro-climate as ideal for producing soft-fruit and began cultivation in the valley. Later on Crawford Castle was erected by the Earls of Crawford, it was replaced by a Baronial stronghold in the seventeenth century, the ruins of which still stand today, also known as Tower Lindsay.

The Clyde flows northwards towards **Abington**, with the M74 following its course. Indeed the local motorway services there are well known to those who frequent this northern section of the United Kingdom's main western road artery. Few will realise however that this is the major departure point on to the A702 north-east at the start of the Clyde Valley tourist route. There is a tourist information centre in the services which can provide the latest information.

Crawfordjohn is a few miles west of Abington by the A74 and B740. There is a 'Heritage Venture' there which includes wildlife

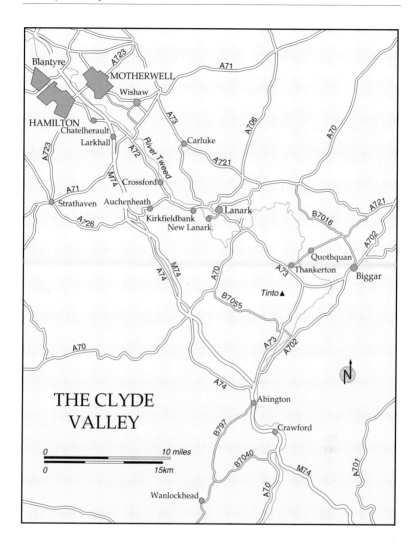

Blantyre
A723
MOTHERWELL
A71
Wishaw
A73
HAMILTON
Chatelherault
A706
A70
Larkhall
A723
A72
Carluke
River Tweed
A721
M74
Crossford
A71
Strathaven
Auchenheath
Kirkfieldbank
Lanark
A721
B7016
A726
New Lanark
A702
A74
M74
A70
Quothquan
Thankerton
A73
Biggar
Tinto ▲
B7055

A70
A73
A702
N

THE CLYDE
VALLEY
Abington
B797
Crawford

0   10 miles
0   15km
B7040
A70
M74
A701

Wanlockhead

photographs, agricultural memorabilia and covenanting tales. Church
enthusiasts may wish to visit 'Old St Brides' at **Douglas**, reached via
the B7078 before turning left on to the A70. The restored fourteenth-
century chancel contains Douglas family tombs, and a clock donated
by Mary Queen of Scots.

The Clyde Valley route proper begins with some 20 miles (32km)
of pleasant driving through the Southern Uplands and along the side
of the Clyde. The A73 runs beneath **Tinto Hill** to the north. This is the

highest point in the area at 2,320ft (707m) and on the top of it there is one of the country's largest Bronze Age cairns. Druids used to hold fertility rights up there. Today there is a good but steep path and conquering the summit is likely to be a 3 hour round trip. Turning right on to the A72, through the village of **Wolfclyde**, Coulter Motte, a twelfth-century castle mound, can be seen on the left. A left turn on to the A702 will bring you to Biggar. **Biggar** is a pleasant market town with a remarkable number of visitor attractions, more than might be expected for a town of its size. This favourable circumstance results largely from the zealous efforts of the Biggar Museum Trust and explains the local saying 'London's big but Biggar's bigger' only a slight exaggeration in terms of facilities. The town is actually located some 2 miles (3km) east of a bend in the Clyde on the A702, and has its own small river, Biggar Water. However it is still part of the Clyde Valley.

Although settlement of the area dates back to Roman times, the current market town grew up under the protection of the Fleming family and was granted its charter in 1451 as a Burgh of a Barony by King James II. Today the population is about 2,000 and it remains an important agricultural centre with regular lamb sales. Strong local traditions are maintained including the annual bonfire in the wide main street on Hogmanay, claimed to be the biggest bonfire in Scotland. A local schoolgirl is still crowned 'Fleming Queen' in honour of the original patron in the town's Gala Week each June.

The world's first public gasworks were established in 1812 by the Gas Light and Coke Company of London. It provided gas light for homes and street lights and was highly successful, leading to the rapid growth of the gas industry. By 1839 towns across the country had their own gasworks and Biggar was no exception. These were improved and expanded over the years, the last improvement at Biggar was made in 1914. In 1973 when North Sea Gas arrived, Biggar did not demolish its redundant gas works, as most towns did, but preserved them in association with the National Museums of Scotland. So the real thing is still available for interested visitors to view and smell.

Biggar's Moat Park Heritage Centre was opened in 1988 and is the best exhibition in the region of the Clyde Valley's development, showing the original geological features that shaped the area and tracing the history of its inhabitants. There are models of past dwellings in the area and a Victorian patchwork quilt measuring 8 x 9ft (2 x 3m) with over 80 figures meticulously stitched into it by a Biggar tailor during the Crimean War.

Those interested in the Covenanting movement will strike gold at Greenhill farmhouse which once stood 10 miles (16km) away in a derelict condition on Tinto Hill; it was moved to Biggar to house a Covenanters' museum. The stone bridge that crosses the burn in front of it is actually quite newly built, but as such constructions are rare these days, has quickly begun to look as old as the house. The exhibition recalls the 'killing times' of the Civil War when men and women who refused to accept political and religious changes following the Union with England were hunted down for worshipping in open fields rather than attending 'state controlled' churches.

Gladstone Court in the town is another reminder of times gone by, containing shops and offices which the elderly may still recall. Shops include an ironmongers, photographers, milliner, printer, bootmaker, watchmaker and dressmaker. There is also a re-created village school and library. Right behind the court is the Albion Archive, housing the complete story of Albion Motors which started on a local farm in 1899 and went on to become the British Empire's biggest truck manufacturer, before being swallowed up by what was then Leyland Daf. Plans are afoot to build a motor museum, and a fund-raising rally is held each August. Biggar's museum list goes on, as the Trust cares for two buildings associated with Scots writers John Buchan, author of *The 39 Steps* and other famous works and Hugh MacDiarmid. There is a display devoted to John Buchan at the old Free Church in **Broughton** (take the eastbound B7016 beyond Biggar), where he met his wife-to-be in 1874 while working there as supply clergyman. Hugh MacDiarmid's home for 25 years, a few miles from Biggar at Brownsbank Cottage is now home to a Writer in Residence sponsored by various public bodies.

Biggar Kirk is apparently one of the few buildings not managed by the Museum Trust but is worth visiting anyway. It was a collegiate church, built in 1545 on the site of an earlier building. The patron was Malcolm, Lord Fleming of Biggar, who was the uncle of Mary Queen of Scots. Biggar's Puppet Theatre, in attractive grounds off the B7016 east of the town, also warrants a mention. This is a complete Victorian theatre in miniature and seats up to 100.

The A73 meanwhile continues west and north for 15 miles (24km) towards Lanark, through the hill farm pastures and frequent 'pick your own,' fruit farms popular in the summer months. The Clyde itself takes a big loop north round by Carstairs Junction and can be followed more closely by taking minor roads through farmland for the dedicated follower.

New Lanark represents both a step forward in industrial technology and, probably more significant, a leap in social justice for the people who lived there at the turn of the nineteenth century. It was in 1785 that Glaswegian industrialist David Dale, having visited the beautiful and powerful Falls of Clyde, thought of harnessing the power of the Clyde and founded New Lanark's mills. Six storeys high, this was one of the largest cotton mill complexes in the world. However true international fame came about when Welshman Robert Owen, Dale's son in law, introduced radical social reforms. These included banning the employment of children under 10 and pauper apprentices, improved sanitation, education and did away with corporal punishment. He did not see his humanitarian philosophy as contrary to capitalist-style employee exploitation, but believed that his measures would be repaid in greater profits. Owen wrote extensively on his experiments and inspired many followers during and after his life.

Today the large mill complex contains numerous attractions; extensive warehouse shop, a classic car collection and a sort of indoor chairlift ride that takes you through mill life in the 1820s. The exhibitions have won numerous awards and New Lanark itself has been nominated a World Heritage Site. It is a short walk from the village to the spectacular Corra Linn, dubbed 'Scotland's greatest cascade of water' in the promotional brochures, and with a good deal of enthusiasm also by past visitors including Turner, Wordsworth, Coleridge, Scott and Dickens.

Lanark itself is a thriving market town which stages the biggest agricultural mart in Scotland every Monday with further plant sales on Thursdays. It is closely associated with Scottish sovereign history, especially prior to the Union with England. The first Scottish parliament is thought to have met here in the tenth century and it was from here that the 'Guardian of Scotland', William Wallace, began his campaigns. The 'Lanimer' festival in the town each June is believed to date from 1140 and includes the crowning as Queen of a local girl at the foot of Wallace's statue. There is also a small local history museum, a country park and 3 miles (5km) west on the A706, a trout and deer farm with pets corner, café and smoke house.

The A72 north-west from Lanark crosses the Clyde to its west bank and reaches **Kirkfieldbank** after about 3 miles (5km). Above this is the National Trust owned **Blackhill** which has a Bronze Age cairn at its 951ft (290m) summit, and the remains of the largest Iron Age fort in Scotland. This is also a very good view point (as Iron Age man would obviously testify) with views as far as Arran and Ben Lomond on a good day, as well as the Clyde Valley. Access is via the B7018.

The A744 goes west from Kirkfieldbank to Kirkmuirhill on the M74. Beyond there on the A726 is **Strathaven**, well worth visiting although there is not space to describe in detail the town and its many attractions here. The John Hastie Museum there houses an internationally important collection of factory made ceramics including Wedgwood, Royal Doulton, Royal Worcester and exhibits from Japan, Bohemia and Scotland. There are also exhibitions on weaving, Covenanting and the popular movement against low living standards in 1820 known as the Radical Rising. A key figure at this time was James Wilson, a native of the town. Weaving was a major industry, probably introduced by Flemish immigrants who were encouraged to settle in the area between the twelfth and sixteenth centuries.

The Town Mill Arts Centre is situated in a watermill built for the Hamilton family in the mid-seventeenth century, which was operational for 300 years. The ruins of Strathaven Castle, originally built by the Earls of Douglas in the fifteenth century but taken over by the Hamilton Dukes later are also here. Five miles (8km) further west of Strathaven is the Drumclog Monument, marking the site of the Battle of Drumclog, won by the Covenanters in 1679, defeating Lord Graham of Claverhouse.

Back on the A72, **Crossford**, a further 3 miles (5km) north of Kirkfieldbank, is the nearest village to **Craignethan Castle**, the fifteenth-century home of the Hamilton family prior to their move downstream (see Chatelherault, Hamilton and Strathclyde Country Park later in this section). It was built by Sir James Hamilton of Finnart, illegitimate son of the first Earl of Arran and thus a kinsman of James V. He was also employed by the king to supervise the remodelling of Falkland Palace. Sir James was executed in 1540 after which the castle was obtained by his half-brother of the same name. The castle was associated with Mary Queen of Scots in May 1568 when she spent her last 'happy' night here. Ahead of her lay defeat at the battle of Langside, her fateful flight to England, years of imprisonment and eventual execution.

The Hamiltons remained faithful however and lost Craignethan to the Earl of Moray, then Regent to Mary's son, the infant King James VI. The Hamiltons arranged Moray's assassination at Linlithgow a few years later and the castle was soon recaptured. The insane third Earl of Arran, who had been a suitor for Mary's hand in 1561, lived there from 1575 to 1579. The castle appears in Sir Walter Scott's book *Old Mortality* as Tillietudlem Castle.

Down in the valley are the 76 acres (30 hectares) of **Clyde Valley**

Strathclyde Country Park is an excellent leisure area

Country Estate (on the B7056, off the A702 by Crossford). This has been established in the grounds of Carfin House, unfortunately demolished in 1957. The coach-house, stables, walled garden and Victorian conservatory have survived however, together with a Victorian footbridge across the Clyde, unused for 50 years but now restored. The estate consists of a garden centre including a Victorian conservatory, bird of prey centre, craft shops, stone mason, frequently changing art displays and a coffee shop with restaurant. There is also an adventure playground, trekking centre, and woodland walks. Railway enthusiasts will be attracted to the narrow gauge railway that operates here. The trains are pulled by a Chance Huntingdon 424 Locomotive named *General Roy* after Carluke's most famous son.

As the Clyde passes Motherwell there is a bird reserve and Country Park by its banks. The RSPB's 265 acre (106 hectare) **Baron's Haugh Reserve** is a haven for wildfowl as the Clyde's floodplain extends over this marshy area. One hundred and seventy three different species of bird have been recorded here of which sixty nine have nested. More than twenty species of wading bird can be seen in the autumn and a similar variety of mammals have also been spotted. **Dalzell Country Park's** arboretum contains one of the most important collections of rare trees in Scotland. It was developed over

300 years by various members of the Hamilton family and now has 700 trees of 50 different species. The oldest is a 600-year-old oak.

Motherwell itself is a large modern town with excellent shopping and leisure facilities which include the Aquatec, a combined ice rink and leisure pool complex and a good civic theatre.

The name of Hamilton is synonymous with one of Scotland's most wealthy and powerful Dukedoms and much of their land in the area has now been divided into large leisure parks, with the Clyde and several rather less attractive motorways and dual carriageways intersecting the former estates as we near Glasgow.

Chatelherault, one of the parts of the estate, was designed as a hunting lodge by William Adam for the fifth Duke of Hamilton (to his grandmother's original vision) and completed in 1744 after 12 years construction. It is set on a hill above the Clyde and the former site of Hamilton Palace, about 1½ miles (2km) south of present day Hamilton town, on the A72.

The building has been restored from dereliction in recent years and an interpretative centre established which shows life as it was in the eighteenth century for all members of the family. The extensive grounds include the Avon Gorge, which stretches for 2½ miles (4km) along Avon water and has carved down 200ft (61m) in to the sandstone at its deepest point. The medieval hunting forest survives, as do the remains of twelfth-century Cadzow Castle. An Iron Age settlement has also been discovered and the original ancient breed of white cattle has been re-introduced.

A definite stop must be made at the remarkable **Hamilton Mausoleum** in the **Strathclyde Country Park**. This is a fine example of how the very wealthy of years gone by would spend huge sums to try to perpetuate their memory after death (whether worth perpetuating or not). This mausoleum was built for Alexander, tenth Duke of Hamilton, who lived from 1767 to 1852 and was a colourful character who was widely travelled and known as 'El Magnifico'. It took 15 years to build and cost £30,000 (a large enough figure today, immense 150 years ago). It has been variously described as a great work of 'architectural sculpture' and as a 'pretentious folly.' It stands 120ft (36m) high and is 110ft (33m) wide and was completed 5 years after El Magnifico's death. He himself was buried in an Egyptian sarcophagus which he had extended to fit him.

The mausoleum is a most impressive building with huge bronze doors, copies of panels on the Ghiberti doors at the Baptistry in Florence, marble mosaic floors and many other fascinating features. There is a tremendous echo which can last up to 15 seconds (some

David Livingstone's birthplace at Blantyre is now a centre dedicated to his memory

claim 22 seconds) and may be the longest in Europe. This rendered the chapel which takes up the main part of the building, operationally useless.

Strathclyde Country Park itself is an excellent leisure area with golf, lake and recreation facilities; unfortunately it is dissected by the M74. Hamilton Palace which dated back to 1591 and was extended and improved in 1705 and early in the nineteenth century to become one off the most magnificent homes in the country, had to be demolished in the 1920s due to mining subsidence.

Hamilton town is well known for its racecourse and famous 'saints and sinners' race each June. The District Museum is housed within the Hamilton Arms Inn, an impressive stop on the road to Glasgow, built in 1696. The collection includes a large transport section and the original eighteenth-century Assembly Rooms have been restored to their original, splendour. A second museum is dedicated to the Cameronian regiment. Exhibitions include regimentalia from the Scottish rifles and items from the Covenanting movement. It is housed within the Duke of Hamilton's former riding school. Another attraction of the town is the Old Parish Church, the only church to be designed by William Adam. It was completed in 1734 and has a pre-Norman ancient Christian Netherton Cross standing in front. The Heads Memorial in the kirkyard is in memory of local Covenanters, beheaded following the 1666 Pentland Rising.

Scotland's most celebrated explorer, David Livingstone, was born at **Blantyre**, just north of Hamilton. His birthplace is now part of a substantial centre dedicated to his memory, which includes a purpose built African Pavilion, whose shape suggests a cluster of African huts. This brings Livingstone's vision of Africa to the present day with a vibrant and realistic view of modern Africa. Livingstone was born in an eighteenth-century tenement which once housed twenty-four families. It is now a museum and exhibition of his life including the famous meeting with Stanley at Ujiji in 1871. Livingstone died 2 years later during an attempt to find the source of the Nile.

The last stop on this journey down the Clyde will be at **Bothwell Castle**, by **Uddingston**, a huge red sandstone fortress which is probably the finest thirteenth-century castle surviving in Scotland. Indeed it was once the largest and finest castle north of the border and its picturesque setting above the Clyde seems rather incongruous against the stark fortifications. Originally the stronghold of the 'Black Douglases' it was restored in the fifteenth-century and because of its prominence played a leading roll in many events of Scottish history, most notably the wars of independence.

The Clyde Valley now widens to accommodate the sprawl of the Glasgow metropolis, its suburbs and now severely depleted Clydeside shipyards. There are however more country parks, leisure centres and much more to visit around **East Kilbride** (a new town which has grown from village to a population of over 70,000 in under 50 years), as well as Coatbridge and Airdrie.

Further Information
— The Clyde Valley —

Places to Visit

Biggar

Biggar Kirk
Kirkstyle
☎ 0899 20994
Open: daily until dusk, Sunday services.

Brownsbank Cottage
Biggar Museum Trust
☎ 0899 21050
Open: all year by appointment only.

Gasworks Museum
Biggar Museum Trust
☎ 0899 21050
Open: 1 June to late September, daily,
2-5pm. Sundays in July and August
opens 12noon.
Admission at other times by arrangement.

Gladstone Court
Biggar Museum Trust
☎ 0899 21050
Open: Easter to end October, Monday
to Saturday, 10am-12.30pm and 2-5pm.
Sundays afternoons only.

Greenhill
Biggar Museum Trust
☎ 0899 21050
Open: daily 2-5pm.

Moat Park
Biggar Museum Trust
☎ 0899 21050
Open: Easter to end October, Monday to
Saturday, 10am-5pm, Sundays 2-5pm.

Puppet Theatre
☎ 0899 20631
Open: all year, Monday to Saturday
(closed Wednesday), 11am-5pm.
Sundays 2-5pm.

Blantyre

David Livingstone Centre
☎ 0698 823140
Open: all Year, Monday to Saturday
10am-8pm, Sunday 2-6pm
(last entry to museum, 5pm).

Broughton

John Buchan Centre
Biggar Museum Trust
☎ 0899 21050
Open: daily 2-5pm.

Crawfordjohn

Heritage Venture
☎ 08644 265
Open: mid-May to mid-September,
Saturday-Sunday 2-5pm.

Crossford

Clyde Valley Country Estate
Carluke
Near Lanark
☎ 055 586 691
Open: daily.

Craignethan Castle
☎ 0555 86364
Open: dates and times as Bothwell Castle.

Dalzell Country Park
Open: daylight hours.
☎ 0698 267676

Hamilton

Cameronian Regimental Museum
☎ 0698 428688
Open: Monday to Saturday (except
Thursday), 10am-1pm and 2-5pm.

Chatelherault Country Park
Ferniegair
☎ 0698 426213
Open: all year, House 11am-4pm
(4.30pm in summer), Visitor Centre
10.30am-4.30pm (5.30pm in summer).

District Museum
129 Muir Street
☎ 0698 283981

Hamilton Mausoleum
Contact details as for Strathclyde
Country Park
Open: Easter to September daily, 45
minute tours at 3pm.
Advance booking recommended. June
to August, additional weekend tours at
7pm. September to Easter, weekend
tours only at 2pm.

Hamilton Park Racecourse
☎ 0698 283806

Strathclyde Country Park
366 Hamilton Road
Motherwell ML1 4ED
☎ 0698 66155
Open: all year.

Lanark
Lanark Market
Weekly livestock on Mondays, plants, vegetables and poultry on Thursdays and implements and sundries sale every third Thursday.
☎ 0555 662281

Museum
☎ 0555 665151
Open: most weekends and Wednesday evenings.

Newmills Trout and Deer Farm
☎ 0555 870730
Open: all year.

Motherwell
Aquatec
Monteith Road
Motherwell ML1 1AZ
☎ 0698 76464

Baron's Haugh RSPB Reserve
9 Wisteria Lane
Carluke
Motherwell ML8 5TB
Open: daily, guided walks on request.

New Lanark
New Lanark Visitor Centre
New Lanark Conservation Trust
New Lanark Mills
Lanark ML11 9DB
☎ 0555 661345
Open: daily 11am-5pm.

Strathaven
John Hastie Museum
☎ 0357 21257
Open May to November, hours vary according to day and month but open most days in the afternoon.

Town Mill Arts Centre
Guided tours by arrangement.
☎ 0357 20014

Uddingston
Bothwell Castle
☎ 0698 816894
Open: April to September, Monday to Saturday, 9.30am-6pm. Sundays 2-6pm. Rest of the year the same except closes at 4pm, and closed Thursday afternoon and all day Friday.

Glasgow Zoo
☎ 041 771 1185
Open: daily, 10am-5pm.

Viewpark Gardens
☎ 0698 818269
Open: May to September only. Monday to Thursday, 12noon-4.15pm, Friday 12noon-3.15pm, weekend 10am-5pm.

Tourist Information Offices

Abington
Welcome Break Service Area
Clydesdale
☎ 08642 436. Open: all year.

Biggar
155 High Street
Clydesdale
☎ 0899 21066. Open: Easter to October.

Coatbridge
Time Capsule Monklands
Buchanan Street
☎ 0236 431133. Open: Easter to October.

Hamilton
Road Chef Services
M74 Northbound
☎ 0698 285590. Open: all year.

Lanark
Clyde Valley Tourist Board
Horsemarket
Ladyacre Road
ML11 7LQ ☎ 0555 662544/ 665709

Motherwell
Motherwell Library
Hamilton Road
☎ 0698 267676. Open: all year.

Strathaven
Town Mill Arts Centre
Stonehouse Road
☎ 0357 29650. Open: Easter to October.

4 • Dundee & Angus

Like Glasgow, **Dundee** has been working hard to change its perception with potential visitors, from a superficially rather dull industrial metropolis to a city of culture with a glorious past and much to see and do. Old attractions have been overhauled and updated, new ones added and the many places to see and things to do in the surrounding countryside are being drawn together in one big promotional push. It works well too. It is a refreshing change to see things that have always been there but were previously forgotten or ignored because Dundee was not seen as a tourist destination, suddenly dusted down and drawn out in to the light. There is a feeling, almost, of discovering the tourist equivalent of buried treasure, rather than just seeing the famous sights tourists have seen before you for decades or centuries before.

Dundee is Scotland's third or fourth largest city depending on whether you take the Dundee view or the Aberdonian one. A wooden hill fort was probably built here by the first settlers but Dundee first came to prominence in trade links with Flanders and the Baltic and was awarded the first of many Royal Charters by King William the Lion at the end of the twelfth century. Fortunes were mixed over the next few centuries with Edward I capturing the city and it was later besieged by Henry VIII's forces. Things took a turn for the worse in the seventeenth century when the city was destroyed twice, firstly by the Royalist Marquis of Montrose and then by Cromwell's army under General Monck.

Despite this rather heavy handed English interference the city, soon only second to Edinburgh, grew great on the three 'J's of jute, jam and journalism. The jute was one of Dundee's former textile strengths and an industry in which it was a world leader.

The jams and marmalades are made from the berry growing areas around the city, and the best products to be found on supermarket shelves around the United Kingdom are still prefixed by 'Dundee'. Dundee is also the centre for 'family' publications such as *The People's*

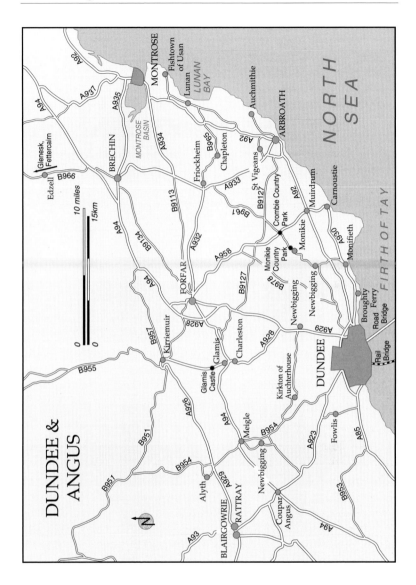

Friend and the great British comic industry that has produced characters such as Dennis The Menace, Desperate Dan, Korky The Cat and The Bash Street Kids. Dundee's historical importance also results from whaling. It was one of the United Kingdom's largest ports for this, then ship-building and railway engineering. The rail bridge which links Dundee with Fife across the Tay and was opened in 1887 is still the longest in the world at just over 2 miles (3km) long. It replaces an earlier one blown over by a storm in 1879 with the loss

A view of Dundee from Fife

of seventy-five lives. The adjacent road bridge is much more recent, opened in 1966.

City status was granted by Queen Victoria in 1889 and 5 years later the city also became a county in its own right. In the past 100 years the huge industries have all but disappeared to be replaced by electronics, light engineering and other developments.

The centre piece of the development project to link Dundee's past with its present was the opening of Discovery Point in 1993. This is a waterfront visitor centre containing the *Discovery*, Captain Scott's ship on which he made his trip to the Antarctic. This was the strongest wooden ship ever built and the visitor centre recreates it's launch in 1901. The *Terra Nova*, captained by Dundee's Harry MacKay is also featured. This was the ship that blasted through the Antarctic ice to free *Discovery* after 2 years ice bound. A third ship, the frigate *Unicorn*, a forty-six gun wooden warship launched in 1824, is berthed at Victoria Dock. The *Unicorn* is the oldest British warship afloat, and the fourth oldest boat afloat in the world.

Dundee city centre is based around the pedestrianised square which once contained the original parish church of St Clements and the Old Town Hall, known as The Pillars, demolished in 1931. Most of the usual chain stores are to be found in the area plus a modern waterfront leisure centre and one of Scotland's leading repertory

Castle Street, Dundee

theatres. For those looking for more original shopping, the indoor Dens Market on Dens Road contains over 100 stalls and is open weekends, Tuesdays and Fridays.

One entry to the old city is through the Wishart Arch on Cowgate, an old gateway that is known to have existed by 1548. It is named after George Wishart, a reformer who is thought to have preached from it during the plague of 1544.

On Barrack Street the city's own natural history museum contains an extensive collection of Scottish wildlife including the skeleton of the Tay whale, a humpback which rather foolishly swam up the Tay in 1883. The Howff is an historic graveyard in the city centre which was once part of Greyfriar's Monastery, gifted to the people of Dundee by Mary Queen of Scots. Until 1788 the nine trades of Dundee met here and the gravestones show a variety of signs and symbols denoting the old craft guilds.

Nineteenth- and twentieth-century Scottish art works are on display in the McManus Galleries in Albert Square. This is an excellent Gothic structure constructed in 1867 built to a design by Sir George Gilbert Scott. It also houses a display of material from Ancient Egypt. Contemporary art work and numerous temporary exhibitions are staged in another gallery on Seagate, the Seagate Gallery and Printmakers Workshop.

St Mary's Tower, a fine square structure in Nethergate, is all that remains of the fifteeth-century church of St Marys. This was the retreat of the city council during General Monck's 6 week demolition of Dundee in 1651. St Mary is the patron saint of Dundee. Next to the tower is a replica of the original mercat cross which stood in Seagate. A new one was carved by John Mylne in 1586 and remained there until 1777. The original shaft of the cross now holds a unicorn sculpture by Scott Sutherland, RSA.

A more complete church, in fact two churches in one, is to be found on King Street where St Andrews, completed in 1772 uses Glasite Church (1777) as its hall. Saint Andrews was paid for entirely by the Nine Trades' Guild of Dundee and the stained glass windows contain trade emblems. The Glasite Church was named after The Reverend John Glas, but was nicknamed the Kail Kirk, as the congregation chose to share soup (kail) together after the service.

The city's cathedral is St Pauls, built in 1853 on the original site of the medieval Castle of Dundee. The spire reaches 210ft (64m) in to the city skyline. There are some fine stained glass windows and a reredos by Salviati of Venice. Guided tours of the cathedral are now organised. St Peter's Church at Invergowrie (A85 just west of the city) was built on the site of the first Christian church on the banks of the Tay. Pictish stones from here are now in Edinburgh's National Museum of Antiquities of Scotland. The present church is sixteenth century.

Also west of the city is the Mills Observatory, the United Kingdom's only full time public observatory. It houses a 10 inch refracting telescope and viewing of the night sky is possible on winter evenings under the guidance of the resident astronomer. In the summer it is used in the daytime for looking out over the Tay to Fife.

The highest point in the city is The Law, the name coming from the old Scots word for Hill. It is 571ft (174m) above sea level and is formed from an old volcanic plug. The original fort about which Dundee grew is thought to have been located here. There are good views from here, as well as the city's war memorial, and four times a year a beacon is lit.

Dundee is surrounded by parks and castles. Dudhope Castle and park is only a 1½ mile (1km) walk from the city centre. It dates from the sixteenth century although there has been a castle on the site since the thirteenth century. Originally the seat of the Scrymgeour Family, in 1683 the castle passed to the Grahams and John Graham of Claverhouse, alias Bonnie Dundee moved in. Since the mid-eighteenth century the castle has contained a woollen mill, later a barracks and now offices, so it can only be viewed from the outside. Nearby is the Duntrune Demonstration Garden where the Council's Parks Department give advice on gardening matters and provide practical horticultural demonstrations. Another place for gardens to call is the University's Botanic Garden on Riverside Drive, 3 miles (5km) west of the city. It was established in 1971 and contains a tropical greenhouse and award winning visitor centre as well as a very wide range of conifer and deciduous trees.

The largest park is on the A923 3 miles (5km) north-west of the city towards Coupar Angus. **Camperdown Country Park** is made up of former lands surrounding Camperdown House, a neo-classical house designed by William Burn and built in 1828 for the First Earl of Camperdown. The park land covers 365 acres (146 hectares) and includes some rare trees, a golf course, horse-riding, award-winning adventure playground and a Wildlife Centre containing indigenous European animals and rather more exotic species.

Just south of the park is another famous Dundee attraction, Shaw's Sweet Factory, where traditional confectionery such as fudges, toffee, coconut ices and boiled sweets have been hand made since 1879. Machinery used dates from the period 1936 to 1956. Also on this side of Dundee is **Clatto Country Park**, where there are 24 acres (10 hectares) of water surrounded by footpaths and beach. Temperton Woods nearby cover 120 acres (48 hectares) and have a woodland interpretation centre and waymarked trails.

Leaving Dundee centre and heading East on the A92 to Arbroath it is 4 miles (6km) to **Claypotts Castle**, just north of Broughty Ferry. This was another former home of John Graham of Claverhouse, Bonnie Dundee, but was originally built in the late sixteenth century for the Strachan family. It is very unusual in tower house design having round towers on diagonally opposite corners.

Broughty Ferry, the 'seaside suburb' on the coast below the castle originated as a Tayside fishing village, clustering round the fifteenth-century castle of Broch. The narrow entry between the castle and Tayport was for centuries an important ferry link to Fife. Many successful Dundee business men built fine houses in the area in the nineteenth century, and now many are clubs and hotels.

Broughty Castle now houses a museum of local history, armair and the whaling industry. In the sixteenth century it was besieged by the English Army and attacked by Cromwell's army, again under General Monck in the seventeenth century and then left ruined until 1861 when it was restored as part of Britain's coastal defences. Its gun battery was dismantled in 1956.

As the A923 leaves north-westwards Dundee it passes north of **Fowlis** and the larger village of Liff. Fowlis Church is probably Scotland's finest surviving small medieval church and still contains part of its original fine rood screen. There are also medieval paintings, alms dish, sacrament house and font. A turning north on to the B954 in the opposition direction from Liff from the A923 leads to **Kirkton of Aucherthouse** which contains another interesting church. The present building dates from 1630 although there is mention of a church on the site in 1275. It contains an octagonal pre-Reformation font, several fine stained glass windows and an eighteenth-century Act of Parliament clock. The local barons are buried in a vault below the vestry.

The A923 then continues on in to Perthshire going first through **Coupar Angus**, once a place of major significance with a Cistercian abbey founded in 1164 which was one of Scotland's largest and most prosperous. It fell in to decay after the Reformation. Further in to Perthshire on the same road come the larger sister communities of Ratray and Blairgowrie. Sitting on the fast flowing, salmon rich River Ericht this is a bustling town that grew up on nineteenth-century textile production.

The A94 north-east from Coupar Angus runs back in to Angus and directly to Glamis and Forfar through the village of **Meigle**. Here a museum that is entirely devoted to ancient stones containing twenty-five sculptured monuments from the Celtic Christian period — the largest collection of its type.

Three miles (5km) west of Coupar Angus, on the A93 (via A984) is Meikleour a beech hedge by the side of the road, planted in 1746 and now 1,968ft (600m) long and 98ft (30m) high.

The road running parallel back in to Angus from Blairgowrie through Glen Isla is the A926. This passes another small village on the Perthshire border, **Alyth**, where there is a folk museum of local history. There are numerous minor roads running north in to the Grampian Mountains and northern Angus' departing every few miles along the A926. All however eventually have to veer west towards the A93 which runs up to Braemar and then goes due east along the Dee to Aberdeen (see Chapter 5 Royal Deeside), or they run east towards the coast. The Grampians themselves are yet to be conquered by roads. The A93 is also easily accessed from the south coming via Perth and can be taken as a route to the Northern Highlands via Braemar, Tomintoul, Grantown and Moray or Carrbridge (see Chapter 6 The Spey Valley). It is a route containing several hairpins, steep gradients and probably deer and sheep on the road; but is still a relatively direct way north avoiding the trunk roads!

Broughty Castle, now a museum of local history

North from Dundee (2 miles/3km) is Mains Castle, built in the mid-sixteenth century by Sir David Graham of Fintry. It remained in his family until the early nineteenth century when it fell in to ruin. However it has now been restored and houses a restaurant.

Four miles (6km) further north, heading for Forfar and Glamis on the A929, is the Tealing Earth House and dovecot. This is a well preserved example of an Iron Age souterrain. The dovecote is rather more recent, dating from 1595.

Glamis Castle is reached by turning off left shortly after Tealing on to the A928, north of the village of **Glamis** which houses the Angus Folk Museum. This is one of the finest collections of its type in Scotland, given to the National Trust in 1974 and housed in a row of six early nineteenth-century cottages with stone slabbed roofs.

Glamis Castle is one of Britain's most important. It is a five storey L shaped block given to the Lyon family by King Robert II of Scotland in 1372. It has been a royal residence since that time. Glamis was redesigned in the seventeenth century and today houses spectacular rooms and a magnificent art collection. The parkland outside was landscaped in the late eighteenth century and contains the 2 acre (1 hectare) Italian Garden enclosed within high yew hedges as well as a more recent nature trail and children's playground. Today the home to the Earls of Strathmore and Kinghorne, the castle was childhood home to Her Majesty Queen Elizabeth the Queen Mother and was the birthplace of Princess Margaret. Shakespeare's play *Macbeth* was probably based on the castle.

The A928 continues north in to Strathmore and passes Forfar to the east en route to the small town of Kirriemuir. The Angus hills are getting higher at this point, with more forestry and new glens appearing in the build up to the Grampian Mountains in the north. Much of **Kirriemuir** retains its eighteenth- and nineteenth-century character when it was a main centre for handloom weaving. Lovers of *Peter Pan* may be more interested to know that this is the birth place of J M Barrie. The dominant tollbooth in the centre of the town marks the town's ancient connection with the Douglas Earls of Angus. Kirriemuir also contains a private RAF museum, and 1 mile (2km) west of the town on the B951 Glenisla road there is an RSPB reserve where Ospreys may be seen.

J M Barrie's birthplace was the site of small local victory in 1937 when there was a proposal that the building be moved to the USA. It was bought by a Mr D Alves however, who then donated it to the National Trust For Scotland along with funds for its restoration. The two storey house is furnished upstairs as it might have been during Barrie's time there; the adjacent house, number 11, is home to an exhibition 'The Genius of J M Barrie' about his literary and theatrical work. The outside wash house is believed to have been his first theatre. The cricket pavilion on the local hill was gifted to the town by Barrie. It houses one of the three remaining camera obscuras in Scotland providing panoramic views over the glens.

Forfar is on the A929 road from Dundee to Aberdeen, but still within the fertile Strathmore area. The town's history is undoubtedly ancient, but regretably much of the detail was lost when Oliver Cromwell's men attacked the town's tolbooth in the mid-seventeenth century, destroying all the local records. What is certain is that Mr Cromwell's army was only the latest in a long line to recognise the value of the area. Bronze Age relics and Roman campsites have been found in the vicinity and King Malcolm Canmore held his first parliament in Forfar in 1057. Apart from the fertility of the land the local Balmashanner Hill was, and still is, an excellent viewpoint to the surrounding area.

A modern tower marks the site of Forfar's original castle, built by King Malcolm III, where King William the Lion convened the Scottish Parliament in the thirteenth century. The castle was destroyed in 1308 when supporters of Robert the Bruce decided to demolish it, no doubt inadvertently neglecting to inform the English troops garrisoned in it at the time of the impending destruction. Forfar is famous, in Scotland at least, for its 'Bridies', traditional semi-circular savouries of minced steak, onions and seasonings encased in pastry.

The A932 runs due east from Forfar towards Friockheim. Soon after leaving the town this road passes south of **Restenneth Priory** (on the B9113) which was at one time almost encircled by the loch. It was built for King Nechtan who ruled way back in the eighth century and was then adapted to become an Augustinian priory 400 years later. The ruins may be visited at any reasonable time. Nearby is Forester's Seat, a local winery.

To the south of the road is the village of **Dunnichen** where a cairn commemorates the battle of Nechtansmere in AD685. This battle resulted in victory for Pictish King Brunei over Northumbian King Ecgfirth and had a major influence on the creation of the Scottish nation. The Northumbrian forces were pushed south to what has since become the accepted border area with England.

A little further on is the larger village of **Letham** which was created by MP George Dempster in 1788 as a centre for handloom weaving. There are walks in the area alongside Vinney Water. Near here is Trumperton Forge where traditional horse shoeing is sometimes demonstrated.

Larger expanses of water are to be found on the north side of the A932 where three sizable lochs follow one another for 5 miles (8km) from Forfar. The last of these, **Balgavies**, is a Scottish Wildlife Trust Nature Reserve, rich in wild fowl. **Pitmuies Garden**, a little further east is a semi formal old walled garden adjoining an eighteenth century house and with particularly good displays of spring bulbs and roses.

Brechin stands on the south side of the River Esk, the old town rising on a steep hill. The river has been bridged since at least 1220 and the current structure is one of the oldest stone bridges in Scotland. This was originally a bustling market town and retains much of the traditional architectural charm of a Scottish burgh, as well as some of the bustle!

Brechin Cathedral is a very interesting building, founded by King David I in the mid-twelfth century. Improvements and renovations have altered its appearance many times over the years, although the latest one has restored some of its original medieval glory. The neighbouring round tower is older than the cathedral, originally free standing it is a stirring example of Celtic Culdee architecture and the last remaining part of a college established around AD990. The only other such tower on the Scottish mainland is at **Abernethy**. Iron Age hill forts have been identified on the white and brown Caterthuns just north of the town and there is a good viewpoint from each.

North of Brechin is the remarkable village of **Edzell**. It is located in the foothills of the Grampians in the North Esk Valley. Visitors instantly know that they are somewhere different when they enter the village through a magnificent archway, the Dalhousie Arch, which stands alone over the road. It was erected in 1887 by tenants and friends of the thirteenth Earl of Dalhousie and his Countess who died within hours of each other in 1887.

Edzell Castle, ancient seat of the Crawford-Lindsays, occupies an important strategic position. The original tower house is early sixteenth century with mansion added in 1580 and the pleasance (walled garden) with summer-house and bath-house constructed 25 years after that. The beautiful walled garden of 1604 remains one of Scotland's unique sites. The walls are decorated with sculptured stone panels and there are alcoves for birds and flower boxes. It was relaid out in the 1930s and the castle preserved from further ruin. Its destruction had begun following the second Jacobite uprising.

The village itself grew up around the church about the same time as the castle. It had a well known market, but did not have its 'boom' until the nineteenth century when the railway arrived (it has since gone again). There are plenty of pleasant walks in the area which has long been popular with royalty for its field sports and country air. The memorial hall in the village was gifted to the community by a former chairman of the London Stock Exchange, the son of a local minister.

The River Esk runs from north and west into Edzell and the dead-end unclassified road into Glen Esk and the Grampian hills is an enjoyable and scenic excursion. The road is reached by crossing the Glannochy Bridge. Originally the river could only be forded here and drowning was common in bad weather. A local farmer built the first bridge in 1732, widened in 1790 it now carries the B966. This also marks the end of Tayside and the start of Grampian region. At **Glenesk** Folk Museum, about 10 miles (16km) into the Glen and a former shooting lodge, there are displays of local life since 1800. At the end of the road is Invermark Castle, strategically positioned with a good view down the Glen. In the sixteenth century the area by Loch Lees was a busy iron and silver mining district.

The B966 continues north-east and merges with the A94 dual carriageway from Dundee to Perth. Just over the border is the Fettercairn distillery, one of Scotland's oldest licensed distilleries, opened in 1824. It was rebuilt around the twentieth century and extended in the 1960s. **Fettercairn** also has an entry arch, this one built to commemorate a visit by Queen Victoria and Albert in 1861. A road departs north from Fettercairn to Banchory on Deeside. It passes Fasque, former home of the Gladstones, and described as 'an excellent example of the Upstairs-Downstairs era'. The contents of the house have been little changed in 170 years and the charm lies in the natural, not museum-like arrangement.

Leaving Dundee and following the east coast roads, the initial choice may be to take the A930 through Broughty Ferry, Monifieth and **Carnoustie** best known for its golf, the local course having staged the British Open five times since 1931 and other major championships. 'Gowff' is reported to have been played on the links in the sixteenth century, but the present courses were begun in Victorian times.

Monikie Country Park is a few miles north of the town and there is a second park at **Crombie** a few miles past that on the B961. The B962 south from Monikie and back towards Monifieth passes the remains of some third-century earth houses. Nearby is the Camus Cross which commemorates the death of a Danish king in 1010 at the Battle of Barry when the invaders were beaten back after a bloody fight. Just north-west of Crombie Country Park on the B961 is the village of **Carmyllie**. This contains a church founded in 1500 as a chapel and has an interesting tower and stained-glass windows. The manse was once home to Reverend Patrick Bell, inventor of the reaping machine in 1828.

Two miles (3km) north-west of **Carnoustie** is Barry Mill, re-opened by the National Trust For Scotland in 1992 following a 3 year restoration programme. The mill had operated commercially for over 300 years before serious damage in the early 1980s put it out of production. It has now been fully restored and working demonstrations are given.

An unclassified coast road leads from Carnoustie to Arbroath, passing by the village of **Panbride**. The church contains iron collars for the punishment of offenders. Nearby is a 'loupin stane' to assist you in 'leaping on' to your horse. and by it a footpath to the neighbouring village of **Muirdrum**. Follow this for a hundred yards and you reach the top of the fairy steps. Make a wish on the third step if you like, it is traditional.

Arbroath is the largest town in Angus and its famous abbey holds a very important place in Scottish history. It was here in 1320 that assembled Scottish nobles swore their independence from England in the famous 'declaration of Arbroath'. The abbey was founded by King William the Lion of Scotland in 1178, who is buried within the buildings. He founded it in memory of his friend Thomas à Becket, martyred Archbishop of Canterbury. The 'Stone of Destiny' was found here in 1951.

Associations with the sea are of course strong. Scotland's second lifeboat station was opened in 1803 and the first harbour in 1394, by order of the abbot. A bell, later immortalised in Robert Southey's poem, was placed on Inchcape Rock and Stevenson's Bell Rock Light House was added in 1811. The mainland signal tower for the lighthouse now houses an award winning museum of local history and industry. There is also a cliff top nature trail and a traditional old fisher cottage part of the town called Fit o' the Toon'. There are many other family attractions including the Keptie pond, boating lake, a leisure centre, art gallery and a miniature one-fifth full size railway opened as long ago as 1935 and running for 400yd alongside British Rails mainline track!

North of Arbroath on the sea-side of the Montrose road is the village of **Auchmithie**. Recognised as being the Musselcrag of Sir Walter Scott's *The Antiquary* this is also the home of the famous 'Arbroath smokie' (lightly smoked gutted haddock, best eaten locally and 'straight from the barrel'). Much of Arbroath's fishing fleet began here before moving down the coast.

The village of **St Vigeans** was the site of a church before Arbroath Abbey and this has been added to and extended over the centuries so that it is now very interesting. A local museum nearby contains Pictish stones from the local vicinity. Further north in magnificent **Lunan Bay** are the remains of Red Castle, parts of which date to the thirteenth century. The castle was used as a manse and a customs post while Lunan Bay was a popular spot for smuggling.

At the north end of the bay is **Boddin**, where a massive lime kiln built in the 1750s was years ahead of its time in agricultural advancement. The cliffs here are quite dangerous, but one headland to the north is worth a closer examination as it resembles a standing elephant! The ruins of the Chapel of Skae and a clifftop graveyard are both here.

Fishtown of Usan, just south of Montrose, was the village from which fresh fish and shellfish were taken to the Royal Court of Scotland when it sat in Forfar in the fifteenth century. Precious stones were once found in the sea, the source probably created and later destroyed by coastal erosion. Some are on display in the Royal Scottish Museum, Edinburgh, as well as local museums.

Montrose is located on the north side of Montrose Basin, a 2,000 acre (800 hectare) tidal basin now a nature reserve and popular with birdlife. In winter in particular thousands of pinkfeet and greylag geese have been recorded. To the south of the basin is the rocky headland of Scurdie Ness, guarded by lighthouse. Nearby Ferryden has had a mini boom thanks to the north sea oil industry.

Montrose itself is a spacious market town with many fine buildings including the public library which contains some early books gifted from Scandinavia. The town grew up when merchants and landowners involved in early Baltic and cross-Channel trading erected homes and public buildings. There are several good antiques shops and the William Lamb Memorial studio which contains busts of Queen Elizabeth II and Princess Margaret as girls.

Three miles (5km) west of the town is the National Trust-run **House of Dun**. It was built in 1730 for David Erskine, Marquis of Dun, to designs by William Adam. The numerous attractions include memorabilia from the reign of King William IV, the father of one of the former occupants, a miniature theatre display and marked woodland walks.

Three miles (5km) north of Montrose on the border with Grampian is the Sunnyside Museum. The name belies an unusual exhibition of artefacts from the building's working past, as this is Scotland's oldest asylum with a 200 year history.

Further Information
— Dundee & Angus —

Places to Visit

Alyth
Folk Museum
Open: May to September, Tuesday to Saturday 1-5pm.
☎ 0738 32488

Arbroath
Signal Tower Museum
Open: November to March, Monday to Friday 2-5pm, Saturday 10.30-5pm. April to October, Monday to Saturday 10.30-5pm, closed 1-2pm. July and August also Sunday 2-5pm
☎ 0241 75598

Brechin
Caledonian Railway
The Station
2 Park Road
DD9 7AF
☎ 0334 55965
Open: Easter and May to August.

Carnoustie
Barry Mill
☎ 0241 56761
Open: Easter and May to October, daily 11am-1pm and 2-5pm.

Crombie Country Park
☎ 02416 360

Dundee
Barrack Street Museum
Barrack Street
☎ 0382 23141 ext 65162
Open: all year, Monday to Saturday 10am-5pm.

Broughty Castle Museum
Castle Green
Broughty Ferry
☎ 0382 76121
Open: all year Monday to Thursday and Saturday 10am-1pm and 2-5pm. Open Sunday afternoons from July to September only. Closed Friday.

Camperdown Wildlife Centre
Camperdown Country Park
☎ 0382 623555
Open: all year daily 10am-4pm.

Clatto Country Park
Dalmahoy Drive
☎ 0382 23281 ext 2558 (Countryside Ranger Service)

Claypotts Castle
Arbroath Road
Open: April to September, Monday to Saturday 9.30am-6.30pm, Sunday 2-6.30pm.

Discovery, Royal Research Ship
Victoria Dock
Open: June to August daily 10-5pm. September to May, Monday to Friday 1-5pm. Saturday, Sunday and Bank Holidays 11-5pm.
☎ 0382 201175

Duntrune Demonstration Garden
☎ 0382 23141 ext 4788
Open: April to October, demonstrations every Wednesday 2-3.30pm and every other Saturday, 10.30am-12noon.

McManus Galleries
Albert Square
☎ 0382 23141 ext 136
Open: Monday to Saturday 10am-5pm.

Mills Observatory
Balgay Hill
☎ 0382 67138
Open: April to September, Monday to Friday 10am-5pm. Saturday 2-5pm. October to March, Monday to Friday 3-10pm. Saturday 2-5pm. Closed Sundays.

Olympia Leisure Centre
☎ 0382 203888

St Paul's Cathedral
1 High Street
☎ 0382 202200

Seagate Gallery and Printmakers Workshop
26-40 Seagate
☎ 0382 26331
Open: Monday to Saturday 10am-5.30pm.

Shaws Dundee Sweet Factory Limited
Fulton Road
Wester Gourdie Industrial Estate
☎ 0382 610369
Open: May to September, Monday to Friday 11.30am-4pm, except last week in July and first in August. October to April open Wednesday afternoons only, 1.30-5pm. Closed Christmas.

Unicorn Frigate
Victoria Dock
☎ 0382 200900
Open: all year, 10am-5pm, Saturday 10am-4pm.

University Botanic Garden
☎ 0382 66939
Open: March to October 10am-4.30pm. November to February 10am-3pm. Sundays and some public holidays 11am-4pm.

Verdant Works
West Henderson's Wynd
☎ 0382 26659

Edzell Castle
Standard opening hours
☎ 031 244 3101

Fettercairn
Fettercairn Distillery
☎ 05614 205
Open: May to September, Monday to Saturday 10am-4.30pm.

Fasque
☎ 05614 569 or 202
Open: May to September, daily except Friday 1.30-5.30pm.

Forfar
Pitmuies Garden
Five miles (8km) east of Forfar
House of Pitmuies
Forfar DD8 2SN
☎ 02412 245
Open: April to October 10am-5pm.

Glamis
Angus Folk Museum
☎ 0307 840288
Open: Easter and May to September daily 11am-5pm (last tour 4.30pm).

Glamis Castle
☎ 030 784 242 or 243
Open: April to October daily from
10.30am.

Glenesk
Glenesk Folk Museum
The Retreat
☎ 0356 670254
Open: every weekend, Saturday and
Monday 2-6pm, Sunday 1-6pm. Open
daily July to September 2-6pm.

Kirriemuir
J M Barrie's Birthplace
9 Brechin Road
☎ 0575 72588
Open: Easter, May to September,
Monday to Saturday 11am-5.30pm,
Sundays 2-5.30pm.

Camera Obscura
☎ 0575 74097
Open: summer months.

Loch of Kinnodry RSPB Nature Reserve
Open: all year from 9am to dusk, except
Saturdays in September and October.

Letham
Trumperton Forge
☎ 0307 62516
Open: May to September daily (except
Tuesday), October to Christmas
weekends only.

Monikie Country Park
☎ 082623 202

Montrose
House of Dun
☎ 0674891 264
Open: House, Easter, May to October
daily 11am-5.30pm (last tour 4pm).
Gardens open all year 10am-sunset.
Salmon fishing available on River Esk.

Sunnyside Museum
Open: Easter to September, Wednesday only 2-3.30pm. For other times
☎ 0674 830 361

Tourist Information Offices

Angus
Market Place
Arbroath
DD11 1HR
☎ 02241 72609 or 76680
Fax 0241 78550

Blairgowrie
26 Wellmeadow
Blairgowrie, Perthshire
PH10 6AS
☎ 0250 872960 or 873701

Brechin
St Ninian's Place
☎ 03356 623050
Open: April to September.

Carnoustie
The Library
High Street
☎ 0241 52258
Open: April to September.

Dundee
4 City Square
☎ 0382 27723 or 23141

Forfar
The Library
☎ 0307 67876
Open: April to September.

Kirriemuir
High Street
☎ 0575 740097
Open: April to September.

Montrose
The Library
High Street
☎ 0674 72000
Open: April to September.

5 • Royal Deeside

K incardine and Deeside is the southerly area of Grampian region that borders Angus in the south. It is one of Scotland's oldest 'tourist' areas, closely associated with the British Royal family since Queen Victoria, but in fact a recreation area for Scottish kings for a thousand years or more. The first 'Highland Games' probably began in this area as Scottish kings looked for a way to find the best men for their service. The Royal connections are very strong to this day. Not only is this the location of Balmoral, the castle to which the Windsors decamp most summers, but driving around you will see many signs of Royal patronage, the colourful Royal 'by appointment' crest above selected shops for example.

The valley itself is greener and less dramatic than many of the more mountainous areas of northern Scotland, there are several market towns and a general feeling of calm prosperity, very different to some of the communities that seem to cling perilously to steep, barren mountain sides on the north-west coast. The mountains at the top of the valley however, are as high and spartan as any in the Grampian or Cairngorm Mountains.

The Dee Valley is also a centre for outdoor sports. A leaflet detailing the numerous golfing options is available from tourist offices and of course there is hill walking, horse riding, pony trekking and fishing. 'Big Foot' adventures are organised from Ballater and gliding is possible from an airstrip near Aboyne.

Braemar is the first sizeable settlement on the salmon rich River Dee after it first rises in the Cairngorms before flowing down to enter the sea at Aberdeen. It is also the first village reached having crossed the border from Tayside in to the Grampian region from the south on the A93 (the ski lifts at Glenshee mark the border). Here the road changes from heading due north to heading due east as it begins to follow the Dee. Braemar is actually two smaller settlements on each side of Clunie Water and has been a favourite hunting resort of Scottish kings for many centuries. There was an old Royal castle at Kindrochit but little remains of that.

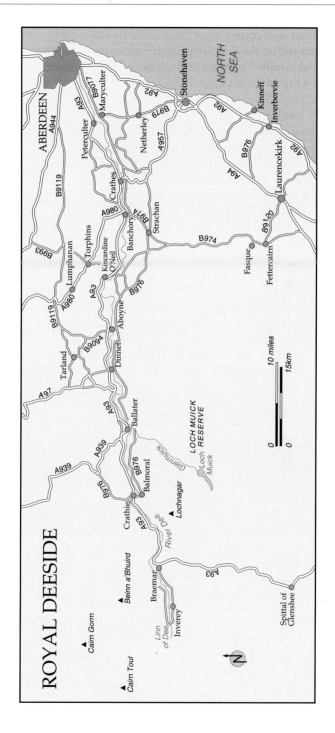

Braemar is of course most famous for its annual 'Highland Gathering', staged on the first Saturday in September and often graced by the Royal family. Gatherings have been held in Braemar since the days of King Malcolm Cranmore, but the current event has been in existence for 175 years. The village is also a key starting place for walkers heading up to the Munros (hills over 3,000ft/915m high) that surround the village. A road leads up to the Linn of Dee, where the bridge over the river was opened by Queen Victoria in September, 1857. The full strength of the river forces its way down a narrow chasm in the rock here. This route includes **Inverey** where there is a monument to John Lamont, a local man who became Astronomer Royal of Bavaria! A short walk also leads to the 'Colonel's Bed' where Colonel John Farquharson hid after escaping from the Battle of Killiecrankie in 1689. The road ends at Allanaquoich where a large circular pot hole is known as the Earl's Punch Bowl as it is said that when the Earl of Mar raised the 1715 Jacobite Rebellion he mixed a bowl of punch for his supporters in this hole.

Braemar has a Highland Heritage Centre, and there is an impressive looking, 'fairy tale' castle ½ mile (1km) north of the village on the main road. It was built in 1628 by the Earl of Mar and attacked and burned 61 years later by the 'Black Colonel' (John Farquharson of Inverey). It was purchased as a ruin by the Farquharsons of Invercauld in 1732 and they renovated it in the latter half of the eighteenth century following its repair by the government and use as garrisons for Hannoverian troops in the 1745 Jacobite uprising.

The road now descends eastwards along the Dee and through the Ballochbuie Forest, with the high peak of **Lochnagar** (3,786ft/1,154m) to the right. The woodland contains elements of the ancient Caledonian Pine forest saved from felling by order of Queen Victoria. Just before Crathie Church, where the Royals go to worship when in residence at Balmoral, a single track (B976) leads northwards to join the A939 via Tomintoul and ultimately to Grantown, 7 miles (11km) north-west in Moragshire. This road contains many challenges for drivers, with spectacular scenery in places as a reward. Drivers of large cars should beware of the very hump-backed bridge by Gairnstial Lodge where vehicles have been grounded in the past. It was constructed in 1751 as part of the old military road from Braemar to Donside. Further north, before Tomintoul, the road passes the bottom of the ski lifts at the Lecht and is usually closed by snow at some point each winter.

Crathie Church was opened on 18 June 1895 by Victoria having been built at a cost of £6,000 raised by public donation, including one

The River Dee

by Victoria herself. Indeed she was enthusiastic enough to allow a 2 day bazaar at Balmoral in September 1894 at which £2,400 was raised towards the cost.

To the south the B976 crosses an old bridge over the Dee and reaches the gates of **Balmoral Castle**. The bridge is most used by pedestrians visiting the castle and parking at a site on the corner of the A93 across the road from the church. It was built at Prince Albert's request by famous engineer, Brunel. Victoria thought it rather dull.

The Queen had visited the earlier castle that stood there in 1848, described as a pretty little castle in the old Scottish style (first referred to as 'Bouchmorale' in 1484). Prince Albert then bought the estate in 1852 on the advice of Queen Victoria's doctor and without having seen it. The new castle was built between 1853 and 1855 by William Smith of Aberdeen, after which the pretty little one was demolished! Queen Victoria, who had laid the foundation stone, was very pleased with the place and her descendants are said to feel likewise. The castle ballroom and grounds are open to the public at limited times in the summer, providing the Royal family is not in residence Although of considerable interest to Royal watchers some people tend to find this large house rather disappointing and the gardens and grounds of other buildings with less important inhabitants not far distant (such as Crathes Castle) much more impressive! From a modern day view point however, Balmoral is probably much more comfortable to actually live in.

Following the B976 on the south side of the Dee from now on may be a good choice. It is generally much quieter and scenic as it passes largely through woodland with glimpses of the Dee. There are also bridges across to the north side at most major places of interest. Just past Balmoral on this road is the Royal Lochnagar Distillery, founded in 1845 by John Begg. Tours are offered to the public as they were to Queen Victoria, Prince Albert and family some time ago and they accepted in 1848, enjoying the visit enough to grant the distillery a Royal Warrant.

Approaching **Ballater** on this south side of the Dee you may be able to catch a glimpse of the pink harled tower house of the Gordons, built in 1550 but not open to the public. Nearer to the town stand the gaunt ruins of Knock Castle. This was built in 1600 and had a bloody history including the murder of the entire resident family by a friendly neighbouring laird.

Ballater is a very pleasant small market town with a lovely green around the church. It was the old terminus of a railway branch line from Aberdeen, destroyed along with most other railways in northern Scotland in the 1960s. This was the terminus for Queen Victoria's Royal Train from Windsor and there is a small display of such railway memorabilia in the local tourist information centre. The old railway line is now a popular 4 mile (6km) footpath to Cambus O'May footbridge, which was re-opened in 1988 by the Queen Mother. The bridge was originally built in 1905 to allow access to the local railway station and had fallen in to serious disrepair by the mid-1980s following the closure of that station. This bridge is shortly before the start of the Muir of Dinnet National Nature Reserve (open dawn till dusk) which contains several picturesque lochs including Davan and Kinford.

Ballater contains a popular confectioners with sweets made in the traditional way on the premises, and a health spa producing bottled water. Indeed the town grew up on a grid pattern of streets in the eighteenth century largely to accommodate visitors taking the waters at Pannanich Wells. Making Treks is a centre for outdoor activity in the area, based at Station Square in the town. They are able to organise all sorts of outdoor sports from cycling, riding, fishing and clay pigeon shooting to off-road driving courses. For those really wanting to get to know the River Dee personally the 'Big Foot' Adventure day may involve canoeing, white water rafting, gorge

A suspension bridge over the River Dee

walking, abseiling, climbing, Tyrolean traversing, orienteering, mountain biking and clue finding. There is also a Victorian Week in the town each August when the residents dress in Victorian costume and many events are organised, culminating in the local Highland Games which began over 120 years ago.

Running south from Ballater into the Grampian Mountains is **Glenmuick**, with the high peak of Lochnagar, first climbed by Queen Victoria in 1848, to the west. It is often snow covered through much of the year. The unlisted road continues for 12 miles (19km) past the Linn of Muick falls to the Spittal of Glenmuick where there is a small visitor centre. Queen Victoria is known to have loved this place in particular and had a cottage built at the remote western end of Loch Muick in 1861, following Prince Albert's death, which she used to escape the increasing numbers of tourists.

North of Ballater the single track A939 winds through wooded Glencairn to meet the B976 from by Crathie Church mentioned earlier. Following this road for 14 miles (22km) leads to **Corgarff Castle**, a sixteenth-century tower house converted in to a garrison post. It was enclosed within a loopholed wall in 1748. The castle was burned in 1571 by Edom O'Gordon and then resident Alexander Forbes and his family died in the flames. Nearby on the A944 to **Strathdon** is Lonach farm, a centre for horse riding and pony trekking.

From Ballater the choice of roads north or south off the Dee remains the same. On the south side, shortly before Banchory, the B974 heads due south for Montrose in Tayside, passing Gladstone's house at Fasque and the village of Fettercairn with distillery and Victorian Arch (see Chapter 4 Dundee and Angus). Before the turn south however there is an option to turn north at Aboyne and follow the B9094 then B9119 up in to the hills north of the Dee. This route takes the driver up past the historic village of **Tarland**, 'The Queen's View', known to be one of Queen Victoria's favourite view points, and an ancient recumbent stone circle of Tomnaverie. The road then passes the Culsh Earth House remains at Craskins. Between Lumphanan and Milton of Auchinhove stands The Peel Ring, a rare example of a twelfth-century 'motte'. Equally interesting is the fact that the local woods were the scene of Macbeth's last stand in 1057. A stone commemorating the spot where he died stands in a field here.

The Alford road (A980) north from the B9119 soon reaches the National Trust run castle at **Craigievar**. This is another 'fairy tale' style castle, which originated as a tower house built by William

Forbes in 1626. The addition of turrets, cupolas and corbelling give the current picturesque effect. There is also a working tannery in the area.

Aboyne itself, located in Glen Tanar, got its name from the Gaelic meaning place of rippling waters. It is a suitable meaning for a picturesque place, much of it laid out in 1676 when Aboyne was recognised as a Burgh by Royal Charter. There are Highland Games held here in early August and attractions include Belwade Farm, the home of an international centre for the rest and rehabilitation of horses. There is also an airstrip here from where gliding has taken place and thrived since 1965. In 1990 a record altitude of 36,500ft (11,128m) was reached by a British two-seater glider. Before Aboyne itself is the Braeloine Interpretative Centre where there is an exhibition of land use and the history of the glen. The plant nurseries in the area specialise in native trees. Boat trips for fishermen are organised on Loch Tanar.

On the B976 just south of Aboyne the Black Faced Sheep craft shop and tea-room specialises in all foods and products genuinely Scottish. North of the Dee the A93 passes the delightfully named Slug of Dess Falls to reach **Kincardine O'Neil**, one of the oldest settlements in Deeside. The ruined church dates from 1233 and past visitors include Edward I with his army of 30,000 men with 5,000 on horseback, certainly putting today's coach parties in the shade. It is unlikely they had to visit by arrangement. Then came David I and then Macbeth on the retreat.

The B993 just past Kincardine leads up to **Torphins** which is believed to have got its name from Thorfinn, greatest of the Orkney Earls and an ally of Macbeth. The current village size results from the former Deeside railway.

Banchory is another pleasant town, larger than those higher up the river and with better facilities and a slightly more 'town like' feel as Aberdeen comes closer. There is a small local museum on Bridge Street and pleasant park lands down by the Dee.

Crathes Castle is 2 miles (3km) east of Banchory and arguably has the best gardens and grounds of all the castles and mansion houses on Deeside. The estate extends to some 600 acres (240 hectares) and contains 15 miles (24km) of well marked trails. The lands, formerly owned by the Leys, were granted to the Burnett family by King Robert the Bruce. The castle includes some exceptional painted ceilings dating from the sixteenth century, but the 4 acre (2 hectare) walled gardens are the major attraction for many. They are in fact a composite of eight separate gardens and yew hedges, giving fine examples of topiary, date from 1702. Just across the road from the castle Crathes Craft Studios and Pottery give demonstrations and sales of work.

Drum Castle, only a few more miles down the road, combines a medieval keep (pre-dating 1290 and one of the three oldest surviving in Scotland) with Jacobean mansion house and Victorian extension. It was lived in by twenty-four generations of the Irvine family until bequeathed to the National Trust in 1976. The original keep was the work of Richard Cementaurius, first provost of Aberdeen and the king's master mason. In 1323 King Robert the Bruce gave a charter of the Royal Forest of Drum to his faithful armour bearer, William de Irwyn, the same year as he gave neighbouring Crathes to the Burnetts. The A93 then continues in to Aberdeen, passing **Maryculter** where the locally famous Storybook Glen is located, having 100 nursery rhyme characters to discover in 20 acres (8 hectares) of scenic grounds.

Stonehaven on the coast is reached by taking the A957 from Crathes (accessed by minor roads from Banchory). The town was begun by Robert Barclay of Ury, a local laird. His wide market square and red sandstone streets contrast completely with the original and irregular housing scheme around the harbour. Robert Thomson, the man we can thank for the invention of the pneumatic tyre, was born here and there are several local attractions including a revived Victorian 'feeing day' market. Each New Year the ancient ceremony of fireball swinging continues in the town. The old ruined chapel of St Mary (1276) is all that remains of the ancient Royal Burgh of Cowie. There are many pleasant walks in the area and there's a museum in the old tolbooth with local history and fishing displays.

South of the town the spectacular and huge ruins of twelfth-century **Dunnottar Castle** stand on one of the large rocky outcrops in to the sea. This was the castle chosen by Franco Zeffirelli when he made his film version of *Hamlet* with Mel Gibson in the early 1990s.

Nearby are several interesting villages. **Kinneff's** old church was the place where the Scottish Crown Jewels were hidden, under the pulpit, for 9 years after being smuggled from Dunnottar Castle past Cromwell's besieging army in 1651. **Crawton** village on the coast was abandoned by its inhabitants and at **Inverbervie** there is a monument to Hercules Linton, designer of famous sailing ship, *The Golden Hind*. The RSPB Reserve at **Fowlsheugh** contains up to 100,000 nesting birds making the cliffs both rather over-crowded and one of Scotland's largest seabird colonies.

Further Information
— Royal Deeside —

Places to Visit

Aboyne
Belwade Farm
☎ 03398 87186
Open: Wednesday 2pm to 4pm, Weekends 11am-4pm, other times by arrangement.

Black Faced Sheep
☎ 033398 87311
Open: daily 10-5pm.

Braeloine Interpretative Centre
☎ 03398 86072
Open: April to September, 10am-5pm.

Deeside Gliding Club
☎ 03398 85339
Open: subject to weather conditions, first come, first flown.

Glen Tanar Loch Fishing
☎ 03398 86451
Open: April to October.

Glen Tanar Nursery
☎ 03398 86590
Open: March to December, from 10am.

Ballater
Dee Valley Manufacturing Confectioners
☎ 03397 55499

Making Treks
☎ 03397 55865

Muir of Dinnet National Nature Reserve
☎ 03398 81667

Pannanich Wells
South Deeside Road
Open: April to October, daily, 11am-3.30pm. November to March, weekends only, 11am-3.30pm.

Spittal of Glenmuick Visitor Centre
Open: daylight hours throughout the year.

Balmoral
Balmoral Castle
Open: May to July, Monday to Saturday, 10am-5pm, except when Royal family resident.

Crathie Church
Open: April to October, 9.30am-5.30pm, Sundays 2-5pm. Services at 11.30am on Sundays.

Royal Lochnagar Distillery
Crathie
Deeside
☎ 03397 42273
Open: Easter to October, Monday to Saturday, 10am-5pm, Sunday 11am-4pm. November to Easter, Monday to Friday, 10am-5pm.

Banchory
Banchory Museum
Open: daily except Thursday, June to September 2-5.15pm.
☎ 0779 77778

Braemar
Braemar Castle
☎ 03397 41219
Open: May to September, daily except Friday, 10am-6pm.

Highland Heritage Centre
Mar Road
☎ 03397 41944

Corgarff
Corgarff Castle
☎ 031 244 3101
Open: April to September, Monday to Saturday 9.30am-7pm, Sunday 2-7pm. October to March, Monday to Saturday 9.30am-4pm, Sunday 2-4pm.

Craigievar
Craigievar Castle
☎ 03398 83635
Open: Castle, May to September, daily 2-6pm (last tour 5.15pm). Grounds open all year from 9.30am to sunset.

Foggielay Tannery & Shop
☎ 033398 83317
Open: Monday to Friday 9am-6pm, weekends 10am-5pm. Please telephone in advance

Crathes
Crathes Castle
☎ 033044 525
Open: Castle and buildings, April to
October, daily, 11am-6pm (last tour
5.15pm). Grounds open all year,
9.30am-sunset.
Crathes Craft Studios & Pottery
☎ 033044 601
Open: daily, all year, 10am-5.30pm.

Drum
Drum Castle
☎ 03308 204
Open: Castle, May to September, daily,
2-6pm. October open weekends, 2-
5pm. Last tour 45 minutes before
closing. Walled Garden open May to
October, 10am-6pm. Grounds open all
year, 9.30am-sunset.

Fowlsheugh
RSPB Nature Reserve
☎ 031 557 33136
Open: always.

Glenmuick
Spittal of Glenmuick Visitor Centre
Open: daylight hours throughout the
year.

Maryculter
Storybook Glen
☎ 0224 732941
Open: daily, March to October, 10am-
6pm and weekends rest of year, 11am-
4pm.

Strathdon
Lonach Farm
☎ 09756 51275

Stonehaven
Dunnottar Castle
☎ 0569 62173
Open: all year, Easter to October
Monday to Saturday, 9am-6pm (last
entry 5.30pm), Sunday 2-5pm.
November to March, weekdays 9am-
dusk, closed weekends.

Tolbooth Museum
Open: June to September, Monday,
Thursday, Friday and Saturday 10am-
12noon and 2-5pm. Wednesday and
Sunday open 2-5pm. Closed Tuesday.

Tourist Information Offices

Aboyne
Ballater Road Car Park
☎ 03398 86060
Open: Easter to September.

Ballater
Station Square
☎ 03397 55306
Open: Easter to October.

Banchory
45 Station Road
Kincardineshire
AB3 3XX
☎ 03302 2066

Bridge Street
☎ 0330 822000
Open: all year.

Braemar
Balnellan Road
☎ 03397 41600
Open: March to November.

Crathie
Car Park
☎ 03397 42414
Open: April to September.

Stonehaven
66 Allardice Street
☎ 0569 62806
Open: April to October.

6 • The Spey Valley

The River Spey is the driving force behind the 'water of life'. The river is the root of the valley's success, bringing it economic life today as much as the water for life through the centuries past. The Spey supports numerous world famous whisky distilleries, water bottling operations as well as the plants, animals, birds and fish which rely on it to create the most fertile valley in the Highlands. People too have farmed and fished here for generations; a land to be fought over by clan chiefs in the past, and now by conservationists fearing that the expansion of leisure facilities will destroy the natural beauty that attracts so many people here in the first place.

The Gaelic translation of the river's name is 'Hawthorn Stream' which would indicate it was named during drought times, or that 'stream' meant something different to what it does today. The Spey can be a mighty river indeed in full flood. Second after whisky production, it is known as a great fishing river where salmon, sea and brown trout, pike, eels and Arctic char may be caught according to the season. Equally significant is the ornithological value of the Spey Valley, said by the RSPB to be most important flood plain in Scotland. They have major reserves at the Insh Marches and Abernethy Forest and have successfully re-introduced ospreys to the area.

On the new A9 from the south, **Dalwhinnie** appears on the left of the road soon after the notorious Drumochter Pass, the longest stretch of dual carriageway on the A9 but still usually closed at least once or twice even in mild winters by snow, land-slips or some other weather-borne extreme! Incidentally the new A9 is the main route north from Perth to Wick and has now been upgraded as far as Dornoch in Sutherland with the three Firths of Moray, Cromarty and Dornoch all crossed by bridges, each cutting out what was a 20 mile (32km) or more drive around each Firth (or a ferry crossing) until quite recently. The new road is largely single carriageway, although some feel it is wide enough to enable them to overtake down the middle with cars coming in the opposite direction, particularly on

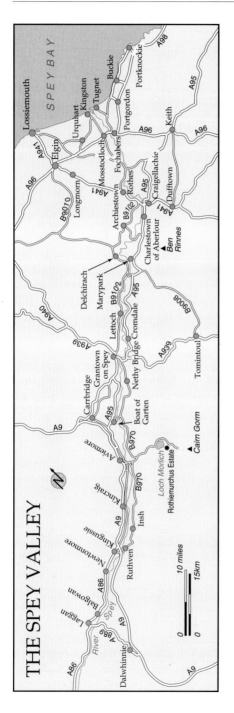

the 100 mile (161km) stretch from Perth to Inverness. This is not advised, indeed the reputation of the road is such that the police have brought out a leaflet specifically to advise drivers on how they should behave and road signs warn of unmarked police cars and the danger of drowsiness for the inexperienced on the long drive. There are dual carriageway sections; these are just far enough apart and short enough in length to be irritating to those in a hurry, and good overtaking stretches to get past the lorries or caravans using the road.

The 'old A9' is the original road that goes through the main streets of all the villages and round the Firths; it is usually signposted with a brown sign saying 'Alternative Route North/South' and is accessed at various points along the new A9. It is certainly a good choice for those not in so much of a hurry to go north as it is generally much more peaceful and tends to go through more rural landscapes according to its natural historical associations with the farms and villages en route rather than through the bleak but most direct route of the new road (although that desolate mountainous landscape is impressive enough). The name Dalwhinnie means 'Meeting Place' and this was the junction of the old drove roads for Highland cattle drivers en route to markets down in Crieff and Falkirk.

Dalwhinnie's distillery stands out clearly above the village looking everything a distillery should, in fact at over 1,000ft (305m) this is Scotland's highest distillery. A particularly good 15-year-old malt is produced here, and there is also a particularly good Visitor Centre for those who want to see the production and try a tipple. The water source for the distillery is the snow-fed Allt an t'Sluic spring, which becomes a source of the Spey itself. The distillery was called Strathspey when it opened in 1897 and has long been a vital ingredient of the famous blend Black & White, created by famous whisky blender James Buchanan. It was only available locally as a single malt until quite recently when owners United Distillers chose it as one of their six classic malts. The whisky's nick name is 'Gentle Spirit' and is known for its remarkable smoothness.

It is about 10 miles (16km) from Dalwhinnie to Newtonmore, the new A9 is most direct but the A889 to Laggan, which joins the A86 Fort William road is a quieter option. The road reaches and crosses the Spey at Laggan from where a minor track follows the river westerly towards its source, petering out at Garva Bridge en route to the Corrieyairack Pass. South of the Spey Dam, located on this road, is the site of the old hill fort of Dun da Lamh.

Newtonmore is a pleasant Highland 'frontier' town, spread along about 1 mile (2km) of the main street. It is well used to tourists and has a number of attractions including a pottery and a heavily promoted water-fountains theatre. A liqueur named 'Stag's Breath', is made here from whisky and comb heather honey, the name coming from Compton Mackenzie's famous book *Whisky Galore* (see Chapter 12 The Western Isles). There is also a small working pottery in the village.

The Clan MacPherson has long been prominent in this area, the ancient Lordship of Badenoch and their museum is located at the junction of the old A9 and the A86 by Newtonmore. The clan still has an annual gathering in Newtonmore each year. MacPherson Museum mementos include a fiddle played by a clan member named James shortly before he was hanged in Banff and a Green Banner which, when present on the battlefield, always assured the clan of victory. The A9/A86 junction is quite an important one historically, with the A86 having come in west from the Great Glen while the old A9 was the main highway north.

Approaching Kingussie from the south, especially on the A9, the prominent fortress-like ruin was in fact **Ruthven Barracks,** last used by Jacobite troops on their way to defeat at Culloden. North of the barracks are the **Insh Marches,** a good spot for bird watchers; wild fowl come here to breed in the spring and migrating whooper swans may be seen in large numbers during the winter.

The hill above the town is Creag Bheag (1,581ft/482m) which can be reached by climbing from Loch Gynack, across the golf course. The Highland Folk Museum in **Kingussie** is a particularly active place, and has ever changing displays of crafts and a season of exhibitions each year within its Iona Gallery. Also of note is the local Bowling Club, which dates back to 1877 making it one of Scotland's oldest.

The 10 miles (16km) between Kingussie and Aviemore continue to appear as a mixture of desolation and forest from the new A9, but two roads run parallel to it on either side of the Spey, both accessed through Kingussie. The B970 on the south-east side passes Insh and Feshiebridge (location of 'Queen's Forest' where there are walks and picnic areas) on its way to Coylumbridge, Boat of Garten and ultimately Grantown. The old A9, now the B1952, stays north-west of the Spey and passes through Kincraig before reaching Aviemore.

Kincraig is located by the edge of Loch Insh and is a popular base for tourers. The Highland Wildlife Park is located just south off the village and is owned by the Royal Zoological Society of Scotland. It covers 260 acres (104 hectares) of natural land and contains animals and birds that are, or once were, indigenous to the region. These include otters, red fox, wild cats, bears and deer. While some more progressive visitor attractions provide a crèche for young children, the Wildlife Park provides free kennels for visitors' dogs!

Insh Church, sited in a prominent position above the loch, has seen Christian worship since the seventh century. Two thousand acres (800 hectares) of marshland at the edge of the loch (frequently flooded in the winter) make up as RSPB reserve where over 120 species of bird are seen annually. The two main providers of leisure activities in the area are the Loch Insh Hotel where there is a dry ski slope and the opportunity of canoeing, sailing, wind-surfing and fishing on the loch and the Alvie Estate which also organises fishing, or photographic safaris and a Bothy Day including lunch with the laird and a clay pigeon shoot — green wellies provided. Pony trekking and bicycle hire are also available locally. Finally the Inshriach Nursery is not to be missed by gardeners, especially Alpine enthusiasts who will find one of the world's largest collections here.

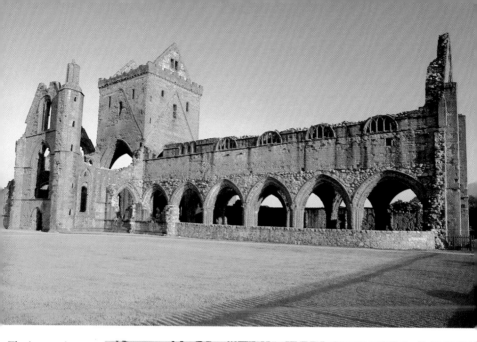

The impressive remains of Sweetheart Abbey (Chapter 2)

Dhoon Bay near Kirkcudbright (Chapter 2)

The rail bridge, linking Dundee with Fife across the Tay, is the longest in the world (Chapter 4)

Gateway to the Grampian Mountains

Scotland's best known ski resort is **Aviemore** and it is difficult to describe the town itself as an attractive place. On the other hand it is lively, there is plenty to do and it is at the centre of wonderful natural scenery and probably Scotland's greatest concentration of organised outdoor leisure facilities. There are numerous places where you can enjoy organised canoeing, windsurfing, sailing, fishing, bird or wildlife watching, golf, clay-pigeon shooting, skiing, go-karting, off-road driving, pony trekking, even ballooning — all within a 10 mile (16km) radius. The expansion of these facilities, particularly the skiing, has worried some environmentalists who have formed a protest group 'Save the Cairngorms' to lobby against development of ski infrastructure and other developments on the hills.

Aviemore's major sore point has for many years now been the Aviemore Centre, fortunately separated from the rest of the town so not immediately obvious unless you drive up to visit the book shop, cinema or hotels up there. This was built in the 1960s in the era of grey concrete rectangular tower blocks on the edge of big cities. Ownership of all or part of the centre keeps moving from one company to another and plans are always afoot to improve it, but it is hard to see what can be done now short of demolition. However individual hotels, such as the excellent Freedom Inn, are spending six and seven figure sums on upgrading.

The centre should not be taken as representative of the feel of Aviemore itself however as there is an awful lot to see and do here. There are about half a dozen ski shops and delicatessen and the award winning fish and chip shop, 'Smiffys' has been voted best in Scotland. Likewise the rather expensive but very nice public toilets, also award winners!

Lovers of steam trains will not want to miss the Strathspey Steam Railway which runs from the farside of Aviemore's railway station (underpass under the tracks). This is a remarkable venture having begun with volunteers but now employing about six and still relying heavily on volunteer support. The train runs 5 miles (8km) to Boat of Garten, although there are long-standing plans to re-open the old line all the way to Grantown, however this would involve the regional council in replacing a railway bridge. Occasional evening trips and lunchtime specials with traditional meals in the restaurant car are provided, as are trips to see the ospreys at Boat of Garten.

It is about 12 miles (19km) from Aviemore through Coylumbridge to the skiing at Cairn Gorm on a good road. The route actually seems more active in the summer as it passes through forest parks, time share complexes and part of the **Rothiemurchus Estate**, each with its own attractions. This is the clanlands of the Grants, who have ruled in the area since the late sixteenth century but had battled over it before with the Cummings, the Shaws and the Mackintoshes. The history of Grant ownership is believed to have begun when a young Shaw chief, then in possession, beheaded his father-in-law for some misdemeanour. As a result the young chief was outlawed and the estate forfeited to the crown. Sensing a bargain in the air, the Laird of Grant put in a successful bid for the estate, moved his son Patrick in. The Grants have been there ever since. The Shaws rather resented this change in fortune. The area begins with low lying fields on the Spey's flood plain and then becomes heather moorland punctuated by areas of birch and Caledonian Pine forest and finally the boulder fields and spartan slopes of the granite Cairngorms. This upper area has been a National Nature Reserve since 1954. There is another nature reserve at Craigellachie, north of Aviemore.

The Rothiemurchus Estate, before the forest park, operates one of the most advanced and comprehensive range of visitor attractions in Scotland. The name means 'Plain Of The Great Pine' in Gaelic. These include a fish farm with some 200,000 trout to visit, a visitor centre, an old school converted into a shop, a farm shop, a shooting ground, estate safari tours, farm tours, forest, river and nature trails, hawking, path-finding, fishing, bird-watching, mountain biking and off-road vehicles. There is also a whisky centre which may have the largest selection of whisky available anywhere (over 500) and a particularly good ski shop.

There are two buildings of particular historical interest on the estate. The castle on **Loch an Eilean** was built some 700 years ago by a Comyn chief. The precise construction date is unknown but it is documented that in 1296 Edward I of England sent messengers to locate it. In 1380 the castle was leased briefly along with the lands of Rothiemurchus to 'Wolf of Badenoch', an illegitimate and rather violent son of Robert the Bruce, by the then owner Bishop of Moray, Alexander Bur. It is likely that the first Grant laird improved the building in the late sixteenth century and it saw action in 1690 when Dame Grizel Mor, widow of the fifth Grant laird, led its defence from defeated Jacobites who laid siege after they lost the battle of Cromdale. The castle fell into ruin in the eighteenth century when a new dam submerged the causeway that linked it to the land. Ospreys nested in the tower through most of the nineteenth century.

The other building of note is the Grant family house on the estate, known as the Doune of Rothiemurchus. Doune is a Gaelic word meaning 'Fort'. It was built below the fort of that name in more peaceful times in the sixteenth century and extended in the eighteenth and nineteenth centuries. The original fort was built by the Shaws and Patrick Grant who built the original mansion house pronounced a curse on any of his descendants who thought about renovating the house.

The mutual animosity between Grant and Shaw is also reflected in the graves surrounding the ruined Rothiemurchus Church not far from the house. The Grants and Shaws are buried separately and it is reported that one Grant family member specifically asked to be buried quite a way from the church so that on judgement day, when the dead will be raised, he would have a good start to make his escape from the Shaw clan. Other points of interest in the churchyard include a monument erected in the 1970s to Seath Mor, one of the most famous Shaws who defeated the Clan Davidson at the battle of Perth in the fourteenth century.

Four miles (6km) from Aviemore and at the edge of the Rothiemurchus Estate, the **Glenmore Forest Park** begins, straddling the road and all but surrounding Loch Morlich, usually a peaceful place although water sports are allowed upon it. The wildlife in the forest includes pine marten, roe deer, wildcat, capercaille, crested tits and crossbills. If you want to be more certain of seeing some deer, Britain's only free-ranging herd of reindeer reside on the northern

The sandy beach at Loch Morlich, surrounded by the Cairngorm Mountains

slopes of the Cairngorms and can be found with the help of a guide at the Reindeer Centre in the forest park.

The road now begins to climb and becomes a one way circuit as the skiing area comes into view, trees end and the National Park begins. There are wonderful views across the Spey Valley from here. The elderly chairlift is open all year, weather permitting. Skiing in Scotland has always been a tricky business. The unpredictability of the snow, like the summer sunshine, means that it is impossible to build a reputation as a serious ski resort by international standards and thus difficult to build a firm economic development strategy.

The key paradoxes of skiing in Scotland are that when there is a good fall of snow it is likely that the wind will be too strong for the chairlifts to operate, and when the wind drops and there is a beautiful blue sky and enough snow to ski on, the slopes will fill to bursting and you will spend a great deal of time standing in the strictly regimented queues for the lifts. Still, when the skiing is good, it is very good.

Back at Coylumbridge a turning on to the B970 follows the Spey all the way to Grantown on its south side, although there are several options to cross, first of all at Boat of Garten 5 miles (8km) away. It is a winding single track road and must be taken slowly. **Boat of Garten** got its name from the old Spey ferry crossing at this point, replaced by a bridge in 1874. Today it is known as the Osprey Village

Canoeing on the calm waters of Loch Morlich

being the closest spot to the RSPB's Loch Garten reserve which the B970 skirts along. The ospreys were successfully reintroduced here in 1959, about 50 years after they had become extinct in Scotland and return to a nesting site closely monitored by hidden cameras year after year. The resulting large public hide and the nest site have been the target of vandals on several occasions — it is difficult to imagine why. A 24 hour watch has to be put on their nest site, and others around the Highlands kept secret from the public, to save them from egg thieves and poisoners. The ospreys however are undeterred and now nest in various parts of Scotland.

Shortly before Boat of Garten on the B970 is a treat for off-road vehicle fans. Highland Drovers gives the opportunity to whizz round trails in 4x4 buggies and 8 wheel all terrain vehicles. Anyone can have a go so long as they are old enough to hold a steering wheel.

Carrbridge gets its name from the ancient stone pack horse bridge that spans the Dulnain river (a Spey tributary) in the heart of the village. The bridge is a little worn at the edges now and serves to fill camera film rather than transport people over the water, but it has the distinction of being the oldest surviving stone bridge in northern Scotland. A popular riverside walk was reopened in 1993, starting at the old bridge and incorporating a refurbished suspension foot-bridge restored the previous summer by volunteers.

The major attraction here for most people will be the Landmark Heritage and Adventure Park, one of Scotland's original natural heritage centres, established in the late 1960s by a gentleman called David Hayes and covering some 30 acres (12 hectares) of natural pine forest. Mr Hayes got some of his ideas from the United States where he worked for the National Park Service. Opened in 1970 by the Duke of Edinburgh, Landmark was awarded the 'Come to Britain Trophy' that year by the British Tourist Authority.

Today the centre continues to expand with new ideas. Although there are attractions for all ages. Children in particular will love the adventure playground, which must be one of the best in the United Kingdom and the treetop walk. There is also a very impressive fully operational steam powered sawmill, as well as a woodland maze, lookout tower and numerous other attractions. Visitors can try their hand at modern or traditional forest work and meet Bob the Clydesdale horse who hauls logs ready for sawing (or try out the state of the art, automated version). Many other sports are on offer either in Carrbridge (such as golf, pony trekking, fishing, sailing, wind-surfing) or near by. There is a craft studio and an antique shop in the village.

Carrbridge was also Scotland's original ski village and is still closely associated with the Cairngorm based industry. Austrian ski instructor Karl Fuchs founded what was Scotland's first professional ski school here. There is a good ski shop and innovative ski tuition is provided by companies such as Ski Pro Personal Performance Courses who employ some of the United Kingdom's best ski instructors to give top quality in-depth tuition for all skier standards, with accommodation as well if required.

The A938, virtually a single track road, leaves Carrbridge en route to Grantown on Spey, meeting the A95 from Aviemore at Dulnain Bridge, north of Nethy Bridge, near to the ruined castle of Roy. **Dulnain Bridge** is close to an award winning heritage centre and garden nursery themed on heather. More than 300 varieties grow in the gardens of Speyside Heather and the centre includes tea-room, craft, gift, fashion and garden shop as well as a visitor centre and information trail.

One of **Grantown on Spey's** most famous visitors was Queen Victoria, and the place has a fairly Victorian feel to it today, architecturally, with many grand buildings, all still in a good state of repair. The Queen recorded a complimentary report on her 'very amusing and never to be forgotten' visit in 1860, which helped to establish the town's reputation as a holiday centre. The town was originally envisaged soon after the Jacobite defeat at Culloden. The

The forest viewing tower at Landmark Highland Heritage and Adventure Park, Carrbridge

Grants, who had lived in the lands since the Norman Conquest of England and who had previously fought for Scotland at Dunbar and Bannockburn, chose to support the Government at Culloden. With new wars to be fought beyond Scotland's shores, wood was required for ships and the Strathspey forests were largely cut down to build them. Grantown's first house was erected on what was barren heath in 1765, planned by 'Good Sir James' Grant. New trees were planted where the old forests had been felled and some remain today from that period, as forestry has continued through the intervening centuries. Sir James had a reputation as a benefactor, bringing improved agricultural conditions, schools, health care and a postal service. Unfortunately however the Industrial Revolution was taking root and Grantown's earlier potential was not reached. A revival followed in the mid-nineteenth century as Grantown became the epitome of Victorian health resorts, endorsed by Queen Victoria. The town's history is recorded in the excellent exhibition organised in the old courthouse by the Grantown Heritage Trust.

Today Grantown is well placed for touring at the junction of the roads from Nairn and Elgin to Aberdeen via Tomintoul and Royal Deeside, or further up the Spey Valley as detailed above. There are plenty of traditional sporting activities on offer in the town, including golf, fishing on the Spey and woodland walks. It is also located just off the famous Malt Whisky Trail. The Grant clan seat overlooks Grantown. Parts of the building date to the fifteenth century. In the eighteenth century the castle park extended to some 4,000 acres (1,600 hectares) and included an avenue of trees, probably the avenue of limes that still exists today.

The seventh Earl of Grant was a great promoter of the Highland railways and the castle once had its own private railway station. Grantown itself lost its entire rail link in the 1960s although this will hopefully change with the Strathspey railway from Boat of Garden which is to be reopened. The seventh Earl is also said to have planted 60 million trees on the estate, however his only child died unmarried in 1884 and the Barony of Grant became extinct. The castle had always been in Grant hands apart from a brief period in 1747 when the then laird, Ludovick Grant tried to stop Jacobites from forcibly persuading his tenants to join their ranks. Ironically the Jacobites arrived and took the castle over in his absence. Robert Burns visited 40 years later in 1787.

The Spey continues to wind its way north-eastwards towards the Moray coast, through an often wooded valley. The mountains gradually subside in to gentler hill country and a land flowing with some of the world's best whisky!

The River Spey near Grantown on Spey

Roads follow the Spey on either bank, the narrower but less crowded B9102 on the north bank, the main A95 continues to the south. Just over the Morayshire border there is the start of the 48 mile (77km) Speyside Way which follows the river to the coast. The bridge here leads to the first distillery on Speyside and on the Malt Whisky Trail coming this way from Grantown, at Glenfarclas, a good place to begin as both distillery and its whisky are very highly regarded by the connoisseurs. In the latter category **Glenfarclas** produces the strongest bottled whisky available, the '105', named after its old British proof rating. It is now marked 60% proof. Its quality surprises many experts as, at 8 years old, it is comparatively young. The distillery also produces 10, 12, 15, 22 and 25 year old malts of equally high pedigree, if lower proof. The distillery itself opened in 1836 and has been in the Grant family for generations, remaining staunchly independent. There is a good Visitor Centre as you would expect, complete with a recreated 'Ships Room' from the *Empress of Australia* ship which sailed between 1913 and 1952 carrying over 1,500 passengers across the world.

Ballindalloch Castle sees both Rivers Spey and Avon flow through its grounds. It is one of few castles still privately owned to have been occupied continuously by one family, the MacPherson-Grants, since 1546, and is an excellent example of the transition from functional sixteenth-century tower house to luxurious Victorian country home. The famed Aberdeen Angus cattle graze outside, the breed having been established by George MacPherson Grant in 1860, and is now the oldest herd in existence. The grounds also contain a rock garden created in the 1900s and a seventeenth-century dovecot. The Inveravon Kirk (1806) nearby contains four early Pictish stones mounted in its south wall.

The Malt Whisky Trail actually continues south on the B9008 along the River Avon, a Spey tributary to the famous distillery at **Glenlivet**. This was the Highlands' first licensed distillery following an Act of Parliament in 1823 which put a stop to years of smuggling and illicit distilling. The Tamnavulin distillery at **Tomnavoulin**, also west of Grantown is included in the 8 distillery 70 mile (113km) trail. The trail leaflet advises you to allow an hour at each distillery, but forgets to advise not to take the dram usually included in your entry fee at each if you are driving. Other distilleries in the area, not included in the trail, are usually happy to welcome visitors.

The remainder of the Spey is within the district of Moray which deserves a historical mention as this was part of the Scottish kingdom made up of united Picts and Scots which largely saw off the Vikings by the eleventh century. At that time it was the land of Shakespeare's *Macbeth* fame, ultimately defeated by Malcolm Canmore. In 1130 however, the House of Moray was overthrown and King David I of Scotland, Canmore's son, planted his own Anglo-Norman supporters in Morayshire. Relative medieval stability followed for two centuries before Edward I of England used the crisis of succession in Scotland to try and take over. His occupation reached as far north as Moray but the former 'Anglos' were now committed 'Scots' and fought back.

The following few centuries were less peaceful as Highland clan leaders passed the time attempting to win the crown of Scotland and, when unsuccessful, sacking castles and villages nearer to home. Notable among these were the Wolf of Badenoch and later the Douglas Earls of Moray who mounted a challenge to King James II. At the end of the Middle Ages however Moray benefited from more peaceful times and has survived the intervening centuries with rather less violence and bloodshed than much of the rest of Scotland.

Today Moray's infrastructure is based largely on agriculture, forestry, whisky distilling and tourism. Two other industries, fishing and oil rig fabrication are on the decline. There are major RAF bases at Lossiemouth and Kinloss, both vital to the local economy, generating almost £100 million a year and employing many local people.

Their presence does not stop the region being one of Scotland's unemployment blackspots however, although the very attractive towns and villages run contrary to the traditional image of an 'unemployment blackspot'. The economic situation helps to make the region one of the strongholds of Scottish nationalism politically.

Staying on the B9102 north of the Spey Valley the road soon passes another distillery, at **Cardhu**, the name coming from the Gaelic meaning 'Black Rock' and having various spellings including Cardow. It is one of three distilleries in the immediate area including Knockando and Tamdhu at Knockando. Helen Cummings, wife of the Cardhu distillery's founder, John, was popular in olden times as she flew a red flag from the distillery to warn local crofters operating illegal stills that the excise men were in the area. Apart from being a malt in its own right, Cardhu produces one of the constituent malts for Johnnie Walker blends.

Shortly afterwards, the road reaches Upper Knockando and a right turn just past the village leads to **Knockando** itself and the Tamdhu Distillery on the banks of the Spey. Founded in 1896, it was closed during the 1930s due to operational difficulties and largely rebuilt in the 1970s. It now produces one of the major Speyside malts, using water from the Tamdhu burn which flows into the Spey. The distillery was one of several originally served by Speyside railway line (specifically sited next to it, with a road being built specially to it) and is a constituent of the Famous Grouse blend. **Archiestown**, 2 miles (3km) further along gets its name from Sir Archibald Grant of Monymusk who founded the village on Ballintomb Moor in 1760. Elchies Forest stretches out to the north.

Several minor roads lead south to cross the Spey at Carron and connect with the A95 trunk road, 2 miles (3km) south-west of **Charlestown of Aberlour**, sited beneath the Conval Hills. It was founded in 1812 by local laird, Charles Grant of Wester Elchies and became nationally famous when the Aberlour Orphanage, built in 1882, opened there. This provided a home for thousands of children until closure in 1967. The area surrounding the former station has been landscaped and named Alice Littler Park after the wife of Mr Sydney Littler who bought the orphanage. There is another distillery here which produces a whisky that scores highly with connoisseurs, who find peppermint and nutmeg in its taste. It was officially recognised in 1826 but probably existed well before. A signposted walk from the distillery leads up to the Linn Waterfall. There is also a visitor centre for Aberlour and a local deer farm. The village store preserves records and products sold there from the 1920s to the early

1970s and is thus an entertaining reminder of the days before the superstore and retail park.

Craigellachie is a major junction on Speyside as the A95 loses its trunk road status here and continues on towards Keith and Banff as a normal A road. Meanwhile the A941 turns north towards Elgin, taking up the trunk road mantle, and south to Dufftown. The B9102 we have been following reaches its end just north of Craigellachie. Rivers meet here too, with the Fiddich running into the Spey.

The village reached its peak in the late nineteenth century when the population quadrupled. There is another distillery here and a large cooperage. The imposing cast iron bridge, now bypassed, was built in Wales in 1814 at a cost of £8,000 to a Telford design. The whisky which shares the village name is a fruity malt in its own right and a component of White Horse blends. The ranger service that operates the ever expanding Speyside way is also based here and there is a visitor centre.

Craigellachie's Speyside Cooperage, a family business for generations, moved to new premises in 1992 enabling the establishment of a visitor centre. This is an interesting addition for those following a distillery trail as it is here that up to 100,000 casks are made or repaired 'in the time-honoured way' each year. The exhibition traces the history of cooperage over thousands of years and recounts how in times past a drunkard wore a cask with holes cut for arms and head, known as a drunkard's cloak. The cask has a working life of 40 years or more and is made from oak imported from Missouri, Kentucky and Tennessee. When a cask finally has 'held its last' it is reduced to shavings which are burned to smoke Scottish salmon!

Dufftown, 5 miles (8km) south, is just outside Speyside, being on the Fiddich River tributary but as it contains many significant features, it is worthy of brief detour. The town was founded in 1817 by James Duff (as you might expect), who was fourth Earl of Fife. He built it to provide employment following the Napoleonic Wars and like many other Moray towns it was well planned with spacious streets converging on the clock tower, completed in 1839 and originally the town jail, now housing the local tourist information centre. The clock has an interesting history as it is known as 'the clock that hung MacPherson' and originally ticked away in Banff. The MacPherson in question, James, was a seventeenth-century outlaw, although apparently regarded locally as a Robin Hood. He was sentenced to death in Banff when caught in 1700. The locals raised a petition calling for a reprieve but as it was on its way at the last minute, the wicked Sheriff of Banff put the clock forward an hour so that MacPherson was hanged shortly before the pardon arrived. The clock was transferred to Dufftown in later years. The clock tower also houses a small local museum.

Balvenie Castle, of courtyard design, dates from the thirteenth century. England's King Edward I is an early entry in the proverbial visitors book, followed by a period of ownership by the Stewarts, Earl of Atholl, from 1459, during which time Mary, Queen of Scots and the Marquis of Montrose each spent a few nights there. It was stormed by Royalists in 1649, occupied by the Jacobites after their victory at Killiecrankie in 1689 and then, for the last time, by government forces when victory was on the other side in 1746.

A second fortification close to Dufftown is the now ruined Auchindoun Castle, set on a steep hillside above the Fiddich river about 1 mile (2km) south-east on the A920. It was built by Robert Cochran, a favourite of King James III but not of the 'Scottish Barons' who hanged him. The castle was burnt down in 1592 although the keep still stands three storey high. The building is unsafe to enter.

Mortlach Parish Church is one of the oldest places of Christian worship in Scotland, believed to have been founded in AD566 by St Moluag, a contemporary of Columba. There are several Pictish stones in and around the buildings which have been extensively modernised through the years. The first improvements are fabled to have been ordered by King Malcolm II in AD1010, an extension of three spears lengths to commemorate victory over the Danes on the grounds below.

The world famous Glenfiddich brand is produced in the distillery at the north end of the town. It is one of only two distilleries to have their own bottling plant (the other being Springbank in Campbeltown). The first whisky was produced on Christmas Day 1887 by William Grant, who used second-hand equipment bought at a bargain price from nearby Cardhu. The Grant family have owned and managed the distillery ever since. It has been greatly extended in recent years and now has an excellent visitor centre. Next door is the Balvenie distillery, owned by the same family.

Dufftown's famous sons include George Stephen, later Lord Mount Stephen who emigrated to Canada and became first President of the mighty Canadian Pacific Railway. The local cottage hospital is named after him and a plaque in the clock tower commemorates his achievements. South-west of the town Ben Rinnes climbs to twin peaks at 2,755ft (840m). From here it may be possible to see from Caithness to the Cairngorms, weather permitting.

The town of **Keith**, is north-east of Dufftown on the B9014 and will not be dealt with in detail here being some distance from the Spey. However the Strathisla distillery, on the Malt Whisky Trail is there, and on the road between the two towns Drummuir Castle Estate. This is the Gordon-Duff family home and contains a spectacular lantern tower. Those who value 'natural' foods will be interested in the walled organic garden and the working meal mill producing organic oatmeal.

At **Rothes**, just north of Craigellachie and the distillery where another famous malt, the Macallan, is produced. The whisky is described by some as the 'Rolls Royce' of the drink and very highly regarded by most of the experts. Rothes was founded in 1766 as a crofting township but boomed in the mid-nineteenth century when Glen Grant, along with four other distilleries, began operations. While the distilleries are still there, the village is dominated by a factory producing animal feed from the distilleries' waste products. The ruins of Rothes Castle can be seen. This was an ancient stronghold of the Leslie family occupied until 1620. The villagers decided to burn it down later to prevent it from being occupied by thieves, then decided to use the stone for their own homes. One huge wall still stands.

The Glen Grant Distillery is the starting point of the Malt Whisky Trail for those coming from the north (Inverness or Elgin). It was built in 1840 by brothers James and John Grant, proud descendants of generations of illicit whisky distillers and smugglers. The spring water used for the whisky comes from the Caperdonich Well in the hillside above and Glen Grant was one of the first distillers to bottle and market a single malt. The two highlanders depicted on the label are James and John.

The B9015 follows the Spey from Rothes to the coast but the main road (A941) continues north-west to Elgin. This road passes Millbuies Country Park, a pleasant beauty spot with peaceful walks and the option of doing a little trout fishing.

Firmly on the coastal plain, **Elgin** is actually located some 8 miles (13km) west of the Spey but, as the Moray county town, cannot be ignored. This busy administrative centre was not planned but grew up on the banks of the River Lossie. Some eighteenth-century buildings and traces of the old medieval street layouts remain leading into the former cobbled market square. All are now fortunately bypassed by the main Aberdeen to Inverness road (A96) which runs through the outskirts of the town centre.

Elgin Cathedral, The 'Lantern of the North' was established in 1224 but burnt down in 1390 by the infamous Wolf of Badenoch after

Sheep roam freely over the Scottish fells and glens

he had a disagreement with the bishop. It was rebuilt and continued in use until the Reformation when it went the way of many cathedrals at that time. The lead went from the roof in the seventeenth century and the central tower collapsed in the eighteenth century. Stone was then removed for building elsewhere. However the remnants went into national care as early as 1825.

At the west end of the High Street are the final remains of the old royal castle (a bit of wall still stands), which was occupied by English King Edward I, who must have liked Scotland as he spent so much time visiting its castles, on this occasion in 1296 when the Scots were trying to send him back south.

Elgin's museum is one of Scotland's oldest, founded in 1836 by a group of local gentlemen. These included Dr George Gordon who corresponded extensively with eminent scientists of the day, including Charles Darwin. Exhibitions include reptile fossils up to 385 million years ago, including Elgin Mirablis, unique to Scotland and found in the same local sandstone of which the museum is constructed. Local wildlife and history displays are to be found, as well as curios collected from the 'New World' of the nineteenth century. Elgin has another museum, dedicated to vintage cars and motorbikes and housed in an old mill building.

Johnstons of Elgin operate a Cashmere Visitor Centre which

shows cashmere in production as well as having an exhibition of cashmere production from the past to the present. Established almost 200 years ago, Johnstons is the only British mill still converting natural raw cashmere into the finished product, using a combination of traditional craft and hi-tec modern machinery. The company uses the purest cashmere from China and Mongolia and chooses to import its lambswool from Australia!

On the western outskirts of the town, off the Inverness Road (A96) is the Old Mills Visitor Centre, a water mill restored to full working order by the local council. The existence of the water mill is documented as far back as 1230. The current building is thought to date from 1794, although previously it had been owned by the monks of Pluscarden Abbey. There is a wood turners business nearby where traditional crafts are on display.

The River Lossie which powers the mill flows northwards through Spynie where the substantial ruins were the home of the powerful Bishops of Moray. In the nearby kirkyard James Ramsay MacDonald, first labour prime minister, is buried. The Lossie reaches the sea at the aptly named town of **Lossiemouth**, Elgin's port after Spynie became cut off from the sea. Now the site of one of Britain's major RAF bases, this has always been a very significant fishing port and several innovations in fishing boat design have been achieved here in the past 150 years. James Ramsay MacDonald was born here. Three miles (5km) south of Elgin on the B9010 is Birnie Kirk, established in 1140 on the site of an earlier church founded by St Brendan. This is one of the few Norman churches in Scotland still in regular use and was for a time seat of the Moray bishops before they adopted Elgin.

Six miles (10km) south-west of Elgin is **Pluscarden Abbey**, which has been undergoing restoration for nearly 50 years. It was originally founded by King Alexander II in 1230, a house of the Valliscaulian Order, and absorbed a Benedictine Order from Urquhart in the mid-fifteenth century, only to see its monastic inhabitants 'disappear' soon afterwards at the Reformation. It was given to another Benedictine community earlier in the twentieth century. They took up residence in 1948 and have been working to restore the abbey ever since.

The Spey flows almost due north from Rothes with only a B road now shadowing its left bank, the B9015. The Speyside Way follows the east bank through wood and farmland. The road crosses the Aberdeen-Inverness trunk road (A96) at **Mosstodloch**. This is close to Cumberland's Crossing, the point on the Spey where 'Butcher' Cumberland crossed the Spey in 1746. What is now the 'old bridge'

The frigate Unicorn, *moored at Dundee harbour, is the oldest British warship afloat* (Chapter 4)

Glamis Castle is one of Britains most important (Chapter 4)

Tossing the caber at Strathpeffer Highland Games (Chapter 7)

Dunrobin Castle, near Golspie, is one of Scotland's greats (Chapter 8)

was erected 48 years later. On the banks of the Spey itself, off the A96, is Baxters, the famous manufacturers of jams, soup and other high quality Scottish food products. The business began as a grocery shop in **Fochabers** in the 1870s and has been developed to its current impressive operation through four generations of the Baxter family. The factory site is now a well developed tourist attraction with a museum, a shop museum, audio-visual display, restaurant, speciality shop, factory tours and outside there is a herd of Highland cattle and Speyside woodland trails. Fochabers itself, created a barony in 1598, is a small and attractive town. However its appeal is almost totally spoilt by having the A96 trunk road, heavy lorries and all, running through its centre. A by-pass is badly needed and the delays in getting one have caused something between local irritation and anger in recent years. There is a folk museum here containing the largest collection of horse-drawn vehicles in the north-east.

Gordon Castle is north of the town although not open to the public. It was once the finest Georgian house in Scotland with a battlemented façade almost 200yd in length and a window for every day of the year. Past residents include Duchess Jane Maxwell who helped to raise the Gordon Highlanders Regiment by rewarding new recruits with a kiss and a shilling.

Having crossed the A96 the B910 on the west side of the Spey, makes its last 3 mile (5km) trek to the sea at Kingston. En route it passes close to **Urquhart**, where there is a stone circle and where once stood a medieval Benedictine priory. It was founded in 1136 by King David I but was eventually absorbed into Pluscarden Priory in 1454.

Garmouth stands by the Spey estuary and was created a Burgh of Barony in 1587 but existed many centuries before that. It is recorded that King Malcolm II made a gift of the land to a Flemish noble in 1160, an ancestor of the local Innes family, whose present home near Urquhart has gardens open to the public (not the house). The village had its heyday as the main port for Moray in the eighteenth century, exporting grain and importing coal and glass.

Garmouth played a vital part in British history when Charles II, having stepped ashore nearby in 1650 on return from exile, reluctantly signed the Solemn League and Covenant. This was a document whose intent was to impose a Scots-style Presbyterianism on Episcopal England. The ancient Maggie Fair (named after a popular member of the Innes family) has been held on the last Saturday in June since 1587 and is one of the few ancient Scottish fairs surviving. The village itself contains houses made of boulders from the beach, held together by clay and straw. That was 200 years ago and they are still standing, as is the old nineteenth-century watertower, no longer in use, but a good viewpoint.

A railway line used to run through here and now a footpath linked to the Speyside Way crosses the impressive Spey viaduct. Two years after it was opened in 1886 the river changed its course and no longer ran through the central arch. The coast and Spey Bay are reached at **Kingston-on-Spey**. This was the spot where Charles II got off his ship. However the 'king' in the title is not Charles II, but the English seaside town Kingston-upon-Hull where two Yorkshire business men who founded the settlement came from. They leased the forest of Glenmore from the Duke of Gordon 200 years ago, felled the trees and floated them down the Spey for export to English shipyards. However they also set up a shipyard of their own here which was substantial for its day. Dunfermline House, a private residence visible from the village, is reputed to have been built originally by monks at Urquhart Priory as a daughter house for Dunfermline Abbey.

The area bordering the shingle beach of Spey Bay is now a Scottish Wildlife Trust Reserve. It was created by the last Ice Age and contains rare flora including the Northern Marsh Orchid and Coralroot Orchid. Off the coast the **Moray Firth** is one of two places in the United Kingdom where bottle nosed dolphins live; there are probably about 200 in the Firth and some may be seen jumping and playing here on occasion in the summer.

The B9104 on the east side of the Spey from Fochabers reaches Spey Bay and its huge 3 mile (5km) stretch of shingle beach at **Tugnet**. Here there is the largest ice house in Scotland, built in 1830 to store ice from the River Spey for packing salmon. It has now been restored and there is an audio-visual display. This is also the starting point of the Speyside Way.

Buckie, past Portgordon 3 miles (5km) east away across Spey Bay, was once the largest town in the old county of Banff. It is made up of a number of small communities and is still a very important fishing port, with weekly fish market. There is a 'hands-on experience centre' here all about the local fishing industry. Traditional wooden fishing boats are still built in the town. Nearby is St Ninian's Chapel, the oldest post-Reformation Roman Catholic church in Scotland. St Gregory's, also nearby, was once the secret headquarters of the Catholic Church in northern Scotland and was later the first post-Reformation church to be built specifically as a place of worship, following the ending of penalties against Catholics.

Further Information
— The Spey Valley —

Places to Visit

Charlestown of Aberlour
Aberlour Distillery
☎ 0340 871204
Open: Monday to Friday, 9.30-11.30am
and 1.30-4.30pm.

**Aviemore
(Cairngorm, Coylumbridge,
Inverdruie, Rothiemurchus)**
Cairngorm Chairlift Company
(ski lifts and summer chair lifts)
☎ 0479 86261
Open: daily, wind permitting.

Cairngorm Reindeer Centre
Reindeer House
Glenmore
Aviemore
Inverness-shire
PH22 1QU
☎ 0479 861228
Open: all year daily from 11am.

Cairngorm Whisky Centre
☎ 0479 810574
Open: all year daily.

Dry Ski Slope
Aviemore
☎ 0479 810310

Glenmore Forest Park
Forestry Commission
Inverness Forest District
Smithton
Inverness
☎ 0463 791575

Rothiemurchus Estate
Aviemore PH22 1QY
☎ 0479 810858

Farm Shop: ☎ 0479 810703
Farm Tours: ☎ 0479 810858
Fish Farm: ☎ 0479 810858
Hawking: ☎ 0479 810858
Mountain Biking: ☎ 0479 810787
Old School Shop: ☎ 0479 810005
Safari Tours: ☎ 0479 810858
Shooting (Clay Pigeon): ☎ 0479
 810858/810467

Tea Room: ☎ 0479 811272
Visitor Centre: ☎ 0479 810858

Strathspey Steam Railway
Aviemore Speyside Station
Dalfaber Road
Aviemore PH22 1PY
☎ 0479 810725
Open: all year, varying times.

Ballindalloch
Ballindalloch Castle
☎ 0807 500206
Open: Easter to end September daily
10am-5pm. Coaches welcome all year
but by appointment from October to
March).

Glenfarclas Distillery Visitor Centre
Ballindalloch
Banffshire AB37 9BD
☎ 0807 500257
Open: winter, Monday to Friday 10am-
4pm. Summer, Mondays to Fridays
9am-4.30pm. Open Saturdays, June to
September 10am-4pm. Closed over
Christmas and New Year holiday
period.

Boat of Garten
Highland Drovers
Croft of Kincardine
☎ 047983 329
Open: daily from 10.30am.

RSPB Abernethy Forest Nature Reserve
☎ 047 983 694 or 047 982 409
Ospreys normally present between late
April and September. Viewing hide
open 10am-8.30pm.

Banff
Museum
Open: June to September, daily except
Thursday 2-5.15pm.
☎ 0779 77778

Carrbridge
Carrbridge Studio
Station Road
☎ 047984 247
Open: normally Sunday to Friday, but
may vary so best to check by phone.

Landmark Heritage and Adventure Park
Open: all year daily from 9.30am. April
to June closes 6pm, July and August at
8pm, September and October at 6pm
and winter at 5pm.

Ski Pro Personal Performance Courses
An Airidh Ski Lodge
Station Road
☎ 0479 841211
Snow or dry slope tuition, advance
reservation required.

Craigellachie
Speyside Cooperage
Dufftown Road
Craigellachie
Banffshire AB38 9RS
☎ 0340 871108
Open: all year, Monday to Friday
9.30am-4.30pm (including Saturdays
from Easter to October).

Speyside Way Visitor Centre
Boat of Fiddich
☎ 0340 881266
Open: May to September.

Dalwhinnie
Dalwhinnie Distillery Visitors Centre
Inverness-shire PH19 1AB
☎ 05282 208

Dufftown
Balvenie Castle
Open: April to September, standard
openings.
☎ 031 244 3101

Glenfiddich Distillery
☎ 0340 820373
Open: January to mid-December,
Monday to Friday 9.30am-6.30pm.
Easter to October also open Saturdays
9.30am-4.30pm, Sundays 12noon-
4.30pm. Closed over Christmas holiday
period.

Drummuir
Drummuir Castle Estate
☎ 0542 810225
Open: tours every Sunday, May to
September at 2pm, 2.45pm and 3.30pm.
Organic Garden open May to Septem-
ber, Sunday 2-4pm. Meal Mill open
Wednesday and Sunday 2-5pm.

Elgin
The Cashmere Visitor Centre
Johnston's of Elgin
Newmill
☎ 0343 549319
Open: 9am-5.30pm Monday, Saturday
(until 6pm Monday to Friday, July to
September).

Elgin Cathedral
King Street
☎ 0343 547171
Open: April to September, Monday to
Saturday 9.30am-6pm. Sunday 2-6pm.
October to March, Monday to Wednes-
day 9.30am-4pm, Thursday 9.30am-
12.30pm, Saturday 9.30am-4pm and
Sunday 2-4pm.

Elgin Museum
1 High Street
Moray IV30 1EQ
Open: April to September, Monday,
Tuesday, Thursday and Friday 10am-
5pm. Saturday 11am-4pm, Sunday 2-
5pm. Closed Wednesday.

Moray Motor Museum
Bridge Street
☎ 0343 544933 (evenings 0343 543713
Open: daily Easter to October 11am-
5pm.

Old Mills Visitor Centre
☎ 0343 540698
Open: April to October, Tuesday to
Sunday 10am-5.30pm. May and
November, Tuesday to Friday 10am-
4pm.

Touch Wood Turnery
Old Mills
☎ 0343 830919 (evenings)
Open: Monday to Friday 9.30am-5pm,
weekends 10am-5pm.

Fochabers
Baxters Visitor Centre
☎ 0343 820393
Open: all year, Monday to Friday
9.30am-4.30pm, Easter to September
weekends from 11am.

Folk Museum
Pringle Church
High Street
☎ 0343 820362
Open: daily 9.30am-11pm, 2-6pm
(closes 5pm in winter).

Glenlivet
Distillery Visitor Centre
Open: Easter to end October. Monday to Saturday 10-4pm.
☎ 08073 427

Grantown on Spey
Grantown Heritage Trust Exhibition
☎ 0479 883193
Open: May and June, Monday to Friday 10am-1pm. July and August, Monday to Friday 10am-4pm. Weekends 2-4pm. September, Monday to Saturday 10am-1pm.

Insh and Kincraig
Alvie Estate
☎ 0540 651255 or 651249

Highland Wildlife Park
Kincraig
Inverness-shire PH21 1NL
☎ 0540 651270
Open: April to October daily, 10am-4pm. June to August to 5pm.

Insh Hall (Dry slope skiing, water sports)
☎ 0540 651272

Insh Marshes RSPB Reserve
The Warden
Zul Bhatia
Ivy Cottage
Insh
☎ 0540 661518
Open: any time all year.

Inshriach Nursery
☎ 0540 651287
Open: Monday to Saturday.

Keith
Strathisla Distillery
Open: mid-May to mid-September. Monday to Friday 9-4.30pm.
☎ 05422 7471

Kingussie
Highland Folk Museum
Duke Street
Kingussie PPH21 1JG
☎ 0540 661307
Open: April to October, Monday to Saturday 10am-6pm and Sundays 2-6pm. Also open March and November,

Monday to Friday 10am-3pm. (Iona Gallery open different hours, mainly morning and late afternoon/evenings).

Knockando
Cardhu Distillery
☎ 0340 810204
Open: all year, Monday to Friday 9.30am-4.30pm, and on Saturdays during summer.

Tamdhu Distillery
☎ 0340 810486
Open: April to October, Monday to Friday 10am-4pm and on Saturdays from June.

Newtonmore
Aonach More Guides
The Retreat
Newtonmore PH20 1DT
☎ 0540 673746
Offer personal guided tours of the remote hills and glens.

Highland Pottery
Church Terrace
☎ 0540 673636
Open: May to October, daily 9am-7pm, November to April daily 10am-5pm.

Clan MacPherson Museum
Open: May to September, Monday to Saturday 10am-5.30pm, Sundays 2.30-5.30pm.

Waltzing Water
Balavil Brae
Inverness-shire PH20 1DR
☎ 0540 673752
Open: late February to New Year daily 10am-4pm. 50 minute shows on the hour. Additional shows April to October at 5pm and 8.30pm.

Pluscarden
Pluscarden Abbey
☎ 034389 257
Open: all year, all reasonable times to 8.30pm.

Rothes
Glen Grant Distillery
☎ 0340 831 413
Open: Easter to September, Monday to Friday 9am-4pm. Open Saturdays during July and August.

Tugnet
Tugnet Ice House
☎ 0309 673701
Open: June to September daily 10am-4pm.

Tourist Information Offices

Aviemore
☎ 0540 661297
Open: all year.

Banff and Buchan
Collie Lodge
Banff AB45 1AU
☎ 0261 812419
Fax: 0261 815807

Buckie
Cluny Square
☎ 0542 834853
Open: summer only (contact Elgin office when closed).

Carrbridge
☎ 0479 810454 (winter)
☎ 0479 84630 (summer)

Cullen
20 Seafield Street
☎ 0542 8407578
Open: summer only (when closed contact Elgin office).

Dufftown
Clock Tower
The Square
☎ 0340 820501
Open: summer only (when closed contact Elgin office).

Elgin
17 High Street
☎ 0343 542666 or 543388
Open: all year.

Forres
Falconer Museum
Tolbooth Street
☎ 0309 672938
Open: summer only (when closed contact Elgin office).

Keith
Church Road
☎ 0542 882634
Open: summer only (when closed contact Elgin office).

Kincraig Promotions
Kincraig Post Office
Inverness-shire PPH21 12NA
☎ 05404 331

Kingussie
☎ 0540 661297
Open: May to September.

Lossiemouth
Pitgavey Street
☎ 0343 8148044
Open: summer only (when closed contact Elgin office).

Tomintoul
The Square
☎ 0807 590285
Open: summer only (when closed contact Elgin office).

7 • The Black Isle & Beauly Firth

The Black Isle is not an isle at all of course, but it must have seemed that way to the residents of its southern shores until the construction of the Kessock Bridge. This bridges the 1 mile (2km) gap between South and North Kessock, previously served by a ferry. It is more than 40 miles (64km) by road round the Beauly Firth. The ferry crossing from South to North Kessock was used for many centuries by pilgrims en route to the shrine of St Duthac in Tain. The fact that Duthac can be confused with the Gaelic word *dubh* meaning 'black' is one explanation of how the area got its name; another is that, because it reputedly has a better climate than the surrounding land, it would stay snow-free in the winter while the surrounding area would turn white.

That the Black Isle has a good climate for its latitude, and that it is also a fertile land compared to much of its surroundings, is certainly also true. The lack of direct road access from Inverness and the south until recently has meant that, although you can now whizz across the Black Isle on the A9 dual carriageway, if you are wise enough to leave this and drive around, you will find winding tree-lined roads reminiscent of rural areas in southern England. The area has been inhabited for some 7,000 years and contains more than fifty prehistoric sites.

To the south of the isle lies the Beauly Firth and it is on the south shore of this remarkable stretch of water, on the traditional overland route into the Black Isle, that this description begins.

The A862 which crosses below the impressive Muirtown Lochs as it leaves the western edge of Inverness is known locally as the 'old A9'. The road was the main road route north from the town before the opening of the splendid Kessock suspension bridge in 1982. Most of the road's users today are therefore tourists, or residents on the south side of the Beauly Firth.

The Muirtown Lochs mark the end of the Caledonian Canal as it steps steeply down into the Moray Firth and then the North Sea. It is

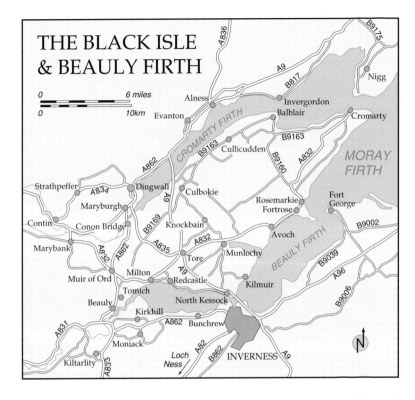

THE BLACK ISLE
& BEAULY FIRTH

common in the summer months to see everything from a small Royal
Naval vessel, to a tall sailing ship or even a car ferry making its way
to or from Loch Ness through the lochs. A road bridge swings open
and resulting tailbacks can stretch back for several miles into the
centre of Inverness.

The road leaves Inverness suddenly ½ mile (1km) later, taking an
S-bend over a railway bridge and for a further ½ mile (1km) runs on
a narrow walled stretch between the railway line and the sides of the
Beauly Firth. The road soon widens out however with lay-bys
appearing from which to sightsee.

The Firth is a remarkable stretch of water 8 miles (13km) long and
up to 2 miles (3km) wide; it is tidal and can drain a large percentage
of its area completely at low tide leaving a haven for wading birds.
Then on the spring and autumn tides the Firth may resemble a
stormy day in the North Atlantic with waves crashing into the walled
stretch of road and sending spray right across. The overall vista as
you leave Inverness, with the mountainscape opening up to the
north and west and the huge stretch of water, is always changing and

often breathtaking, especially at sunset on a clear day with a be-calmed Firth. Apart from bird life the Firth is also a haven for seals and sometimes dolphins, crannogs (2,000 year old man-made islands) can sometimes be seen at low tide, as can some seventeenth-century fish traps known as cairidhs.

The first village reached, 2 miles (3km) from Inverness, is **Bunchrew** a small collection of attractive roadside houses. Shielded from view by trees, however, as you enter the village is the seventeenth-century mansion of Bunchrew House, built by Simon Fraser, eighth Lord Lovat, in 1621, whose marriage to Jean Stewart in the same year is commemorated by a stone lintel above the fireplace in the drawing room. The house is now a comfortable hotel with a high calibre restaurant. It has its own mineral water spring.

The A862 continues westerly to Inchmore, a further 5 miles (8km) on. The road passes through **Lentran**, where little is visible except for a candle-makers studio called Northern Lights where wondrous wax creations can be seen in production. In **Inchmore** itself the prominent Inchmore Hotel is to be found, known until quite recently as the Bogroy Inn. The hostelry dates back to at least the sixteenth century and was closely associated with smuggling. One anecdote recalls how a barrelful of whisky, previously confiscated, was stolen from a room at the Inn where it was being guarded by excisemen. The smugglers obtained inside information from a servant girl and bored a hole through the ceiling of the room below and into the bottom of the barrel, confiscating their whisky back, minus the barrel. Whisky is no longer stored upstairs in the hotel. Across the road from the hotel is a converted church which is now home to Highland Aromatics, manufacturers of a popular range of fine hand-made soaps.

Just by the hotel and perfumery there is a staggered crossroads, giving drivers the chance to take the B9164, a very quiet road through the little village of **Kirkhill** which emerges close to Beauly, or the left turn up into a network of unclassified single tracks that criss-cross the high ground above Loch Ness and the Beauly Firth on a triangle between Drumnadrochit, Inverness and Beauly. Many spectacular views are possible by taking this route, but few junctions are marked with driver priority and there are still fewer signposts, so a good map and good map reading skills are advisable.

The back roads are one way of getting to **Moniack**, a further 2 miles (3km) west, where there is an excellent choice of woodland walks in little Reelig Glen. The 'high' and 'low' walks are well prepared and each about 1 mile (2km) long through beautiful forest. If you take the forest walk you may see that some of the birch trees

Children will enjoy a day at Cluanie Deer Farm Park, near Beauly

are being tapped for their sap, and nearby is Moniack Castle, home of Highland Wineries where free tours and tastings are organised. Wines are made of local juices and saps. Unlike many attractions in the Highlands, the wineries are clearly marked from the main road.

Three more miles (5km) west from Moniack the A833 turns off south to Drumnadrochit on Loch Ness side, passing by the Lovat Estate and the village of **Kiltarlity** after a couple of miles. The village has a strong local community and grew up alongside the Lovat Estate. Lord Lovat built the local parish church and the villagers then built their own Free Church. There are also two pubs and two shops in Kiltarlity, as well as a successful garden centre, Highland Liliums, which has an excellent selection of Alpine flowers. A talented wood carver also works on the outskirts of the village and has a studio where visitors are welcome. The village has a regular programme of events such as ceilidhs, many of them to raise funds for a proposed new village hall. Information on these and most other Kiltarlity matters can be obtained from the Post Office. Over the A883 from Kiltarlity is **Belladrum**, another old estate with excellent walks in the woodlands above. A glass engraver works in the area and visitors are welcome by pre-arrangement. The Lovat Estate, which includes the salmon rich Beauly River, dominates the area and a mineral water bottling operation was recently begun on the outskirts of the village. This has quickly proved highly successful with the local water certified some of Europe's finest and the big supermarkets all selling 'Lovat Spring'. There is a free visitor centre at the plant.

The plant is reached by driving through Kiltarlity and towards the River Beauly. This will bring you in to the beautiful areas of Strathglass and Glen Affric which are well worth spending time in. On the south-east side of the river, a single track road winds along with usually very little traffic likely. On the other side the A831 is a little busier.

The A831 can be reached directly by staying on the A862 from Inverness rather than turning down to Kiltarlity. A mile (2km) after that turning there is a narrow humped backed bridge over the Beauly River after which the A831 goes straight ahead while the main road, the A862 bends round sharply to begin heading due north and into Beauly. This junction marks the end each June of a famous endurance race of 50 miles (80km) from the west coast through Glen Affric where participants run across the hilltops for 20 miles (32km) then relax and cycle the remaining 30 miles (48km). The event is known as The Highland Cross and raises huge sums for charity.

Around the Aigas Forest, a few miles along the A831, is Cluanie Deer Farm Park, where numerous rare breeds are on show, and there is a cuddle corner for children. Nearby is Aigas House and Field Centre where there is a named tree collection and art and sculpture exhibitions of local interest. There is also a salmon ladder by the Aigas Hydro-electric dam.

Beauly, on the Ross-shire border and at the end of the Firth that bears its name, is a very attractive town. Centred on a large rectangular square, now part road, part car-parking, this is a bustling little community with an active commercial centre. Throughout the summer months there are flowers everywhere and the town has won awards for its floral displays.

Approaching the town from Inverness the Made in Scotland shop and exhibition centre on the left as soon as you go over the railway bridge is arguably Scotland's best craft shop. This is because it is the headquarters of a 'semi-autonomous' umbrella group, set up to promote Highland and Scottish crafts. Work on sale varies in price from a few pence to works of art that may reach a thousand pounds. Trade buyers from around the world visit the centre, as well as ordinary holidaymakers. There is also a small display on Beauly's past at the rear of the building. Other shopping opportunities in the town include The Highland Tweed House, by appointment to the Queen Mother, who have been famous for tweeds, especially sporting tweeds, since 1858.

At the north end of the Square is Beauly's main attraction however, the ruined abbey. This was founded in 1230 and completed by 1280, probably on the site of an earlier chapel dedicated to St Michael. It was one of three established that year in Scotland by the Order of Valliscaulians, named after their original house at Val des Choux in Burgundy. This was a particularly harsh order whose rules included near silence, uncomfortable clothing, straw beds in rooms no bigger than 6ft by 4ft (2m by 1m) and very little food. It is unlikely that there were ever more than ten monks at any one time. At the Reformation the priory's lands and fishing rights were sold to Lord Lovat and then annexed to the Crown under an act of King James in 1587. After that the building was used as a supply of ready-cut stone for locals and Cromwell's troops engaged in the construction of a fort in Inverness in 1652. Mary Queen of Scots had visited the priory on her most northerly journey in August and September 1564. She is reputed to have been much impressed and said, 'Oui, c'est un beau lieu.' Legend now has it that the name Beauly comes from 'beau lieu'. The doctor's surgery in Beauly Square sells a booklet containing ten or so walking itineraries in the Beauly and Kiltarlity area ranging from quite easy to rather more strenuous.

Muir of Ord, 2 miles (3km) further along the road, has a popular golf course. The main place of interest however is the Glen Ord Distillery, on the A832, a sharp left turn after crossing the railway bridge on the road through the town. The distillery was established in 1838 and conducted tours are given regularly on week days. You have now crossed the border into Ross and Cromarty, another geographically huge region of the Highlands stretching from west to east coasts and generally divided in to Wester and Easter Ross. The communities on each side are different in many ways (although similar in others), with Easter Ross having grown up with strong Norse influence and benefiting in recent decades from the oil boom, while Wester Ross remains primarily of Gaelic influence and economically is more reliant on fishing and fish farming.

Muir of Ord is also famous for the huge and remarkable Black Isle Show which is staged here on one Thursday each summer. This remains primarily an agricultural show but apart from endless displays of prize animals there are flower shows, market stalls, helicopter rides and all the makings of a major festival.

The A832 runs easterly out of Muir of Ord to link the 'old A9' with the 'new A9' dual carriageway at Tore roundabout (a very pleasant diversion through Milton and Redcastle along the north coast of the Beauly Firth right back to North Kessock, across the bridge from Inverness is possible this way). From Tore the A832 continues

A tartan and tweed shop in Beauly

through the heart of the Black Isle to the historic towns of Fortrose and Cromarty which are described later in this chapter. Travelling north-west in the other direction from the Muir of Ord, past the distillery, the road leads to the A835, the 'new road' to Dingwall and Ullapool that runs above the A832 from Tore roundabout.

This stretch of the A832 is worth taking, but it is subject to flooding near to the junction with the A835 and is closed on average once a year, usually in springtime, by high water. This is the access route to the beautiful valleys of **Strathconon** and Glen Orrin however, each reached by long narrow single track roads from Marybank. The road in to Strathconon is about 30 miles long from the village and top speed on the road should not be more than 30 miles per hour (48kph), so a good half day is required for this worthwhile excursion. Remember to pull over to let locals who know the road come past you. This area has not been developed or promoted for tourists and is as 'off the beaten track' as you will find anywhere in Britain.

Once on the new A835 it is little more than 30 minutes drive to Ullapool; but turn right on to the A834 at Contin, a 1 mile (2km) along this road, and quickly reach Strathpeffer, a popular destination for over 100 years. The only attraction prior to this that should be mentioned although officially just beyond the coverage of this section, are the **Falls Rogie**. This is a few miles beyond Contin on the

A835, good car parking, pleasant woodside walks, and an excellent waterfall which is an impressive torrent in the spring and a good place to see the salmon leap in summer.

Strathpeffer had a tourism peak in Victorian times when its spa water was first discovered by a Dr Morrison of Kincardineshire. His writings about the healing properties of the waters emanating from Ben Wyvis caused the local 'Water Rush' bringing visitors in search of cure-alls. Several grand old hotels, bear testimony to this past glory. At one time five spas were operating and a rheumatic hospital was founded. The town remains a popular destination today however and there are several worthwhile attractions.

Newest of these is the Highland Museum of Childhood, part of the beautifully restored old railway station which also includes craft and gift shops. The museum itself aims to bring to life the story of childhood in the Highlands and includes a dressing up area for today's 'wee bairns'.

The peace and tranquillity of a bygone era are actively promoted by local tourist agencies, with well kept public floral displays and wonderful themed 'Victorian Days'. Sporting activity ties in well with this healthy image and there is a popular 18 hole golf course, and some of Scotland's best fishing on the Conon river. For the more active, hill walking and climbing on mighty Ben Wyvis (3,433ft/ 1,047m) is a popular pastime. The introduction of downhill skiing to this mountain, which often spends a large part of the year snow-capped, has been considered. International mountain biking championships have also been held in Strathpeffer in recent years.

At the south side of Strathpeffer stands the Eagle Stone, richly decorated in Pictish symbols. It is fenced off and firmly embedded in concrete because the Black Isle's Brahan Seer, predicted that if it were dropped three times, the valley including Strathpeffer and Dingwall, would be flooded, and ships would tie up to the stone.

Another stone near Strathpeffer should be mentioned, an erected memorial to Highland writer Neil Gunn who lived for 80 years from 1891, mostly in various houses around the Black Isle. He wrote over a dozen novels based on Highland history and tradition, several of which won major literary prizes as well as popular acclaim. The memorial viewpoint is sited above the Dingwall road (A834) at the Heights of Brae.

Taking the A834 through Strathpeffer, the A835 back east from Maryburgh, or staying on the 'old A9' (A862) through Muir of Ord all bring you to **Dingwall**, Ross-shire's commercial capital and the reputed birthplace of Macbeth. The name comes from the Old Norse

Bagpipers and throwing the hammer are part of Scottish tradition at the Strathpeffer Highland Games

word 'Thingvollr', meaning 'Parliament' or 'Meeting Place'.
There are some interesting shops close to the town's pedestrianised centre, and the small leisure centre, which has housed everything from badminton tournaments to Royal Shakespeare Company
performances includes a pleasant swimming pool. On the outskirts
of the town centre there is also a small park which contains an
exceptionally well equipped modern play park for children under 9
years of-age and a second adventure park area for older children
which is also extremely good.

A Royal Charter was bestowed on the town in 1226 and the stones
of the original castle (Macbeth's birthplace?) were incorporated in
the eighteenth-century tollbooth tower in the High Street. All that
remains of the old castle is a flanking tower at the bottom of Castle
Street. Incidentally the depiction of *Macbeth* in Shakespeare's play is
largely false because the great bard's source material was incorrect
and he used quite a lot of dramatic licence and political bias (with
successful results). The real Macbeth lived around 1005 to 1057 and
probably had about as much right to the Scottish throne as did
Duncan. They were both grandchildren of Malcolm II, who had in
turn murdered Kenneth III to seize control of Scotland. Macbeth did
not actually murder Duncan as depicted in the play anyway, he
engineered a civil war, and Malcolm was killed in a resulting battle.
A thousand years ago it was accepted that anyone with 'regal
standing', which normally meant control of an army, had a fairly
strong 'right' to claim kingship in any case. Macbeth's behaviour was
probably quite honest in comparison to many and it was unlikely he
needed much encouragement from his wife! He is also known as a
benign and successful King, holding the throne for 15 years.

A later resident of the town was Sir Hector MacDonald who was
born of humble parentage at Rootfield, Urquhart in 1853. He joined
the Cameron Highlanders in 1870, distinguished himself in the
second Afghan War , won a commission and went on to fight in
Egypt and South Africa. He commanded a regiment in Ceylon but
was 'found shot' en route back to London where he was due to
appear on 'grave moral charges'. However a memorial was put up to
'Fighting Mac' on Mitchell Hill above the town.

Other historic buildings in the town are restored Tulloch Castle,
once the seat of the Baynes and Davidsons. It was refurbished in the
1920s by the well known Scottish architect Sir Robert Latimer. The
town house on the High Street dates to the nineteenth century.
Dingwall Museum contains a wide variety of displays including an
old smiddy, 1900s kitchen, militaria and old printing techniques.

Haggis, the legendary Scottish meal

Returning to the traffic island at Maryburgh and taking the A835 back towards Inverness, or continuing along the last stretch of the old A9 (A862) to the end of the Cromarty Firth Causeway where it finally meets the new A9, takes the driver eastwards and into the Black Isle proper. The B9163 is reached either by a right turn off the A835 soon after leaving the Maryburgh roundabout, or by another right turn off the new A9 soon after crossing the Cromarty Firth causeway, both en route back to Inverness. This is a long, largely straight road that runs above the Cromarty Firth along the north coast of the Black Isle to Cromarty.

Cromarty Firth is a natural deep water harbour and is usually full of oil rigs in for repair; a surreal rather than particularly ugly sight to most minds, with the huge rigs standing above the water, mainly on the north side of the Firth, against the Highland scenery and towering above the little white cottages. The Firth is also a stopping place for international cruise liners, which then transfer bus passengers down to Inverness and Loch Ness, sometimes to the irritation of the Ross and Cromarty Tourist Board, who would prefer they stopped to look at some of the local attractions. The Firth was also used as a harbour by the British Fleet during World War I.

On the hills across the Firth and above the village of **Evanton** you can see Sir Hector Munro's Monument, which was commissioned by the General in 1781 when he returned to the area having distinguished himself in an Indian Campaign. It is an exact replica of the Indian Gateway at Seringapatam and is said to have been created in a generous gesture to provide work for the locals. Below it, by the village of Evanton, is the Black Rock Gorge, a remarkable geological freak being only a few feet wide but reaching depth's of nearly 200ft (61m) in places. Not surprisingly there are rumours of inhabiting ghosts.

Cromarty is probably the major attraction of the Black Isle, although neighbouring Fortrose and Rosemarkie are also historically significant. It was once a thriving seaport and trading centre, on the Pilgrims Way. A ferry still crosses the Cromarty Firth from here to Nigg, the crossing is known to have been made by kings such as James IV and Robert the Bruce en route to Tain. When the large fabrication yard at Nigg was opened in 1972 it was the world's largest dry dock. A British Alcan aluminium plant in neighbouring Invergordon employed 1,000 during the 1970s before vanishing as quickly as it had arisen, typical of the history of large-scale industrial development in the Highlands as a whole.

Cromarty is more than 700 years old and has always relied on the sea and the fertile Black Isle lands for its prosperity. It was particularly successful in the late eighteenth century when cargoes of flax and hemp were imported from St Petersburg in Russia and spun in mills within the town. Cromarty harbour and the entire Cromarty Firth is reached by passing between two headlands known as the Sutors of Cromarty. These comprise older and harder rocks than the surrounding land (at least 700 million years old). The two were split apart 10,000 years ago when ice building up from the west in the last Ice Age carved out the Cromarty Firth while pushing against the hard rock and eventually broke through forming the entrance to the North Sea.

'Sutor' is Scots for 'shoemaker' and local legend has it that there were two giant shoemakers who shared their tools and threw them across from one side to the other. In 1914 the young Winston Churchill visited the south Sutor and authorised the building of forts and gun emplacements which were later extended in World War II. An enormous metal net was stretched across under water to catch submarines. However, on 30 December 1915 *HMS Natal* mysteriously blew up in the Firth with the loss of over 400 lives. Some of the seamen's graves can be seen in the churchyard of the Gaelic chapel in the town.

Local coastal attractions include MacFarquhar's Bed, reached by

*An oil rig in
Cromarty Firth,
awaiting repair*

a track through Cromarty Mains Farm. This is a sheltered bay with caves, a natural arch and rich plant life. The drooping cave, over the rocks east of Cromarty got its name from the stalactites hanging from the roof. It is supposed to be guarded by a mermaid and eighteenth-century sea captain John Reid is supposed to have caught her and only let her go after she granted him three wishes, although there seems to be no record of what the wishes were or whether they came true.

A sign on the road into Cromarty announces that this is the hometown of one Hugh Miller. He was a famous geologist, fossil hunter, writer and theologian born in the town in 1802. His home is now a popular attraction, run by the National Trust For Scotland. It was built by Miller's great grandfather in 1711 and opened to the public as early as 1890, before being given to the Trust in 1938, making it one of their older properties. Miller eventually moved to Edinburgh where he became editor of the Free Church of Scotland's newspaper, *The Witness*, building it up to become the country's second best seller of the time.

A few yards further along Church Street is the more recently renovated Cromarty Courthouse, an excellent exhibition with interactive displays recreating life in the courthouse and Cromarty as a whole around 200 years ago. The museum won the National Museum of the Year award in 1991 soon after opening and contains effective talking animated figures, specially constructed in Florida. It is possible to sit in the recreated court room and watch a poor young girl be banished time and time again for some relatively minor misdemeanour.

There are plenty of interesting shops and cafés in Cromarty. Much of the town was rebuilt by George Ross who acquired the local estate in the 1760s. He established one of Scotland's first factories to carry out the weaving work, as well as a brewery, the harbour, courthouse, Gaelic Chapel and Cromarty House. Most of his architecture survived and it has led to the town being said to be 'the jewel in the crown of Scottish vernacular architecture.' He had obtained the estate following recent ownership by Sir Thomas Urquhart, a noted eccentric who claimed to have traced his own direct lineage from Adam and Eve. He also invented a universal language and wrote great works on mathematics which no one else could comprehend. He was nonetheless an important literary figure and his credits include a rather wild and raucous translation of the works of Rabelais from French to English, the first to be made. Visitors can meet Sir Thomas, or at least an animated version of him, in the Cromarty Courthouse, where he will expound his knowledge of six different specialist subjects at the press of a button.

Turning south-west down the Black Isle's coast and along the Pilgrim's Way, the coast runs in a line with the Great Glen that contains Loch Ness and was indeed created by the same mighty geological forces. A path to the coast by Upper Ethie between Cromarty and Rosemarkie leads to Ethie Bay where Miller conducted his early fossil hunts.

This area of the Black Isle is particularly rich in Pictish and religious remains, with plenty of accompanying myth and legend. One of the major figures in this area was the so-called Brahan Seer, also known as Coinneach Odhar Fiosaiche or Kenneth Mackenzie, whose memorial can be seen at Chanonry Point, a peninsular largely covered with Fortrose Golf Course, at the end of Rosemarkie's Bay, 10 miles (16km) south of Cromarty. Born in the Inner Hebrides he lived most of his life in the Black Isle. Of the many versions of how he gained his 'second sight', most original is the story that his mother was advised by the ghost of a dead Norwegian king that a blue stone

Hugh Miller's cottage, Cromarty

she would find in a lake could be used by her son to foresee future events by meditating upon it.

His predictions include the advent of the Caledonian Canal and a belief that the streets of Inverness would 'run with fire and water' — so far interpreted, perhaps rather conveniently, as the advent of street lighting and a sewage system. His prediction of big trouble in Inverness once the River Ness was bridged nine times has yet to come true, although there is some disagreement over how many bridges there now are. The Friars Bridge, built in the mid-1980s to relieve traffic congestion caused some anxiety as it was thought to be the ninth. There have been no major disasters as yet beyond a big flood that brought down the railway bridge bringing the total back down to eight, until it was rebuilt. It has been argued that two footbridges which cross the Ness in stages, with an island in between, count as one bridge, so there have in fact only ever been eight bridges.

The Brahan Seer's foresight did not save him from a sticky end when he reluctantly advised Lady Seaforth what her absent husband was getting up to in Paris. This particular vision landed him in hot water, or burning tar to be precise, he was executed in a spiked barrel of it in Fortrose, accused of being a witch.

Rosemarkie has a very pleasant sea front with a park area and a small beach made up of rocky coves. The coastline all along here is rich with bird and animal life, as well as fossilised remains and geological evidence of the Ice Age. It is not uncommon to see bottlenose dolphins 'playing' in the off-shore waters, the colony in the Inner Moray Firth is the United Kingdom's largest.

The fishing village itself is the centre of the Black Isle's mystical tradition. The best place to immerse yourself within this is Groam House Museum, an eighteenth-century building full of Pictish remains including the 1,200-year-old Rosemarkie Cross Slab. This and other remains indicate the importance of Rosemarkie as a Pictish Christian centre, thought to have been evangelised by St Boniface (Curitan) in the early eighth century. Photographs of all of Ross and Cromarty's major Pictish stones are located here.

Rosemarkie kirkyard has been in use far longer than the oldest stone there, which dates to 1691. A stone dedicated to Provost Alexander Houghton from 1766 contains the skull and cross-bones symbol amongst others, which refer to shortness of life and was later borrowed by pirates of the period. Nearby is the tomb of the Leslies of Raddery, where watchers used to guard the newly dead from the Resurrectionists. Those entombed here include Dr William Bryden, the only British man to escape alive from the massacre of the army retreating from Kabul in 1841.

It is thought that Rosemarkie may have been created a Burgh as early as 1216 by Alexander II, but that it went into decline soon after with the decision to build the new cathedral in Fortrose around 1240. It was made part of the Royal Burgh of Fortrose in 1455 and had no trade or market day until 1552. The market cross erected after that time was knocked down by a horse and cart in 1830 and not replaced, the market ceased again around 1850.

The Fairy Glen at the north end of the town is very picturesque and has interesting geological deposits of boulder clay and rich bird and plant life. Celandine, wood anemone, bluebells and primroses all flower here each spring. Folk tales tell of the Fairy Well, surrounded by white pebbles and rustic seats, decorated with flowers by village children. There is also a darker tale of an old witch who made a clay model of an enemy in voodoo style and held it under the waterfall each day until it, and her enemy, wasted away.

Rosemarkie almost runs into Fortrose, a little over a mile away. This place was once called Chanonry, or 'Place of Canons' and was the busiest centre in the diocese of Ross. The grassy Kirk Green in Cathedral Square, where stand the remains of the once impressive cathedral, is a very tranquil place today. All that remains of the cathedral dedicated to St Peter and St Boniface is the south aisle, built in the late fourteenth century from pink-red sandstone quarried in nearby Munlochy Bay. Tombs surviving include that of Euphemia, Countess of Ross, who is thought to have paid for the aisle's construction, those of two pre-Reformation bishops and also of several members of the Mackenzie Clan, including Humberston Mackenzie, the last Lord Seaforth, and his four sons who pre-deceased him as per another cheerful and correct prediction of the Brahan Seer. The seer was about to be placed in a spiked barrelful of burning tar by Lord Seaforth at the time of this prediction. The cathedral was started in 1250 but fell into decline after the Reformation of 1560 when permission was granted for the lead to be stripped. Bits of the stone borrowed by locals for their own homes remain clearly visible as you walk about Fortrose.

Fortrose was created a Royal Burgh by James II in 1455; many of the town's buildings are historically significant, and there are a particularly large number of religious establishments, many still operational today. These include St Andrew's Hall, thought to have been the first meeting place for Episcopalians until burned down by troops after Culloden. It may have been rebuilt by Sir Alexander Mackenzie whose marriage stone dated 1788 is set above the lintel. It was renovated again early in the twentieth century by the rector of nearby St Andrew's Episcopal church in order to have a place to hold Sunday schools. Fortrose Academy is the major educational establishment in the area and has been for many centuries. It was formed from the old grammar school in 1791. The old building now standing dates from 1896, greatly extended in the late 1960s. It was still too small to house the increasing roll however and the primary section was moved to Avoch. Fortrose Castle probably stood at the top of Deans Road, but was razed by Cromwell in the 1650s, who then removed much of the stone to build his Invernessian citadel, presumably mixing it with stone from Beauly Priory and elsewhere.

Fortrose has a pleasant little pink sandy beach, at its best when the wind is from the east (beach lovers should opt for Rosemarkie when the wind is from the west). The harbour is one of the many feats of engineering by Thomas Telford. The huge battlements visible across the firth from this stretch of Black Isle coast is Fort George, a good physical reminder of the massive and ruthless suppression of Highlanders following the Jacobite defeat at Culloden. It was begun in 1748, has had a military presence ever since, but a shot has never been fired in anger there.

A few miles further on the A832 is **Avoch** (pronounced simply 'Ock'), another little fishing village where some of the local people still speak a distinctive dialect. The Heritage Association here operate a visitor centre close behind the Station Hotel in the summer months.

The A832 now bends inland to skirt the north side of Munlochy Bay, a popular spot for ornothologists, before rejoining the A9 a few miles from the Kessock Bridge and Inverness. Just past the Munlochy turn-off is a wishing well or 'clootie well' festooned in rags, an ancient pagan custom. At **Drumsmittal**, across the A9 from North Kessock there is a waterfowl country park which contains lots of animals to stroke, and baby chicks are hatched weekly.

North Kessock, the traditional port for ferries across the firth to Inverness before the Kessock Bridge was opened, is a pleasant place to visit, now bypassed by the main road. It is another good spot for dolphin spotting and for views of Inverness.

Further Information
— The Black Isle And Beauly Firth —

Places to Visit

Avoch
Avoch Heritage Association
☎ 0381 220587 or 20152
Open: July to September, most days except Sunday.

Beauly
Aigas Dam Fish Lift
Open: June to October, Monday to Friday, 10am-3pm.

Aigas House and Field Centre
Inverness-shire
IV4 7AD
☎ 0463 782443

Made In Scotland
The Craft Centre
☎ 0463 782578
Open: Monday to Saturday, 10am-5.30pm, Sunday 12noon-5pm.

Belladrum
Highland Crystal Craft Craigievar
Belladrum
Kiltarlity By Beauly
☎ 0463 741678
Open: Tuesday to Saturday, 10.30am-5.30pm. Advisable to telephone first.

Cromarty
Cromarty Courthouse
☎ 03817 418
Open: all year. April to end October 10am-6pm. Other dates 12noon-4pm.

Fishertown Craft Centre
Shore Street
☎ 03817 254
Open: all year Sunday to Friday 10.30am-5.30pm. Saturdays from 2.30pm.

Hugh Miller's Cottage
☎ 031 226 5922 (National Trust For Scotland Headquarters) Open: every day April to September, 10am-1pm and 2-5pm (Sundays, afternoons ony).

Dingwall
Leisure Centre
☎ 0349 864226

Museum
Open: May to September, 10am-5pm.

Inchmore/Kirkhill
Highland Aromatics
☎ 0463 83625
Open: Monday to Friday, 10am-4pm.

Kiltarlity
Cluanie Deer Farm Park
☎ 0463 782415
Open: May to October, 10am-5pm.

*Lovat Mineral Water Bottling Plant
    Visitor Centre*
Fanellan By Kiltarlity
☎ 0463 741620
Open: April to October, Monday to
Friday, 9.30am-4.30pm. Open rest of
the year but probably more limited
hours.

Woodcarving Studio
Tigh Bea
Kiltarlity IV4 7JH
☎ 0463 741425

Lentran
Northern Lights Candles Workshop
☎ 0463 83332
Open: Easter to Christmas, Monday to
Friday, 12noon-6pm and daily in July
and August, 10am-7pm.

Moniack
Highland Wineries
Moniack Castle
Kirkhill
Inverness
☎ 0463 83283
Open: Monday to Saturday, 10am-
5pm.

Muir of Ord
Glen Ord Distillery Visitor Centre
☎ 0463 870421
Open: Monday to Friday, 9.30am-5pm.

Waterfowl and Country Park
Drumsmittal
☎ 0463733 656
Open: all year 10am-dark.

Rosemarkie
Groam House Museum
☎ 0381 20961
Open: May to September 11am-5pm
daily and 2.30-4.30pm Sundays. Open
each weekend throughout the year.

Strathpeffer
Highland Museum of Childhood
☎ 0997 421031
Open: March to November, most days,
variable hours. Open other dates by
arrangement.

Tourist Information Offices

Inverness
Castle Wynd
☎ 0463 2234353
Open: all year.

North Kessock
☎ 0463 73505
Open: all year.

Strathpeffer
☎ 0997 421415
Open: Easter to October.

8 • The North-East Highland Coast

One of northern Scotland's most historically significant towns is **Tain**, now more than 920 years old and for centuries one of Scotland's major places of pilgrimages. This early importance results from the fact that St Duthac was born here around AD1000, a very significant figure in Celtic Christianity whose many miracles included the carrying of hot coals without being burnt. His chapel down in the churchyard was sadly destroyed by fire in 1427. One of Scotland's greatest kings, Malcolm Cranmore, had established a sanctuary here in the eleventh century and the holy relics, which included Duthac's skull set in silver, were guarded by a hermit monk. The saint actually died in Ireland and it was 200 years before his relics were returned in 1253. Among many distinguished visitors, James IV visited here annually and Robert the Bruce's wife and daughter were captured here in 1306.

The St Duthac Memorial Church was built in the fourteenth and fifteenth centuries by William, Earl of Ross. Its sixteenth-century pulpit was a gift from the Earl of Moray, regent to the young King James VI. A panel displayed in the church represents the six Craft Guild members of Tain. There are several other buildings of historic interest in the town. The first tower built in 1630 formed Tain's original tolbooth, it was replaced by the present substantial structure in the early eighteenth century. This holds the curfew bell and below is the Mercat cross, a place of markets and public humiliation! There was known to be a music and grammar school in Tain in 1634. By 1780 Latin and book-keeping had been added to the curriculum and when the Royal Academy opened in 1813 the lessons included navigation and 'The Elements of Fortification and Gunnery'.

The town's museum houses district and Clan Ross memorabilia including Tain silver. There are also some unique old photographs on display. The towns many other attractions include a golf course, a rose garden laid out to commemorate the 900th anniversary and a fine Highland Cheese Factory.

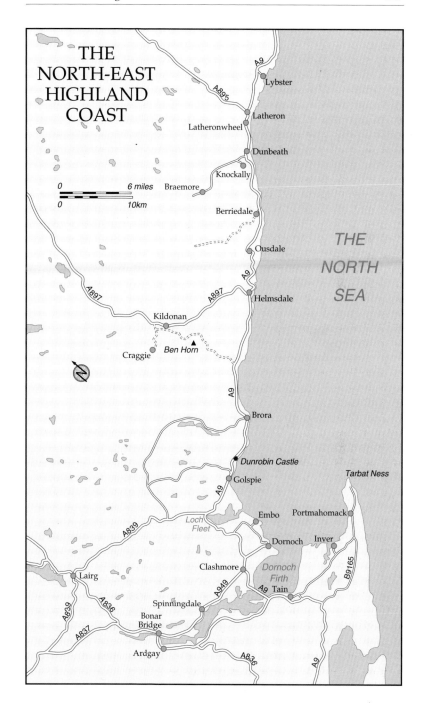

THE
NORTH-EAST
HIGHLAND
COAST

Lybster

Latheron

Latheronwheel

Dunbeath

Knockally

0   6 miles

0   10km

Braemore

Berriedale

Ousdale

THE

NORTH

SEA

Helmsdale

Kildonan

Ben Horn

Craggie

Brora

Dunrobin Castle

Tarbat Ness

Golspie

Embo

Portmahomack

Loch
Fleet

Dornoch   Inver

Clashmore

Dornoch
Firth

Lairg

Tain

Spinningdale

Bonar
Bridge

Ardgay

Last but by no means least on Tain's list attractions is the Glenmorangie Distillery. Glenmorangie is one of the best selling malts in the world and was one of the earliest to be sold as a single malt, in the 1920s. The character of the whisky is such that a French perfume house was able to identify twenty-six fragrances in the spirit, including almond, cinnamon and wild mint. The distillery itself is very highly regarded by the experts.

East of Tain a road extends for about 10 miles (16km) in to the Fearn Peninsular to the headland at Tarbat Ness, site of Britain's second highest lighthouse (not open to the public). It passes the test bombing range of Morrich More, which is also a site of special interest for students of coastal erosion and development. The picturesque fishing village of **Portmahomack** is a popular excursion as it has excellent sandy beaches and a couple of good pubs.

Leaving Tain and heading westwards along the south shore of the Dornoch Firth the new traffic island and bridge across the Firth soon appears. It is from here also that a peninsular extends in to the Firth, the site of the former Ferry Point from which travellers took the Meikle Ferry across the Firth prior to even Bonar Bridge being built. That bridge was in fact constructed as a result of a ferry disaster on the Meikle crossing in 1809 when ninety-nine people lost their lives. The bridge was built 3 years later.

A few miles after the bridge turning the village of **Edderton** contains a distillery, open to the public. There are several ancient remains around the village including chambered cairns and a sandstone obelisk of pre-Christian Pictish origin. It dates from around AD600 and may mark the site of a battle with Viking invaders. The parish church in the village (1743) is on the site of a much earlier Christian foundation and a Christian Pictish stone stands in the graveyard.

Further on at the head of the firth is Ardgay at the head of beautiful Strathcarron. Minor roads lead up in to the Strath and reach **Croick** where there is a church. This was made famous in 1845 during the clearances when people cleared from Glencalvie sheltered in the churchyard. Some scratched their names in the glass of the church's east windows, these are still visible today. By **Ardgay** itself there is a rare breeds animal croft and there is also the remains of an ice house, built to preserve salmon prior to transportation south following the arrival of the railway.

It is from **Bonar Bridge** that a wonderful road, large single track (A836), begins to run northward reaching Lairg, from where the choice is to continue through the very heart of northern Scotland to

Tongue (see Chapter 9 The North Coast), to follow the shores of Loch Shin to Laxford Bridge and Kinlochbervie on the A838 or to take the A837 westwards towards Lochinver. Combining any two of these roads makes for an excellent circular route of 100 to 200 miles (161 to 322km), easily possible on a long spring or summer's day.

Shortly before Lairg, by crossing over the River Shin and getting on to the B864, the spectacular Falls of Shin with salmon ladder may be viewed. Nearby is Carbisdale, the last true castle built in Scotland, commissioned by the Dowager Duchess of Sutherland but only completed 2 years after her death in 1914. It is now a youth hostel. Also in the area is Andrew Carnegie's Aultnagar Lodge, built in 1902 and now a luxury hotel.

The A949 runs east from Bonar Bridge towards Clashmore. A tight corner is required to get through **Spinningdale**, 4 miles (6km) from Bonar Bridge on this road. This village was founded in 1790 by George Dempster of Skibo who established a cotton mill in a bid to tackle unemployment. The venture was unsuccessfull, partly due to high transportation costs, and the mill was not rebuilt after it was destroyed by fire in 1806, 6 years before the first bridge was built. Four miles (6km) further on there is an 11ft (3m) high standing stone, probably dating to the Bronze Age.

Dornoch suddenly became half an hour closer to Inverness and the south when the Queen Mother opened the Dornoch Firth bridge in 1991. It has been a popular destination for visitors since Victorian times when the railway arrived. Like many other northern towns the railway has now gone and the existing mainline north is now a much slower and less direct route than the road. A campaign has been running for several years to have a railway bridge across the Dornoch Firth. This is the county town of the huge area of Sutherland, which takes in much of the west and north coast of Scotland right over to Cape Wrath, as well as this stretch of the east coast. Dornoch first appears in records of King David I who in 1140 asked the Earls of Caithness and Orkney to protect the town's monks. It became a Royal Burgh in 1628 by order of Charles I.

The charming town centre contains a small cathedral, founded in 1224 by St Gilbert de Moravia. He was local bishop at the time and a magnificent stained glass window to him was unveiled by Prince Charles in 1989. Much of the cathedral had been left in a ruinous state for over 250 years following a raid in 1570 by the Earl of Caithness, with the MacKay clan and Sutherland of Evelix. Restoration began in 1835 at the expense of the dowager Duchess of Sutherland. There is a good view of the area from the cathedral tower. The Bishop's Palace across the road is now a first class hotel.

A small cathedral in the charming town centre of Dornoch

Dornoch has several excellent beaches and many other fine old buildings including the library, gifted by Andrew Carnegie, and the nineteenth-century court house, jail (now a popular craft centre) and Drill Hall. The Witch's Stone in a Carnaig Street garden recalls a less happy time in the town's history when a poor woman named Janet Horne was put on a trial and burned as a witch. This was the last witch-burning in Scotland and took place in 1722.

The town may be best known to many for its Royal Dornoch golf course, ranked eleventh in the world, dating from 1616 and third oldest in Scotland. Many great players have done a round here, and many golf-course designers have visited too. Donald Ross, a Dornoch man took his own skills to America and designed over 500 courses there.

North of Dornoch on the coast lies the village of **Embo**, linked by a railway branch line until the 1960s. This was the fishing village of Dornoch parish, but evidence of settlement can be found here dating back to 3700BC in the form of burial cairns located at the entrance to the local caravan site. The present village was formed in 1820 when the residents were cleared from the surrounding fertile lands and deposited on the coast to make way for sheep. Many of the local population emigrated to North America and Australia or New Zealand. The town holds an 'Independence Day' recognised by the Queen.

A mile or so north is the site of the Battle of Embo, a bloody encounter that followed the arrival of a marauding force of Vikings in 1245. Sir Richard de Moravia on orders of William Earl of Sutherland took his forces to fight the Norse invaders and was all but defeated when Sir William's reinforcements arrived from Dornoch and helped to win the day. The story goes that Earl William led his troops himself and was disarmed in battle but, keeping his wits about him, grabbed a severed horse's leg and bludgeoned the Viking chief to death with it. Sir Richard too was killed and has a memorial to this day in Dornoch Cathedral. The battle is commemorated by the horseshoe in Dornoch's coat of arms.

Sir Richard's castle at **Skelbo** is up on the shores of Loch Fleet. It was probably originally (and rather ironically) a site chosen by invading Norsemen in the ninth century as suitable for their fleets. The castle is first mentioned in a charter of 1211 as being gifted to Richard's brother Gilbert de Moravia, later Bishop of Caithness, that year. It was probably of earth and wood construction at that time. The castle also played a part in the tragic tale of Margaret, Maid of Norway (see St Margaret's Hope, Chapter 13 Orkney Isles). It was here that the envoys of Edward I stayed en route to meet the young princess and with the intention of bringing her to London to marry the English king's son.

The A9 crosses **Loch Fleet** on the third and oldest north-east coast causeway, which may not be recognised as such by drivers crossing the loch which appears to be mainly marsh land rather than a deep firth such as Cromarty or Dornoch. This causeway, at 3,001ft (915m) long is a similar length to the other two however, but is in effect more of a dam, being constructed by Thomas Telford in 1812 with finance from the House of Sutherland. The idea was to reclaim 400 acres (160 hectares) of land and although this part of the project was unsuccessful, a haven for wildlife was created, and the alder groves on the landward side are now a National Nature Reserve. The Sutherlands were heavy investors in local road and rail links to the south and north and later financed the branch rail line to Dornoch in 1902 which closed 58 years later.

The first sight of **Golspie** comes with the statue of the first Duke of Sutherland, who died in 1836, looking down from the top of Ben Bhraggie. This is the administrative centre of modern day Sutherland, containing a high school, local newspaper, library and some of the best leisure facilities in the county (if you exclude the natural facilities throughout the region). There is an indoor swimming pool and a go-karting track as well as a fine golf course. There are many excellent walks around the area including a path along the side of the Big Burn from north of the village, one of the most picturesque gorges in the area. Golspie also boasts first class beaches and a stoneware company specialising in the creation of natural stone products. Their premises include an exhibition of geology and fossils.

A mile north of Golspie stands the stunning **Dunrobin Castle**, one of Scotland's greats. It is also the largest house in northern Scotland, having 189 rooms. The original castle dates back to the thirteenth century and has been occupied continuously since then. It was much rebuilt during the nineteenth century in the French style and is now of 'fairy tale' appearance. Much of the castle is open to visitors and it is certainly well worth exploring, being rich in treasures of all kinds expertly displayed throughout. The room where Queen Victoria

*The picturesque
Big Burn gorge,
by Golspie*

*A monument in
Dunrobin Castle
grounds*

stayed has been restored to the way it would have been at the time of her visit. The Sutherland family reached the height of their power in the eighteenth and nineteenth centuries when they owned almost all of Sutherland, (1,300,000 acres/520,000 hectares), the largest area owned by anyone in Western Europe. At this time the family were responsible for many improvements in infrastructure and farming methods, but also for the 'clearing' of 5,000 people from their ancestral dwellings. The castle is surrounded by beautiful gardens and grounds with prepared walks through them. The former summer house contains a collection of artefacts reflecting the family's wide ranging interests throughout the centuries. This ranges from Pictish stones to 'big-game' brought back from safari. Just north of the castle is the well preserved Iron Age broch of Carn Liath.

The next settlement of any size is **Brora** which, difficult though it may be to believe, was once one of the north's foremost industrial centres. The pleasant seaside village housed one of Scotland's earliest coal mines. It still contains a first class woollen mill at Hunters, which has fought hard to maintain business in recent lean years and there is also the Clynelish distillery and an ice-cream maker. There is another highly regarded golf course (laid out by James Braid) and yet more fine beaches. The Brora River on which the village stands is famous for its salmon. Between Brora and Helmsdale stands the Wolf Stone, marking the spot where the last Scottish wolf is reputed to have been killed in 1700.

Helmsdale, at the mouth of another great salmon river, owes its existence mainly to the herring industry. There are still fishing boats in the harbour but not as many. The award winning Timespan Heritage Centre located beside Thomas Telford's twin-arched bridge tells the tale of Highland heritage from times long past, including the notorious Highland clearances. Outside the centre there is a fascinating herb-garden containing many rare species. Helmsdale has more great beaches and another golf course.

Local estates have also put together an operation called Hidden Hills, giving visitors the opportunity to explore the remote landscape of the area with a guide who lives there and works on the land himself. The tours look at the rich heritage of archaeology including why Pictish farming methods in Sutherland gradually gave way to a cattle based economy in the centuries prior to sheep arriving with the clearances. Today the land has a mixed use including forestry and field sports. Indigenous birdlife, wildlife and aspects of botanical interest are also explored.

The railway line leaves the coast here and follows the Strath of Kildonan west and north up towards the north coast near Dounreay. A single track road also follows the **Strath** which saw the 'Great Sutherland Gold Rush' of 1869 when men from all over Britain descended on the area. Gold is still panned here today, but mostly by tourists!

The A9 continues to follow the coast, climbing in to the Ord of Caithness around some single-track hair-pin bends with good views north along the Caithness Coast and sometimes of the oil rigs working out in the North Sea. On a clear day it is possible to see as far south as the Moray Coast to the south with the Grampian mountains beyond.

The village of **Ousdale** is famous for its weavers, who export their designer standard materials to major fashion houses around the world. The population of **Badbea** a little further north exported themselves, mainly to America and New Zealand, as the monument erected there in 1911 states. The ruined croft houses perched on the cliffs are all that remain of this community, cleared from the fertile

The small fishing harbour of Helmsdale

Straths Valleys. Tradition has it that the sit was so exposed that children, as well as livestock, had to be tethered down to ensure they were not blown over the cliffs. **Berriedale** has pleasant gardens and cottages, there is also a puffin colony here in the early summer and a llama farm with other rare breeds including raccoons and chip munks.

Dunbeath Strath, which contains several ruined brochs, reaches the coast at **Dunbeath**, birthplace of local author Neil M Gunn. The castle here remains privately owned but can be seen from the harbour. The village itself contains a Heritage Centre with audio visual displays of natural and social history. There are also art and crafts galleries. A road up the Stath to Braemore gives excellent views across the Caithness hills. Just north of the village is the **Laidhay** Croft Museum, a traditional longhouse croft with straw roof dating from around 1842 and containing artefacts from the early years of the crofting era.

Adjoining villages of **Latheron** and **Latheronwheel** are home to the Clan Gunn Heritage Centre where the clan's history is traced from its Norse origins. Evidence is also put forward that the Scots discovered America nearly 100 years before Columbus. Pony trekking and riding is a popular pastime in the area and there is also a good harbour. The A895 departs due north to Thurso from here while the A9 begins its last leg as a trunk road across the flat coastal plan of Caithness.

Lybster is another village with a fine harbour, as well as a 9 hole golf course and a Celtic cross in its church yard. There are a number of ancient monuments between Lybster and Wick, including the Grey Cairns of Camster, reached by a minor road just north of the village. These date back to between 3000 and 4000BC and are still accessible, but visitors must be prepared to crawl in. The Hill O' Many stanes contains twenty-two rows of stones, averaging eight per row and dating from Bronze Age times. Nearby rock of a different kind can be seen being made, lettering and all, at Kyleburn Confectionery.

Further Information
— The North-East Highland Coast —

Places to Visit

Ardgay
Corvost Rare Animals Croft
☎ 08633 3117
Open: daily at 11am.

Berriedale
Kingspark Llama Farm
☎ 05935 202

Brora
Clynelish Distillery Visitor Centre
☎ 0408 621444
Open: Monday to Friday, 9.30am-4.30pm (last tour 4pm).

Dornoch
Dornoch Craft Centre
Town Jail
Castle Street
☎ 0862 810555

Royal Dornoch Golf Club
☎ 0862 810219

Dunbeath
Preservation Trust
Open: May to September. Monday to Saturday 10am-5pm. Sunday 11am-6pm.
☎ 05933 233

Edderton
Balblair Distillery
☎ 086282 273
Open: Monday to Thursday, 10am-12noon and 2pm-4pm.

Golspie
Dunrobin Castle
☎ 0408 633177
Open: May, Monday to Thursday, 10.30am-12.30pm, June to September, Monday to Saturday 10.30am-5.30pm and Sundays 1pm-5.30pm; October is same as summer but closing an hour earlier.
Last tours 30 minutes before closing.

Orcadian Stone Company Limited
Main Street
☎ 0408 633483
Open: daily from 9am-6pm.

Helmsdale
Hidden Hills
☎ 04312 640

Timespan Heritage Centre
Sutherland
☎ 04312 327
Open: Easter to October, Monday to Saturday 10am-5pm, Sunday 2pm-5pm. Open until 6pm during July and August.

Laidhay
Croft Museum
Open: daily during the summer.

Latheron
The Clan Gunn Heritage Centre
Open: June to September inclusive,
Tuesday to Saturday, 10am-1pm, 2-
5pm and a few days over Christmas
☎ 05932 229

Lybster
The Lybster Gallery
Caithness
KW3 6BN
Open: June to September, Tuesday to
Saturday 10am-1pm, 2-5pm and a few
days of Christmas
☎ 05932 229

Ousdale
Ousdale Weaving Limited
☎ 04312 371

Tain
Glenmorangie Distillery
☎ 0862 892043 for opening times.

Highland Fine Cheeses
Blairliath
Shore Road
☎ 0862 892034
Open: Monday to Thursday, 10am-4pm.

Tain and District Museum
Open: Easter to September, Monday to
Saturday, 10am-4.30pm.

Tourist Information Offices
Caithness
Whitechapel Road
Wick
KW1 4EA
☎ 0955 2596
Fax: 0955 4940

Dornoch
The Square
Sutherland
IV25 3SD
☎ 0862 810400
Fax: 0862 810644

North Kessock
Inverness
IV1 1XB
☎ 046373 505
Fax: 046373 701

Offices below open Easter until
September or October

Bonar Bridge
☎ 08632 333

Helmsdale
☎ 04312 640

9 • The North Coast

While charity fund raisers hop, skip and jump along the A9 to John O'Groats on the east coast, and fish lorries negotiate the single tracks to Kinlochbervie near Britain's north-westerly tip, few people, it seems, think of taking the drive from the north-west to the north-east corner of Scotland and Britain. Those that do may remember the journey for a long time: desolate hill country of northern Sunderland giving way to the Caithness flow country; remote villages on the west and comparative suburbia in the east; empty sandy beaches, magnificent cliffs, stacks and caves; unbeatable wildlife and, in the middle of it all, the eerie surrealism of the Dounreay nuclear power plant.

A true north coast guide must begin at **Cape Wrath** although, from a driver's perspective, mainland Britain's most north-westerly bit of road ends on the bank of the Kyle of Durness — a stretch of water 10 miles (16km) east of the cape. Only a passenger ferry crosses this kyle and from there a summertime minibus takes visitors through the remote land — popular with huge colonies of seabirds and larger, faster metal 'birds' from NATO forces, who use the area as a permanent test bombing range (the mini bus does not operate when they are in action!). The main place of interest at Cape Wrath is a lighthouse constructed in 1827 by Robert Stevenson, but ornithologists may be more impressed by the nearby sandstone cliffs of Clo Mor, mainland Britain's highest at 920ft (280m). The Kyle is reached via an access road about 1 mile (2km) south of Durness, signposted to the Cape Wrath Hotel (which is actually on the public road side of the kyle).

Durness itself is deceptively dull when first approached. There are the remains of two old brochs just south of the village that date to Pictish time. Picts farmed the lands in this area for centuries before the arrival of the Gaels. But for those arriving with no knowledge of the village, the only visible point of interest is the fact that the road bends round to the right and you know you have finally stopped heading north and must now go east. But Durness is certainly worth a stop.

Where the main road bends right there is a side road off to the left and this should be taken first. Half a mile (1km) down you will approach the famous and curious Balnakeil Craft Village. This is a collection of buildings erected as part of the 'Early Warning System' in the hay day of the Cold War. In the event the camp was outdated for that purpose virtually before it was complete and it was taken over in an enlightened move by the local council who sought to make it into a craft centre.

The buildings, which symbolise a tiny victory in the war of sense over insanity, have been made a little more attractive by the inhabitants, who are skilled in marquetry, patchwork, printing, toy making, pottery, wood and leatherwork, painting, traditional wines, weaving, knitwear and renting out mountain bikes. More unusual products to try include longbows and hats. Danish born Lotte Glob, an artist working in ceramics who has exhibited across Europe and sold work to the Museum of Fine Art in

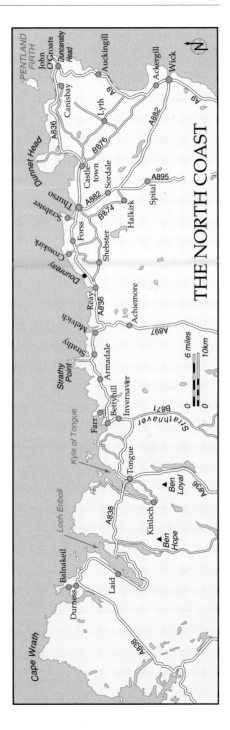

THE NORTH COAST

Copenhagen amongst others, has a studio here. There is a hotel which serves wholesome meals within the settlement and a teashop too.

More of Durness's hidden delights are to be found by persevering to the end of the road on which **Balnakeil** is situated. Crossing a cattle grid you will come to a grassy parking area with a beautiful long beach stretching out ahead of you to Faraid Head. If you walk onto this headland you will find more cliffs filled with seabirds, including puffins, in the season, and idyllic white sandy coves in between. On a clear day the cliffs of Cape Wrath can be seen from the end of the headland.

Also at the end of the road is the ruined Balnakeil church which dates from 1619 and was itself constructed on earlier religious buildings going at least as far back as the eighth century. The original church was established by St Maelrubha who brought Christianity to Lairg and Durness. Balnakeil actually means 'Place of the Church', and records of the church, dating back to 1190, are in the Vatican. The graveyard contains a monument to Rob Donn, a famous Celtic bard. Although himself illiterate he might have been pleased to know that his poems were printed 2 years after his death, and soon afterwards translated into English with an introduction by Sir Walter Scott. Another interesting monument is the Gothic-looking stone within the ruined church building, the tomb of Donald MacLeod, a notorious local murderer and robber. He is said to have bought his own tomb to avoid enemies defiling his remains after his death.

Driving back through Durness and finally heading east, perhaps the village's main attraction is **Smoo Cave**. This is a huge, dramatic limestone cavern with a beautiful waterfall cascading down into the back of it, reached by a raised walkway. Boat trips can be arranged into the floodlit inner caverns. In wintertime the stream leaving the caverns mouth and flowing to the sea can become a torrent, making access which is normally very easy from the car park above, virtually impossible. The cave is well looked after with toilet facilities above and prepared steps down. Across the road from the car park the stream which forms the underground waterfall can be seen and there is a footbridge above it, from which you can watch the water rush foaming into the ground.

Sports lovers will find three surfing beaches in Durness at Ceannabeinne, Sango and Balnakeil. Although not quite Hawaii, and subject to weather conditions, surfing is popular here with home grown British surf enthusiasts. There is also a 9 hole golf course down by Balnakeil church and plenty of fishing opportunities — mainly for brown trout from April to September.

The ruins of Balnakeil church, near Durness

The single track from Durness to Tongue (30 miles/48km), the next settlement of more than a few houses, winds its way around the coast with a barren landscape inland and a typical mixture of beautiful sandy beaches or cliffs on the seaward side of the road. The distance is perhaps twice as long as it might otherwise be if nature had not decided to lay Loch Eriboll between the two villages, causing a substantial detour.

Loch Eriboll was better known as 'Loch 'Orrible' by the servicemen who were stationed here during World War II with little to do but wait for their role in the battles to begin. Indeed the loch has historically been used as a naval anchorage, including Vikings sheltering here before sea battles centuries earlier. One of the few specific points of interest is to be found on the western shore by the settlement of **Portnacon**. If you can find it (and there is no obvious sign), two small cairns (piles of rocks) on the sea side of the road mark the entrance to an Iron Age underground food storeroom. Enter at your own risk. A few miles further south is **Choraidh Croft** which has rare breeds, live shellfish displays, crafts, tearoom and a pets corner. Near to here the very last old style British mainland pay phone was taken out of service in the early 1990s. It was first introduced with A and B buttons 70 years earlier. Some still survive on the islands.

The rugged cliffs of Faraid Head, Durness

Once finally round Loch Eriboll you will be shocked to find yourself back on a road wide enough for two vehicles, complete with white lines down the middle! There is also a short burst of greenery around a few houses known as **Heilam** in the shelter of Ben Arnaboll. The road crosses a narrow bridge over River Hope here before winding steeply uphill and off due east to Tongue. Experienced walkers who are happy to tramp over boggy heather on no real paths will be rewarded by parking the car and heading north at this point to **Whiten Head** a good 5 miles (8km) away. In addition to the scenic attractions, the caves beneath the head are the only known remaining grey seal breeding ground in mainland Britain (obviously timing is important here).

Those who are not keen walkers but are ambitious drivers have the second alternative of turning south once again along the ungraded road to Altnaharra. This is one of those roads with few passing places and grass growing up the middle in places, so great care is needed. On the other hand the rewards are access by car to places remoter still than the remoteness through which you are already passing on the A838.

Those taking the ungraded road will get their best reward along the first 10 miles (16km) or so when the road follows the shore of Loch Hope beneath the magnificent **Ben Hope** (3,040ft/927m), Scotland's most northerly munro (mountains over 3,000ft/915m high). The land here is comparatively rich and agricultural, in contrast to that through which the coast road takes you. At the end of the loch is the Allt-na-caillich waterfall. Past the shelter of Ben Hope the land returns to more familiar desolation. The driver's efforts are rewarded about 15 miles (24km) along the track, however, with the appearance of **Dun Dornadilla Broch** by the roadside. Nearly 23ft (7m) high and 2,000 years old this is Caithness and Sutherland's best preserved Iron Age broch. It is another 15 miles (24km) before you reach the A836 which will take you back up to Tongue.

An alternative route is to carry on and cross over that road onto the B873 which runs along the side of Loch Naver, and then follows the loch's outflowing river back to the north coast. This is better than the unclassified road only in that it has slightly more passing places and a better surface. Otherwise it is still very winding. Those who choose to take the B873 should look out for the rare great northern diver and even an osprey taking fish from the river. The Naver Valley is also notorious in Highland history for some of the most brutal clearances of the local population in the nineteenth century. The lack of much habitation within the valley now is therefore food for thought. Even more so as one of the few houses that do remain is Syre Lodge which was the home of Patrick Sellar, the brutal factor hated across the Highlands for having orchestrated the harsh clearances. There is a good amount of information on the local clearances at the Strathnaver museum in Bettyhill.

In any event, if you are feeling peckish or thirsty the only establishment within a 20 mile (32km) radius is the friendly Altnaharra Inn, about ½ mile (1km) south of this crossroads. The A836, although still single track, should provide light relief for the driver who will find himself often able to see miles ahead with a reassuring string of white diamond shaped passing place signs between himself and any oncoming traffic. Those who have stuck to the north coast road and the A838 will find themselves rewarded with the luxury of the two lane road all the way over to Tongue, but little else to inspire them as the stretch from Loch Hope to the Kyle of Tongue is relatively featureless. Lest drivers become too excited by the improved road conditions a notice warning 'Road Liable to Subsidence' heralds one of those stretches when the road itself makes a loud booming noise as you drive over it, wondering if the strange sound indicates some problem with your car. The main features to see out of the window are bits of old single track road slowly sinking into the peat.

The **Kyle of Tongue**, unlike Loch Eriboll, has a causeway across

Loch Eriboll lies between Durness and Tongue

it, an achievement in itself for so remote a community. The old road, now unclassified, does still run around the Kyle. A few miles south of Tongue on this old road is a stone to Ewan Robertson, known as Bard of the Clearances. Driving around the Kyle, which appears to be full of sand banks, events of 250 years ago may be recalled. It was here that a ship, previously captured from the English by the Jacobites and renamed *Prince Charles*, ran aground while being pursued by the English navy. The ship contained stores and more than £10,000 in gold. 'Bonnie Prince Charlie', in Inverness prior to the final battle at Culloden, sent 1,500 men to recover the treasure, but they were captured on the way by soldiers of the Earl of Sutherland and Lord Reay.

Tongue itself is a pleasant place to stop, there are two good hotels and an excellent village store — the type that sells everything and even has a small government 'job centre' board in its window, should you decide to stay permanently. A private house here has reputedly the world's most northerly palm tree growing in its garden. Another claim to fame is that John Lennon managed to have a car crash when visiting here in 1969.

A footpath from the village leads down and across a stream before going up to the ruins of fourteenth-century Varrich Castle, owned by the Clan Mackay but which may previously have been a Viking stronghold. There is also a church in Tongue where the 'Lairds Loft' is a local attraction. Fishermen will find fourteen lochs in the area accessed by the local angling club.

The A838 merges with the A836 which has come up through the middle of northern Scotland and eventually arrives at the north coast on the outskirts of Tongue. From then on the road is officially the A836 although it is that road which today meets the A838 at a T-junction.

Further on there is an unlisted road up to the coast itself at **Skerray**. This road is worth taking if you have time and like to pass beaches and small lochs. There are scattered areas of deciduous woodland in places — a Highland rarity. The road also takes you by the Torrisdale nature reserve. A boat operates from the pier at Skerray and trips can be arranged to some of the small islands off the coast. Otherwise the A836 continues to meander on to **Bettyhill**, 12 miles (19km) further on.

There is disagreement over whether Bettyhill was named after Elizabeth, first Duchess of Sutherland or the Betty who owned the pub at the top of the hill. The village is similar in layout to Durness and Tongue, although lacking the splash of greenery of the latter. It is likely that the locals prefer the second explanation of where their village name comes from because, unlike Durness, Bettyhill suffered badly in the clearances. Elizabeth, First Duchess of Sutherland did have a good reputation herself but was married to the Marquess of Salford, who became Duke when he married her. He was responsible for the removal of 1,200 people from the area. There is the chance to inspect the remains of a cleared village by turning right as signposted just after crossing the narrow bridge over the River Naver on entering the village. The remains of the village *Rossal* have been excavated after they were re-discovered by the Forestry Commission who were preparing to plant trees on the site. Settlement there has now been traced back to the earliest available records in the thirteenth century, but ended abruptly one day in 1830.

More can be learned of the brutal removal of indigenous families at the Strathnaver Museum within the former village church. The museum contains displays charting the history of the clearances as well as artefacts from Highland living in the past and is well worth a visit. Access is easiest from the small car park in front of the tourist office in the village. This building also contains a craft and coffee shop. The graveyard outside the church-turned-museum contains a ninth-century Celtic cross called the Farr Stone, which is a very good example, intricately carved. Plans are afoot to move the cleaned stone inside the museum, where it will join artefacts dating as far back as a 4,000-year-old cist removed from an ancient burial site in the area.

Beach lovers will also be delighted by the choice of Torrisdale and Farr beaches by the village. **Torrisdale** beach, which some consider to be Scotland's best, is popular with archaeologists as it contains cairns, ring stones and brochs. To the back of the beach is the Invernaver nature reserve which has a good selection of flora and fauna. The alpine plants in the area are reputedly very fine specimens. **Farr** beach is also very attractive. There are plenty of fishing opportunities.

The ruins of Borve Castle, destroyed by the Earl of Sutherland in 1555 are also to be found here. The castle was a former stronghold of the Mackay Clan famous in the area. There is a Mackay Clan room in the Strathnaver Museum, which attracts visitors from all over the world.

From Bettyhill onwards the landscape becomes positively urban, with at least a house every mile or so and a number of small settlements. The road becomes increasingly confused as to whether it is a single-track or two-lane road and drivers should keep on their toes (or clutch/brakes) as one stretch switches to another.

Various short tracks off the A836 take you north to the coastal villages. **Armadale** is famous for a heroic lifeboat team and a little further on **Strathy Point** is yet another bird sanctuary with nature reserve status and beautiful coastal scenery. There is a nature trail to follow.

Melvich, where the road decides it definitely will become two-way from now on, is an attractive village where there are good views out over the Halladale Estuary to the **Pentland Firth** and the Orkneys on a clear day. There is a Tourist Information Point and the bay is popular with surfers.

A few miles past Melvich by **Drumholiston** you may spot a large rock by the roadside that has been split in two. This is the 'Devil's Stone' that was supposedly split by the Devil's tail. Whether he was chasing an old woman, or heading off in a huff to Caithness having failed to tempt the people of Melvich, depends on which version of the story you are told.

Shortly before entering Caithness you have the option of turning south onto the single-track A897 along Strath Halladale, which follows the Caithness border and the small river, and eventually meets up with the railway that heads for Wick and Thurso. This road cuts through the 'Flow Country' too, the site of many a verbal battle.

Shags and other seabirds are common on the north coast of Scotland

On the one side are the environmentalists who want to preserve what is left of the peaty bogs of Britain and their unique flora and fauna. On the other side are the people who have lived in the area for generations and feel that they have been told what they can and cannot do by outside interests for too long.

Back on the A836 you will soon pass Sandside Bay which has a reputation for sailing and windsurfing. Sportspeople preferring dry land may care to visit the 18 hole golf course at Reay a little further on.

You are now entering Caithness and will notice that the land is generally much flatter. You may also see that dry-stone walls are often replaced by thin upright slab 'fences' made of local stone. These flagstones were exported widely in Britain and Europe during the early nineteenth century. **Reay** has a fine harbour and the famous 'Reay Stone' set in the west wall of the chapel at the old burial ground. This is a cross slab dating from the tenth century. Cross slabs are thought to have sanctified local areas. The key to the chapel is available at the Post Office.

A mile (2km) further on from Reay at Isauld an ungraded road cuts inland slightly and off towards Shebster. In **Shebster** there is another ungraded road crossing the first and you should turn north back up towards the coast. You will soon pass two grass covered cairns known as Cnoc Freiceadain. The south cairn, at 230ft (70m) long is one of the largest known. There are three rounded mounds at the site which were given the name 'Na Tri Shean' (The Three Fairy Mounds) by the locals.

Directly beyond the cairns you can see the nuclear research establishment of Dounreay in stark contrast to the prehistoric cairns. If you follow the ungraded road you will emerge back on the A836 just past the site and must turn left/west to go back to it if you wish to. It should be noted that the unclassified road from Reay forms the north-westerly extremity of a network of similar single-track roads that criss-cross the Caithness peatlands. These are of interest to explore for anyone with a good map but is not towing a caravan!

Dounreay must have taken up more airtime on the Highland's TV and radio stations for the past three decades than any other building in the area. Admission to the exhibition centre is free and there are plenty of parking spaces and even a picnic site. The exhibition has two floors of information, models, videos and hands-on exhibits. Tours of the prototype fast reactor are available from the centre but visitors must be over 12 years old.

Interestingly Dounreay's most obvious landmark, the white dome, held an earlier reactor which is no longer there but the dome will remain as it is now a listed building — like many of the red phone boxes you will still see dotted around the Highlands.

Back on the A836 and shortly before Bridge of Forss a minor road leads off north to the sea and to **Crosskirk**. Here are the remains of a twelfth-century chapel dedicated to St Mary, one of Scotland's oldest. The architecture is of a Norse design, only to be found otherwise in Orkney, Shetland or Ireland, not elsewhere on the mainland.

Thurso may come as something of a culture shock for those that have avoided Dounreay. The town has clearly benefitted economically from being close to the nuclear establishment. There are good shopping facilities and a leisure centre in the town. Thurso was historically important before Dounreay however. It was once an important Norse settlement and was noted for trade with Scandinavian countries as long ago as the fourteenth century. The importance of this trade is underlined by the fact that King David II decreed that the Caithness pound weight should become the standard for all of Scotland. This was at a time when Scotland's southern border was beyond Newcastle in the south. In the seventeenth and eighteenth centuries Thurso enjoyed a considerable trade in animal products.

One of the town's more famous sons, Sir John Sinclair, lived towards the end of that period. He was born in Thurso East Castle, the one before the ruined castle there now, which was built in 1872. There is a statue of him in the town centre, and Sir John's Square, an ornamental garden, was given to the town by his grandson, Tollemache. Sir John was educated at Harrow alongside Sir Robert Peel and Lord Byron, the latter later describing him as 'the prodigy of our school days'. Upon finishing school he did not return straight to Thurso but popped over to France where he was arrested as a spy and dragged up before Napoleon. He managed to persuade the Emperor that he was not involved in espionage and was, rather surprisingly, set free.

Sir John was later to become the driving force behind many agricultural 'improvements' including dry-stone walling across Caithness, crop rotation and the arrival of sheep to replace people. In 1790 he instigated *The Statistical Account of Scotland*, a sort of mini-*Doomsday Book* went into great detail about every area in Scotland — the minister for each parish being obliged to report on statistics of population, schools, businesses and so on as well as the local population's collective attitude to entertainment, work or alcohol!

Other episodes from Thurso's history that should be recorded are the food riots of the mid-nineteenth century. These occurred following the introduction of new farming ideas, including the potato. The blight that caused the infamous Irish potato famine in 1845 moved on to Scotland in 1846. A hundred special constables had to be mobilised to protect grain being loaded on ships for sale in the south.

There are many minor roads criss-crossing the flow country between Thurso and Wick; some have long straight stretches which are a rare treat in most of Scotland. The A882 and the railway line cut the north-east corner off Scotland and go directly the last 20 miles (32km) to Wick. The A836 continues to meander around the coast taking about 50 miles (80km) between the towns.

Following the coast road the first headland passed is Harald, about 2 miles (3km) from Thurso. Nearby is Harald Tower, dating from the eighteenth century and the burial place of the Sinclairs of Ulbster. The clan's burials here go back much further however. Harald, Earl of Orkney was buried here after losing his life at the battle of Claredon in 1196. A little further around the coast is the Stoer lighthouse from where a difficult 2 mile (3km) walk extends to the old Man of Stoer, a famous sea stack.

Castletown offers another opportunity for a south-easterly turn to Wick, this time on the B876. The harbour here was built to support

Dunnet Head, the most northerly point of mainland Britain famous for its colonies of sea birds

the Caithness flagstone industry but today the town is best known for being home of Norfrost, surprisingly perhaps one of the United Kingdom's major producers and exporters of freezers and a vital local employer, testimony to the ease of communications from the far north.

As the cliffs get ever more spectacular yet another haven for ornithologists opens up with the rare species of the flow country running into the teeming colonies of sea birds nesting on the cliffs. One of the most famous places for seeing them is **Dunnet Head**, reached by a turning north at Dunnet on to the B855. There is an abandoned services base here and a working lighthouse. The head is particularly famous for its colonies of puffins and for being the most northerly point of mainland Britain. The B855 passes through **Brough** where there is a fine quality knitwear workshop open to visitors.

Before the turning for Dunnet Head the sand dunes (and parking area) on the coast side of the road hide the magnificent sandy beach of the huge **Dunnet Bay**. There is a nature reserve behind the dunes and the Dunnet Bay pavilion contains a display explaining the natural history of the area. In Dunnet itself the local kirk has a medieval west tower.

Back on the A836, the village of **Mey** has grown up by the castle of the same name, favoured summer residence of the Queen Mother. It was built between 1566 and 1572 by the fourth Earl of Caithness. Generally it is not open to the public although the gardens are, occasionally, in aid of charity. The Castle Arms Hotel in Mey contains a 'Royal Gallery' housing unique photographs of the royal family's visits to the area.

So on to world famous **John O'Groats** along the south side of the famous Pentland Firth that joins Atlantic Ocean to North Sea. A final pause perhaps at Canisbay where the church dates to the fifteenth century, although there is reference to a building from 1222.

The actual north-east tip, and furthest point from Lands End, is **Duncansby Head** where there are some spectacular coastal features and a lighthouse. Yet charity fund raising cyclists, runners, walkers, roller-skaters, pogo-stickers *et al* rightly count their journey from Cornwall complete when they reach the famous signpost pointing back to the opposite corner of Britain, 876 miles (1,410km) away. Most of them no doubt take the high-wire walk along the cliffs to Duncansby. As is well known John O'Groats got its name from a Dutch man, Jan De Groot, who settled in the area getting on for 500 years ago.

The place has become a little less disappointing of late with some modern craft units selling candles and pottery. The assortment of last and first shops (depending on your point of view), last houses, last fuel station, last bus-stop in Britain and so on have been around a lot longer. Whatever commercial ventures come and go though, and whatever you feel about the place from that perspective, it is difficult not to feel a sense of achievement reaching the end of the land. The road ends and the view out to Stroma and the Orkneys beyond is a reward in itself. Maybe it is the publicity of the place or the shape of the land, but in the north-west you just round the corner, here you feel almost a mild shock that the A9 which has served you for so long, just has to stop!

The **Isle of Stroma**, close to the mainland and clearly seen on all but the foggiest of days, was abandoned in the 1950s mainly due to a lack of utilities. It is hard to imagine now that such facilities could not be provided, especially with the advent of wind turbines. At the time of the evacuation however, facilities on the mainland, so close, must have been very tempting. The former inhabitants do return to tend the graves of relatives by the abandoned church.

Just beyond the Isle of Stroma in the Pentland Firth a famous whirlpool appears every now and then. It has taken the lives of sailors down through the centuries. The Norsemen who named it

The world famous John O'Groats

Svelgr, now Swelkie, believed it was created by a magic mill, churning out the salt in the sea, after a sea-king's boat containing the mill was sunk on the spot by the weight of the salt. King and boat are gone but the mill keeps churning away.

The main road south from John O'Groats (A9) runs straight across the peat land, following the east coast. **Freswick**, 5 miles (8km) south, contains a seventeenth-century fortified tower house, built on the foundations of a twelfth-century Viking structure. It is not open to the public. The original owner's neighbour 800 years ago lived 1 mile (2km) down the road at Bucholie Castle. He was Sweyn Asliefson, a famous Norse pirate. The current name has come from Aberdeenshire owners in the more recent past, who brought it with them from their own estates in Grampian. Viking remains, including that of the only long-house in Scotland, have been found in the locality at Freswick Bay.

At **Auckingill** there are Three Follies — the first (on the left) was a boat's lantern, the second held a barometer and the third, Mervin's Tower, was built for a small local boy, no doubt called Mervin. The motto inscribed means 'Hasten Slowly'. The village also contains the John Nicholson Museum, which houses displays on the archaeological history of Caithness, especially brochs. John Nicholson was a Victorian antiquarian who lived in the village.

A few miles further on at **Kneiss** a castle once stood, but all that remains is a tall slim tower on the cliff tops, now more than 300 years old. A newer castle dating from the nineteenth century is still in use.

The B876 turning back north-west a short distance from Kneiss leads to the village of **Lyth** and the remarkably popular (considering its remote location) Lyth Art Centre. This manages to stage a huge variety of theatrical and musical productions for its seventy-five seat auditorium and also arranges exhibitions of art work of all kinds.

The more direct road from Thurso to Wick (A882) passes **Halkirk** (on the B874 west), a lovely little village where the locals once roasted alive the local bishop, Adam, because he was a bit heavy handed with his taxation policy. That was back in 1222 however.

For those bypassing Wick the A895 goes due south to Latheron. It passes **Spittal** a few miles after departing the A882. This is named after the Hospital of St Magnus. The surrounding countryside contains numerous flagstone quarries where important fossil remains have been found, as well as flagstones. Examples of both are to be found in the local Fossil Centre.

Just north of Wick is Noss Head with a lighthouse and cliffs filled with yet more seabirds. Down below in **Sinclair's Bay** are the two castles of Girnigoe and Sinclair, built in the fifteenth and sixteenth centuries and former strongholds of the Sinclair family, Earls of Caithness.

In days gone by this was not a particularly pleasant family. The Sinclairs possibly reached their hereditary lowpoint in 1576 when the fourth Earl imprisoned his own son in the dungeons at Girnegoe for 6 years, accusing him of plotting against him. In a fit of brilliance the Earl then ordered his son be given a feast of salted meat, but nothing to drink. A while later the younger man died of dehydration.

The last clan battle in Scotland was fought near here by a later generation of Sinclairs and the Campbells in 1680. By that time Girnegoe and Sinclair castles were already abandoned and they were reported in ruin as early as 1700. A Celtic cross marks the site of the battle on the B874 by the Wick river, a few miles east of the A9, just north of Wick. The Sinclairs lost the battle, having too bad a hangover from a serious whisky drinking session the night before and thereby lost the Earldom, but moaned and skirmished to have it returned 7 years later.

Ackergill Tower, also in Sinclair's Bay, dates from the fifteenth century and stands a good 70ft (21m) high. It was much modernised about 150 years ago and is run partly as a luxury retreat for paying guests.

The Royal Burgh of **Wick** was once Europe's biggest herring fishing port. The name Wick (Vik) comes from the Norse meaning a creek or a bay. The town became a Royal Burgh by order of King James IV of Scotland in 1589 and there were many celebrations 400 years later to commemorate the event. Wick does not share ThursO's cosmopolitan feel but instead exudes a sense of strength and endurance, the Victorian stone buildings having seen prosperity in former boom years and remaining unchanged through leaner times.

Those 150 boom herring fishing years began in the late 1760s, with 32 'sloops' fishing from the port by 1790. By 1795 there were 200 boats and a few years later Thomas Telford was employed to build a new harbour and a purpose-designed village to house workers arriving in their hundreds. Expansion was so rapid, thanks partly to war with France, that a new harbour was needed within 15 years and by the 1860s a total of 1,122 boats were registered at the harbour. The town benefited at this time from a new public library, court house, banks, post office and other public buildings.

The old parish church dates from the boom years of the (early nineteenth century). It was built on the ruins of an older structure and is reputed to have the widest unsupported roof span of any church in Scotland. In the churchyard is the ruined thirteenth-century chapel of St Fergus, patron saint of Wick. The Roman Catholic Church of St Joachim (1835) was built on land donated by Wick townspeople to Father Lovi in thanks for his efforts during an outbreak of cholera in the town. Scotland's most northerly mainland distillery is also here, producing an 8-year-old single malt 'Old Pulteney'.

The multi-award winning Heritage Centre is a major attraction in the town. Constructed within harbourside houses built in 1810 by Telford, it takes you into a restored nineteenth-century fisherman's home, a cooperage and a working fish kiln. The centre also includes the famous and amazing Johnston photographic collection of 115 years of history and an art gallery with terraced gardens.

Much publicity in the region goes to the Caithness Glass Factory and visitor facility where glass making skills are on display. The product is internationally famous.

Wick's Golf Club is the north's oldest, formed in 1870. It is a largely flat course by the beach a few miles north of Wick off the A9. The second hole has a burn particularly close to the green which apparently resembles the first at St Andrews!

Old Wick Castle (or the Castle of Oldwick), south of the town, is believed to be Scotland's oldest, dating from the twelfth century. There is one other contender in Argyll. It still stands 40ft (12m) high.

Further Information
— The North Coast —

Places to Visit

Auckingill
John Nicholson Museum
☎ 0955 3761 ext 242
Open: June to August, Monday to
Saturday 10am-12noon, 2-4pm.

Bettyhill
Strathnaver Museum
☎ 06412 421
Open: Monday to Saturday, Easter to
September, 10am-1pm and 2-5pm.

Brough
Brough Knitwear Workshop
☎ 084785 695

Dounreay
Dounreay Exhibition Centre
☎ 0847 802701
Open: Tuesday to Sunday inclusive.
Admission free.

Durness
Balnakeil Craft Village
Open: 10am-6pm in summer. Some
shops closed on Sundays.

Choraidh Croft
Loch Eribollside
Laid
Durness
☎ 0971 511235
Open: May to October 10.30am-9pm.

Lyth
Lyth Arts Centre
☎ 095584 270

Spittal
The Fossil Centre
☎ 0084784 236

Wick
Caithness Glass Visitor Centre
Airport Industrial Estate
☎ 0955 2286
Open: Monday to Saturday all year,
9am-5pm. Open Sundays Easter to end
September, 11am-5pm.

Wick Heritage Centre
☎ 0955 5393
Open: June to September 10am-5pm,
Monday to Saturday.

Tourist Information Offices

Dornoch
The Square
Dornoch IV25 3SD
☎ 0862 810400

Wick
Whitechapel Road
Wick KW1 4EA
☎ 0955 2596

Seasonal Offices (Easter to end October)
Bettyhill ☎ 06412 342
Durness ☎ 00971 511259
John O'Groats ☎ 0955 81373
Thurso ☎ 0847 62371

10 • The North-West Highlands

W hile Scotland's north-west coast can no longer be claimed to be tourist free, the numbers that venture north of the Kyle of Lochalsh are few compared to those who travel to the lower reaches of the west coast. That being said, there are fewer indigenous people about, so strangers do tend to stand out. Spring and autumn are the best times to visit and avoid both tourists and midges. The snow-capped mountains and desolate moors have still greater atmosphere in the winter, when few venture out (and travelling is certainly inadvisable when the weather is really bad), unfortunately much of the tourist accommodation tends to close down then though.

There have been few great industrial experiments on this stretch of Scottish coast, probably the most inaccessible even today; although the excellent and constantly improved roads from Inverness to the Kyle of Lochalsh and to Ullapool (continuing almost to Kinlochbervie), have aided communications immensely. Instead the traditional employment has been in fishing, remarkably, some of Europe's biggest fishing ports are here. In recent years fish farming and tourism have also become main players.

This is a land of high mountains beloved of climbers, hill walkers, deer and sheep; stunning sandy beaches, huge estates and tiny crofting communities huddled on the coast, often the remnants of larger and more agriculturally successful villages that were 'cleared' in the eighteenth and nineteenth centuries to make way for the then more profitable sheep. The 'national' identity of the Highlanders was suppressed at that time too and only in the latter half of the twentieth century is public funding appearing alongside the political will to re-assert Gaelic traditions and language. Large tracts of land and many off-shore islands remain privately owned however, and the lives of their inhabitants is often very much still left to the economic circumstances or other whim of the land owner; be it an individual or a large pensions company.

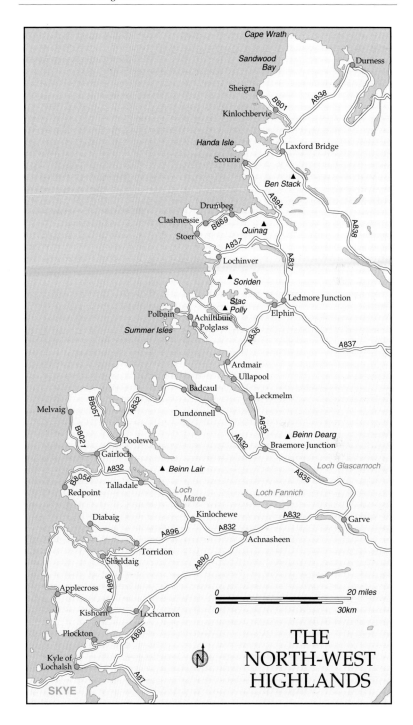

Cape Wrath

Sandwood
Bay

Durness

Sheigra

B801

A838

Kinlochbervie

Handa Isle

Laxford Bridge

Scourie

▲ Ben Stack

A894

Drumbeg

Clashnessie

B869

▲ Quinag

Stoer

A837

Lochinver

A837

▲ Soriden

Ledmore Junction

▲ Stac Polly

Elphin

Polbain

Achiltibuie

Polglass

A835

A837

Summer Isles

Ardmair

Ullapool

Badcaul

Leckmelm

Melvaig

B8057

A832

Dundonnell

A835

▲ Beinn Dearg

Braemore Junction

B8021

Poolewe

A832

Gairloch

Loch Glascarnoch

A832

▲ Beinn Lair

A835

B8056

Talladale

Loch
Maree

Loch Fannich

Redpoint

Diabaig

Kinlochewe

A832

Garve

A896

A832

Achnasheen

Torridon

A890

Shieldaig

Applecross

A896

0   20 miles

Kishorn

Lochcarron

0   30km

Plockton

A890

Kyle of
Lochalsh

**THE
NORTH-WEST
HIGHLANDS**

A87

SKYE

The **Kyle of Lochalsh** grew up around the short ferry crossing to Skye and has several good shops and hotels.

A minor road leads north up the coast to the peaceful fishing village of **Plockton**. The whole peninsular is largely covered by the National Trust's Balmacara Estate and Lochalsh Woodland Garden which is best accessed from the main A87 trunk road. There are several good view points, prepared walks and a display in the coach house. The informal woodland garden here contains giant beeches, oaks and a variety of pines, many planted about 200 years ago.

The minor road through Plockton joins on to the A890 as it climbs up to the border with Wester Ross, where it becomes single track to follow the side of magnificent **Loch Carron**. Shortly after beginning its ascent from the A87 there is a car park and excellent viewspot off the A890. Near to the junction with the Plockton road is **Achmore**, where the West Highland Dairy is situated, and local cheeses (ten sorts), yoghurts and ice-cream are produced in a sheltered glen. The dairy has its own milk ewes and also uses local goats' and cows' milk. Courses in cheese, yoghurt and ice-cream making are organised.

A single rail track and a single roadway are all that can fit between the Loch Carron's Shore and the towering cliffs; the latter are heavily restrained by wire netting. Local people have kept their children from school in the past, because of fears of falling rock. At the end of the cliffs is **Attadale**, the name a remnant of Viking times amongst a predominantly Gaelic influence in later centuries. Here privately owned Attadale House opens its doors one or two afternoons each year under the Gardens of Scotland Scheme. There are 5 acres (2 hectares) of rhododendrons and other shrubs as well as formal and water gardens.

Lochcarron village at the end of the loch has been inhabited for at least 1,300 years, with the Celts arriving around AD600, probably finding the Picts already in residence. St Malruba of the now predominant Scots arrived from Ireland in AD673 to found a monastery at Applecross and the Norsemen were next, 120 years later. In the nineteenth century the main industry was fishing and it is to some extent today, along with tourism. Rivalry is usually friendly between fish farmers, shell-fishers and trawlermen. There is also a local tartan weavers workshop with sales outlet. The ruins of Strome Castle can be seen at North Strome, former stronghold of the McKenzie barons of Kintail.

Kishorn is back on the west coast having turned left at Lochcarron around the north side of the loch, while the improved A890 continues easterly to Achnasheen, Garve, Dingwall and Inverness. The land from here northwards is one of desolate mountain scenery for much of Scotland; many peaks are over 3,000ft (915m), beloved of 'Munro Baggers' who attempt to climb all the high peaks in Scotland during the course of their lives, or, in the case of some record attempts, in the course of a few weeks. The only roads follow the sides of the largest lochs and the sea coasts, linking tiny fishing and crofting communities. The only substantial fertile land is miles away to the east.

The Applecross peninsular can be reached with a left turning a few miles beyond Kishorn. As a large warning sign states at the bottom of the road, this is not a route for learners, caravanners or indeed any faint hearted driver who does not like the sound of a succession of steep hairpin bends on single track roads with precipitous drops below and minimal crash barriers between! This is the Bealach na Ba pass (or Pass of the Cattle) around the magnificent peak of Beinn Bhan (2,936ft/895m). The problem is that the coastal route is a good 30 miles (48km) round.

Applecross, in a sheltered bay, is well worth visiting. It was one of the earliest Christian settlements in Scotland; the followers of St Maelrubha, who arrived here from Ireland in AD673, are buried in the churchyard. The village is actually made up of a number of tiny hamlets including Toscaig, Culduie, Camustiel and Camusterrach — but it is difficult for the visitor to be able to spot the difference. Applecross's name comes from 'Apor Crossan' which means the Estuary of the River Crossan, but has also become A'Chomraich in Gaelic which means 'The Sanctuary'. Much of the land in the area is owned by the Applecrosss Trust, who control 30,000 acres (12,000 hectares) of what was the Applecross Estate. There are several footpaths offering a variety of terrain. At low tide the wide sandy Applecross estuary is exposed and is a great place for beach combing. Maelrubha travelled widely during his 50 years in Scotland and founded many churches in the area.

The A896 meets the Applecross coast road in a leafy glen before **Shieldaig** on the shores of Loch Shieldaig, a part of Loch Torridon. This is a peaceful fishing and crofting village beneath Beinn Shieldeig. The small island just off shore is also called Shieldaig (which is a Norse word meaning Herring Bay) and is owned by the National Trust For Scotland. Its 32 acres (13 hectares) are almost entirely covered by Scots Pine which once clad much of Scotland in the huge and ancient Caledonian Forest.

The A896 now follows the southern shores of Upper Loch Torridon past Balgy Falls to **Torridon** itself, another small village on the edge

Upper Loch Torridon and the high peaks of Beinn Damh

of the huge 16,100 acre (6,440 hectare) Torridon Estate which has been administered by the National Trust since the late 1960s. It includes more excellent mountain scenery including the seven peaked mount Liathach (3,456ft/1,054m). Apart from climbers, naturalists and hill walkers, the area is of interest to geologists as Liathach is composed of 750 million-year-old sandstone, but its tops are partly white quartzite, a good 150 million years younger and containing some very early fossils.

For those who just want to get out of the car, there is a visitor centre which includes displays of Highland wildlife and a deer museum. A minor road runs along the north side of the loch beneath Beinn Alligin (3,230ft/985m) to **Diabaig**, a scattered crofting village with natural harbour. There are some good coastal walks here along with spectacular views out to the Applecross peninsular, Skye and the Western Isles. It is possible to walk northwards up the coast to Redpoint. The walk is about 10 miles (16km), a fifth of the distance round by road.

The A896 now heads north-easterly to **Kinlochewe**, at the intersection of three glens, two of which contain the A832. It is another small peaceful village, but historically was the home of a MacKenzie Clan who were rather put upon for a long period by an unsavoury band of Camerons who came over to thieve cattle and be generally violent.

Loch Maree

The north-westerly road follows the southern shores of **Loch Maree**. It is a fast two-carriageway stretch of road with good views of Slioch (3,211ft/979m) across the loch, although the strip of woodland between road and loch, containing birch, alder, oak and Scots pine, obscures much of the view so you must stop and park. A mile or so from Kinlochewe is the Aultroy Visitor Centre where exhibitions explain naturalist and conservation work being carried out in the local Beinn Eighe Nature Reserve and neighbouring estates. There are also several prepared footpaths.

St Maelrubha, established a cell on **Isle Maree**, one of the islands on the loch itself, now in the care of Scottish Natural Heritage. A later visitor was Queen Victoria in 1877 and a memorial commemorating the occasion is displayed at the Loch Maree Hotel. Presumably the Victoria Falls at Talladale were named after her. Talladale is also the starting point for a walk along the northern end of the Loch to Poolewe, as the road departs due west for Gairloch on the coast.

Before arriving in Gairloch however, the 15 mile (24km) excursion to **Redpoint** along the winding single-track B8056 is well worth the excursion. After 3 miles (5km) the road skirts the delightful harbour at Badachro, popular with yachtsmen, and then climbs to give magnificent views south to the Applecross peninsular and beyond. Redpoint itself has a wonderful sandy beach with huge dunes and is often completely empty.

Gairloch has excellent beaches (especially the one behind the golf course) and has been a tourist destination for many years, as some of the grand old holiday accommodation will testify. The village school is a key part of the community and pioneering work has been done here in maximising the potential of information technology in a rural community.

The Heritage Museum in the village has won awards for its exhibitions of life in prehistoric Gairloch through to the present day. The interior and exterior of a traditional croft house have been maintained. The museum also houses a gallery and outside there are two restored fishing boats and the reconstructed top section of the original local light house. The collection is housed in a former farm steading building around a cobbled courtyard. Gairloch is a haven for crafts shoppers, with 'Ewe and Me', The Nature Shop, Kirkhand Weave and a local bookshop. This is also an excellent centre for all sorts of water sports from yachting to sea angling.

The A832 now takes a short cut from Loch Gairloch to Loch Ewe, but there is a B road on each side of the peninsula. The first (B8021) passes the coastal communities of Big Sand and North Erradale before arriving at Melvaig. A private road from here goes on to the now automated Ru 're' Lighthouse (the original lamp is now in Gairloch Museum). This offers the opportunity of a good cliff top walk, especially for sea bird lovers.

The second B road on the other side of the peninsular is the B8057 to Inverasdale and Cove, where there are some caves once used as a place of worship, however access is possible but difficult.

Poolewe is another popular holiday spot, although many overlook it as they drive on to the remarkable Inverewe Gardens on the edge of the village. However Poolewe itself was a centre for early ironworking in Scotland when a gentleman called Sir George Hay started a business in 1610. The remains of the old red smiddy can still be seen on the banks of the River Ewe. For many years this was the main port for ferries to the Hebrides, and until about 150 years ago, livestock were forced to swim ashore from boats anchored in Loch Ewe. The local church of Scotland was a Thomas Telford project, completed in 1828. There are several pleasant footpaths to follow and a visit to the 'everything' store of Taylors should not be missed. Greengrocery, bread baked on the premises, toys, newspapers, health foods, postage stamps, camping equipment and whisky can all be purchased here.

Inverewe is one of Britain's greatest gardens and all the more remarkable given its location and history. It was begun by Osgood

Crofts can be found scattered all over the northern areas of coastal Scotland

Mackenzie in 1862 and continued by his daughter. Although favourably placed to receive the benefits of the Gulf Stream, the gardens had to be protected from sea spray and a great deal of fertile ground had to be brought in. There is a huge variety of rhododendron here, along with South African and South American plants, in fact plants from all corners of the world. Run by the National Trust For Scotland there are guided tours, a very good shop, plant sales and a restaurant.

Aultbea and its neighbour Mellon Charles (an Anglicisation of meallan meaning hilloch) were important in World War II as Russian convoys used to assemble here. The island in the loch is, not surprisingly, called the Isle of Ewe; it is unlikely that this pleasant double entendre is anything other than accidental.

There is an excellent sandy beach at Mellon Udrigle, on a minor road from Laide. **Laide** itself is thought to have been the site of a chapel for St Columba in the sixth century, but the only ruins there are from a later date. This is the edge of Gruinard Bay, famed for yet more excellent coastal scenery and as a good place to spot the rare black-throated diver in late summer.

The Ardessie Falls at **Dundonnel** almost spill across the road. This village has a frontier feel to it, being on the edge of some of the most beautiful, wild and treacherous mountains in Wester Ross. There is a volunteer mountain rescue force based here. Dundonnel House is privately owned but its excellent gardens are open to the public three or four times a year under Scotland's Garden Scheme.

The A832 now passes north of spectacular An Teallach (3,483ft/ 1,062m) and some regimented forest plantations. This stretch is known as Destitution Road as it was built to provide employment for those suffering in the potato famine in the nineteenth century. The A832 reaches its junction with the A835 from Inverness at Braemore Junction, around the top of the River Broom, which runs within the mile long **Corrieshalloch Gorge**. This is a spectacular geological feature accessible from either road, but there is more substantial parking and a shorter walk on the A835. The gorge is one of Britain's finest examples of a box canyon and is up to 200ft (61m) deep. The suspension bridge a little way down stream was built by John Fowler in the 1860s. He bought the local estate of Braemore in 1867 and was also the man who designed the rather more substantial Forth Railway Bridge. The gorge is owned by the National Trust For Scotland.

The A835 runs down the 12 miles (19km) towards Ullapool, cutting in to the steep hillside which banks on to Loch Broom. On the way down this hill is the Forestry Commission's Lael Forest Garden, which covers 17 acres (7 hectares), contains 150 different trees and dates from the 1870s. There are several steep walks trails of up to 2 miles (3km). Six miles (10km) further on, a few miles before Ullapool at **Leckmelm**, there is a shrubbery and arboretum which includes a $2\frac{1}{2}$ acre (1 hectare) arboretum laid out in the latter half of the nineteenth century. It was left unattended for 45 years until 1985 when restoration work began.

As you near the town there are excellent views of the white fronted houses along the harbour which juts out in to the loch. There may also be many large fishing boats, although the days of the great Soviet factory fishing fleets sheltering in the loch have probably now passed.

Ullapool did not grow up in the way many settlements do but was planned and built to a grid system by the British Fisheries Society in 1788. They wanted to develop the herring industry in the Minch and Loch Broom. Decline in the nineteenth century followed this boom, but today Ullapool is is the main departure point for ferries to Stornoway on Lewis, the Western Isles capital, and the fishing industry is again as healthy as it is anywhere. The shopping facilities in the small town tend to reflect the needs of sailors, and several small stores are stocked full of low price electrical consumer goods, whisky miniatures and digital watches bought in large numbers by sailors about to depart for their homelands, or sometimes bartered for goods more valuable over here.

A peaceful spot near Smoo Cave, Durness (Chapter 9)

Sango Bay at Durness is ideal for surfing enthusiasts (Chapter 9)

The beautiful scenery surrounding Ullapool (Chapter 10)

Ullapool is the main departure point for ferries to Stornoway on Lewis (Chapter 10)

Ullapool is regarded by many as a base for excursions to the numerous natural attractions in the near vicinity, or as a seemingly traditional white-washed fishing village to wander through, but there are two museums here to visit. Ullapool Museum on West Argyll Street includes exhibits illustrating life around Loch Broom for the last 200 years, while the small Loch Broom Museum concentrates on artefacts from ancient times to World War II, and has an excellent collection of geological specimens. This is a great centre for sea anglers and walkers, with one of the most popular and desolate trails beginning by following the Ullapool river upstream.

The A835 road north-west from Ullapool climbs steeply towards the Assynt Hills, and as you round the corner, there is a good view of the north coast and the ancient mountains, some of Scotland's oldest, ahead of you. These coastal mountains of Stac Polly, Cul Mor and Ben More Assynt are not especially high, although they rise steeply enough, but they have been formed in to individual identities, giving each more character than your 'average' mountain.

The road dives down again towards sea level at Ardmair with spectacular coastal scenery and many small islets in view, then turns north-easterly towards Kylesku, Kinlochbervie and Durness. The largest and nearest island is **Isle Martin** which contains the ruins of an extensive fish curing operation and the chapel of St Martin.

The most remarkable mountain coming in to view now is **Stac Polly** (Stac Pollaidh) at (2,009ft/612m) with its strange cylindrical and apparently inaccessible summit. It is rather depressing to learn it is actually a comparatively an easy peak to conquer for those aware of the path round the back. The road which turns west and runs beneath Stac Polly's towering slopes and Loch Lurgainn is well worth taking. It is single track and bendy in parts but has good stretches for the careful driver and very rewarding scenery for those who do not have to watch the road. This is the route to the coastal villages of Reiff, Polbain, Polglass and, most notably, Achiltibuie. It is also the nearest point to the **Summer Isles** which were the ones previously seen from Ardmair.

The isles are a paradise for nature lovers, with about thirty varieties of sea bird to be seen. It is possible to take a boat across to Tanera Morr, one of the largest isles, which had quite a thriving fishing community 200 years ago. It was also the home of famous naturalist Fraser Darling. **Achiltibuie** itself has a smoke house with a reputation for good smoked food and a hydroponicum with a reputation for good tropical food. A hydroponicum is essentially a giant greenhouse where plants feed on a liquid nutrient solution, their roots in liquid rather than earth. Harnessing the Gulf Stream, the hydroponicum has successfully grown many varieties including bananas. Figs, lemons, passion fruit vines, vegetables, flowers and herbs grow in a choice of three climates: Hampshire, Bordeaux or The Canaries. A gentleman called Robert Irvine has created a strange building, looking incongruous in the bleak Highland landscape; yet the philosophy and some might say eccentricity is nonetheless very much in keeping with human history in the Highlands and of course this could be a key to maintaining the ever decreasing rural population in the region. The craft shop at **Polbain** contains a wide variety of local hand crafts including knitwear.

It is possible to reach Lochinver by taking a north turn off this minor road to Achiltibuie just past Stac Polly. The road is badly in need of repair, with grass growing up the middle in many places. It is a road worth taking, once again, as it passes many small, remote and beautiful lochs as well as giving glimpses of rocky coves and islets in Enard Bay before descending in to Lochinver. This road crosses the border in to Sutherland at the River Kirkaig although there is of course no sign to announce either river or border. There is, however, a book shop, which must be Britain's remotest.

Inverkirkaig, further on this road, is a crofting township which gets its name from a Culdee religious settlement of 112 monks who lived there in the eleventh century. Although allowed to marry, they could not live with their wives who instead lived in Badnaban, 'the village of the nuns'.

For those who have stayed on the main A835 road the Knockan Visitor Centre at the heart of the **Inverpolly** Nature Reserve will be an option, located 12 miles (19km) north of Ullapool. The reserve covers 27,000 acres (10,800 hectares) of very wild land right over to the West Coast. For those who do not fancy venturing out in to much of it there is an exhibition and a short nature trail at the centre.

A little further along is **Elphin**, where there is a mini tourist industry, being a centre for hill walkers. It has a crafts centre and also an Animal Visitor Centre with pets corner. Species include soay lambs, Hebridean ewes, muscovy ducks and Scots Dumpy hens. Soon after Elphin comes Ledmore Junction where the A835 meets the A837 and drivers can choose whether to head north or return on a different route south-easterly along the famous salmon River Oykel.

The next National Nature Reserve now begins at **Inchnadamph**. This area is of particular interest to geologists having ancient rock formations. Cavers also enjoy the limestone caverns, one of which was occupied by 'Upper Palaeolithic Man' at the end of the last Ice Age.

The stark ruins of Ardvreck Castle, near Inchnadamph

Ardvreck Castle, further on, is a ruined shell of a fortress built in 1597 by the Laird MacLeod and it was here, 53 years later, that the Marquess of Montrose, James Graham, turned himself over to the MacLeods, having been defeated in his attempt to regain Scotland for England at Carbisdale, south of Lairg. He was then handed over to the Scottish Parliament in Edinburgh who hanged and dismembered him in the standard charitable fashion of the time. In 1691 the Seaforth Mackenzies laid siege to the castle in a bid to get the MacLeods to pay up some overdue rent and eventually evicted them. By 1736 it was the newly installed Mackenzie Laird who was badly in debt himself and the castle passed to the Earl of Sutherland by 1757.

The ruins of Calda House result from similar disputes. It was constructed by the Mackenzie laird in 1695, shortly after the family had moved in at Ardvreck; later the Earl of Seaforth and Earl of Sutherland had a violent disagreement over ownership connected with the Ardvreck Castle rent dispute. Calda House was burnt down, the Seaforth Mackenzies were accused, but nothing was proven. Opposite Ardvreck Castle is the Alt a'Chalda Beag crushing mill, a very large mill wheel that was probably originally ox driven. A small quarry near the wheel provided limestone which was crushed and then used as road material or to improve agricultural land.

At Skiag Bridge the A894 departs due north for Kylesku while the A837 continues around Loch Assynt to head west for Lochinver. **Lochinver** is another attractive fishing village grown up once again on the herring industry, and was a major port for this trade in the seventeenth and eighteenth centuries. Its sheltered waters were valued at least as far back as Viking times. Fishing remains relatively strong with the Regional Council investing nearly £7 million in recent years to upgrade its facilities and attract business, including some from France and Spain. Most of the fishing done today is for shell and white fish.

There are a couple of comparatively sizable and successful local craft industries in Lochinver. Most notable is Highland Stoneware, established in 1974 and now employing over twenty people with an additional outlet in Ullapool. Pottery visits are leisurely and you can see a wide range of manufacturing and decorating techniques as well as purchase from the substantial selection of products. The Sutherland Gem Cutters are also in the village, locally producing many jewellery items.

The B869 which follows the coast north of Lochinver, is a remarkable single track road. At its far end near Kylesku a sign warns off inexperienced drivers and those towing caravans; the reasons for this are soon apparent with hair-pin bends and sudden steep ascents. Some caravans have made it along the road however, huge static ones are permanent homes in some places and one can only assume these floated in on the tide or were dropped by helicopter.

There are many fine views from the road to the islands of Eddrachillis Bay on the north side and the mountains beyond, there are also some fine sandy bays such as those at Achmelvich, Clashnessie and Clachtoll, to be found if you are prepared to look.

A left turn, shortly after **Stoer** where there are the remains of an Iron Age broch, leads to the Point of Stoer where the spectacular Old

A panoramic view of Lochs Glencoul and Glendhu

Man of Stoer rock stack stands an hour's walk from the car park. The lighthouse at Rhu Stoer was built in 1870 but has been automated since 1976. It flashes every 15 seconds and can normally be seen for about 24 miles (39km). The road eventually rounds the north side of mighty Quinag (2,654ft/809m).

The main road from the south is now rejoined at Newton, this is the A894 which progresses with excellent views of Lochs Glencoul and Glendhu (and their fish farms), with surrounding forest, to the famous award winning curved bridge of **Kylesku**, which replaced a free ferry. It is worth stopping to take a boat trip, however, as that is the easiest way to get to see the local seal colonies and Eas-Coul-Aulin waterfall, which at over 656ft (200m) is the highest in Britain. There is a strenuous 2 hour overland route for the experienced walker.

The A894 now follows the coast northwards towards **Scourie**, departure point for the RSPB island reserve of **Handa**, famous for its puffins, as well as the more violent Arctic and great skuas. No dogs are allowed on the island.

Boats make a shorter crossing from the village of **Tarbet**, which is closer to Handa and reached by taking a minor road off to the west. On this same minor road loop is Fangamore, on the shores of Loch Laxford where again boat trips operate regularly in the summer to view the wildlife.

The famous award winning curved bridge of Kylesku

At **Laxford Bridge**, which spans the river of the same name, famed for its salmon fishing, the great loop of the A838 begins, having come up from near Lairg in the south-east and gone up the centre of northern Scotland from there to Tongue, then west to Durness and back down to Laxford Bridge. Although category A it is mainly single track, but with many long straight stretches.

It is hard to believe that **Kinlochbervie's** fish lorries have to use such roads. This is the third largest fishing port in Britain and with a population of over 400, the most populated village on Sutherland's western coast. It is reached via the B801 turning north-west at Loch Inchard. This was once part of church lands belonging to the Bishops of Caithness and has, like Lochinver, seen investment in its fishing industry in recent decades. An enormous new fish market was opened in 1988.

This B801 reaches its end at Sheigra where there is a splendid sandy beach at Oldshoremore. However **Sandwood Bay**, regarded by many to be the greatest beach in Britain (as well as one of the most isolated), is a 4 mile (6km) walk, cross country from near Sheigra. There is a small freshwater loch behind the beach and a ruined old bothy, supposedly residence of the ghost of a bearded sailor. The A838 continues northward through spectacular desolation to arrive at the Kyle of Durness some 15 miles (24km) further on. This is described in Chapter 9 The North Coast.

Highland cattle can be found throughout the north-west of Scotland

Further Information
— The North-West Highlands —

Places to Visit

Achiltibuie
Hydroponicum
☎ 085482 202
Open: March to October, daily, 75 minute tours at 10am,12noon, 2pm and 5pm.

Summer Isles Foods
☎ 085482 353
Open: all year, Monday to Friday, 9.30am-5pm (Saturdays from May to September).

Achmore
West Highland Dairy
Deilfearn
Achmore
Stromeferry
☎ 059987 203
Open: dawn till dusk every day, but those wishing to see specific aspects of production should phone first.

Elphin
Knockan Gallery and Craft shop
☎ 085486 261
Open: Easter to October, daily.

Scottish Farm Animal Visitor Centre
☎ 085486 2204
Open: May to September, daily, 10am-5pm.

Gairloch
Ewe & Me
Strath
☎ 04445 2181
Open: evenings in July and August.

Gairloch Bookshop
Strath
☎ 04445 2181

Heritage Museum
Open: Easter to September, Monday to Saturday, 10am-5pm.

Kirkhand Weave
Strath
☎ 0445 22375

The Nature shop
Strath Square
☎ 0445 2316

Laxford
Laxford Cruises
☎ 0971 2409
Open: 2 hour cruises depart Easter to
mid-September 10am, 12noon, 2pm,
4pm, Monday to Saturday.

Lochcarron
Lochcarron Weavers
North Strome
☎ 05202 212
Open: all Year, Monday to Friday,
9am-5pm. Also Saturdays
from April to October.

Lochinver
Highland Stonewear
☎ 05714 376
Open: all year, weekdays (Saturdays in
summer season).

Sutherland Gem Cutters
84 Torbreck
Lochinver
☎ 05714 312

Polbain
Coigach Craft Shop
☎ 085482 346 (Evenings)
Open: June to September, daily, 10am-
11pm and 2-5pm. Limited
opening low season.

Torridon
Countryside Centre
☎ 044587 221
Open: May to September, Monday to
Saturday 10am-6pm, Sundays 2-6pm.

Ullapool
Highland Stoneware
☎ 05714 376
Open: all year, weekdays (Saturdays in
Summer season).

Leckmelm Shrubbery and Arboretum
Open: daily, April to September, 10am-
5pm.

Loch Broom Museum
Open: Easter to October Monday to
Saturday, 9am-6pm

Ullapool Museum
West Argyll Street
Open: April to October, Monday to
Friday, 10am-5pm. Open 7-9pm from
June to September.

Tourist Information Offices

Dornoch
Sutherland Tourist Board
The Square
Sutherland
IV25 3SSD
☎ 0862 810400
Open: all year.

North Kessock
Ross and Cromarty Tourist Board
☎ 046373 505
Fax: 046373 701

Lochcarron
☎ 05202 357
Open: Easter to October.

Lochinver
☎ 05714 330
Open: Easter to October.

Ullapool
☎ 0854 612135
Open: Easter to October.

11 • South of Fort William

L eaving Fort William on the A82, be ready for a very winding
stretch of road before the landscape opens up. There are excellent views of Loch Linnie and across to the Ardgour hills and mountains. After 6 miles (10km) the road passes Corriechurachan Forest where waymarked trails have been laid out, and there are more walks to the waterfall at Inchree, a few miles further down the road.

Passing the village of Onich (filling stations and shops) there is the option of continuing southwards on the A82 over the bridge at North Ballachulish, or taking the worthwhile 18 mile (29km) detour east here on the B863 around Loch Leven (signposted Kinlochleven). This takes you over the Ballachulish Bridge, opened in 1974 and past the pointed mountain, Sgurr Na Ciche, known as the Pap of Glencoe, marking the entry to this stunning valley. At the far end of the bridge a large piece of granite on a plinth marks the spot where James of the Glen was hung on a gibbet after the murder of the Red Fox of Appin, part of the story made famous in Robert Louis Stevenson's book *Kidnapped*. The Red Fox in reality was Colin Campbell, local factor, who was shot when out collecting rent in 1752. James was apparently innocent of the murder and it remains a mystery today who the culprit was. **Ballachulish** was famous for many years as the quarrying point for slate which covered the roofs of many of the buildings in the country. A display in the local tourist office charts the development of the industry. It is also possible to walk around the old quarry, now landscaped.

Kinlochleven's industrial heritage was in the aluminium industry, the metal has been smelted there for over 80 years and has been exported throughout the world. The streams and rivers rushing in to Loch Leven from the surrounding mountains have been used for decades to generate hydro electricity to power what was originally the world's largest smelter. There was also the climate and access to the sea, essential for transportation in the early years of the twentieth

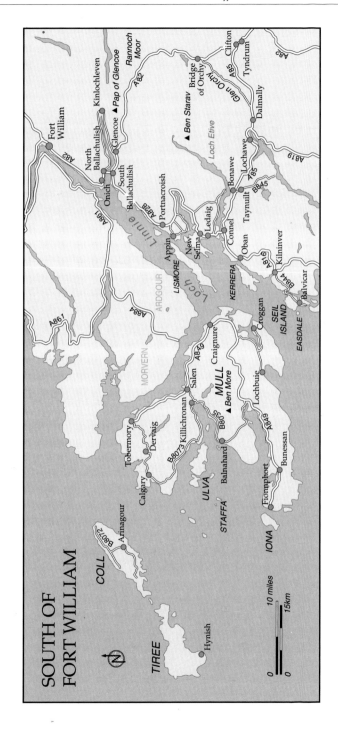

century. The local community grew up around the construction of the hydro power plant, the smelter and then the aluminium industry; an interpretative centre now charts this development. The West Highland Way touches the road network here. The small island of Eileen Munda in Loch Leven contains the graves of many and the ruins of a chapel where St Munda built a chapel in the seventh century. Back on the A82 a roundabout soon after the bridge gives the option of going east and south on the A82 (signposted Glasgow) or towards Oban on the south-westerly and coastal A828. The route through Glencoe, site of the famous massacre, is one of Scotland's most stunning drives. There is spectacular desolation here as the mountains tower above on either side of the road. Much of the valley (14,200acres/5,680 hectares) is owned by the National Trust who operate a visitor centre, which appears on the left soon after entering the valley. The exhibition here includes a history of mountaineering in the area. This is an excellent area for climbers, and popular too, hence the existence of a local volunteer mountain rescue team.

There is a particularly good 3 mile (5km) walk through Forestry Commission lands from **Glencoe** village and a small museum of local, Jacobite and clan interest open in the summer months. Among the natural inhabitants of the valley are golden eagle, golden plover, wildcats, red deer and ptarmigan. Fishing permits for Loch Achtriochtan are available at the centre.

The presence of the MacDonalds is remembered at Signal Rock, an old look out point (there is also a memorial in Glencoe village). Another geological feature with historical connections is Ossian's cave, located high on the face of Aonach Dubh. Ossian was a famous local bard. The southern section of the valley is guarded by Buachaille Etive Mor or 'The Great Shepherd Of Etive' (3,345ft/1,020m) and to the north-east the 'Devils Staircase' leads walkers on the West Highland Way up behind Glencoe to Kilochleven.

Soon afterwards on the road south is the White Corries Chairlift of Glencoe ski area, site of the original Scottish ski lifts (although since replaced by a newer chair) and one of the more popular destinations for dedicated Scottish skiers. The road continues south across Rannoch Mor through more desolate scenery, passing Loch Tulla on the right before reaching Bridge of Orchy at the end of Glen Orchy. A minor road (B8074) follows the glen south-westerly to meet with the A85 running due west to Oban. This is a worthwhile shortcut on our route as the river has some spectacular stretches, especially so with the spring melt waters. Otherwise continue on towards Tyndrum (tourist services), but turn west on to the A85

The mountains of Glencoe as seen over Loch Leven

(signposted Oban) shortly before. **Tyndrum** is located beneath several major peaks. One of them is Ben Challum (3,354ft/1,022m), to the west, marking the start of tributaries that ultimately flow in to the mighty River Tay on the east coast.

The A85 runs about 30 miles (48km) due east to Oban following the River Lochy, the Awe and then the south side of Loch Etive. These are largely wooded and abandoned glens between high hills. Above **Dalmally**, 10 miles (16km) from Tyndrum, stands a monument to Duncan Ben MacIntyre, a celebrated Gaelic poet. At the northeastern corner of Loch Awe, one of Scotland's longest, deepest and most picturesque lochs, the A819 turns off south to Inverary . The original **Inverary** town and castle were demolished in 1744 and rebuilt ½ mile (1km) away. The numerous visitor attractions include a restored West Highland township, early nineteenth-century jail, spectacular castle, wildlife park and an Episcopal church containing the second heaviest ring of ten bells in the world.

This road junction was guarded by Kilchurn Castle, a midfifteenth century tower house now in a ruinous state. This was built by Sir Colin Campbell and was last garrisoned during the 1745 Rising, becoming derelict later that century. The nearby village of **Lochawe** contains St Conan's Kirk (1881) decorated by symbols only recognisable to Masonic initiates.

To the north now the mighty Ben Cruachan rises to 3,689ft (1,125m). Anyone wishing to climb it will be assured of wonderful views across most of western Scotland. This is known as the 'Hollow Mountain' as it houses a hydro electric power station near **Taynuilt**, operated by the Scottish Power electricity generating board and with exhibition and visitor attractions. The road is now cutting through the Pass of Brander, to the south side of which a battle was fought between the MacDougalls and Robert the Bruce by the Awe Dam.

Loch Etive which lies with its north-east end beneath Ben Starav (3,541ft/1,080m), home of golden eagles, up in Lochaber is another steeped in local legend. Where the A85 first reaches it, the remains of the Bonawe Iron Furnace can be seen. This was founded in 1753 by a partnership of Cumbrian ironmasters and is the most complete surviving charcoal-fuelled iron works in Britain. The local forests provided the charcoal and Loch Etive the means for transporting the iron by boat. As you get closer to the sea look out for forest walk options at Fearnoch and seals on the rocky islands in Loch Etive Bay. This route now meets with the A828 that has followed the coast from Ballachulish so that road should be described before the final 4 miles (6km) to Oban are detailed.

The A828 from the Ballachulish roundabout goes back to the bridge but passes underneath it this time along the shores of Loch Leven. The road is very pleasant, following the lochside with woodland on the south and east side. After about 2 miles (3km) it reaches the village of **Kentallen**. The hotel and restaurant here are built on the site of the old railway line that used to run from the Ballachulish slate quarries to Oban. The murder site of the Red Fox is near here, on a minor road to the coast before the village.

A mile and a half (1km) past the village of **Duror** is Keil Kirk where James of the Glen is buried. Soon afterwards you cross the border from Lochaber region and enter Argyll and Bute. The road now bends easterly to follow the edge of Loch Creran and passes through Strath Appin. Shortly before the loch begins, and after a stretch of rhododendron and woodland lined road, the A28 rounds a bend and descends past **Portnacroish** and the site of the battle of Stalc in 1468. Here you have a great view of **Castle Staker**, possibly the second most photographed castle for postcards and brochures after Eilean Donan, south of Kyle of Lochalsh. The castle stands on a tiny islet of its own and is thought to have been built at the order of James V around 1540 for the Stewarts of Appin. In the mid-seventeenth century it passed in to Campbell hands, then back to the Stewarts in 1686, but was lost again 4 years later after the usurpation of William

Rugged mountain scenery around Glencoe

of Orange. It became derelict early in the nineteenth century but has since been restored to become a private residence.

It is possible to get a ferry to **Lismore** from Port Appin and the west Highland's largest garden nurseries are also to be found here in the pleasant surroundings of Kinlochlaich House. The road then winds sometimes tortuously around Loch Crenan, the collapsing bridge that can be seen across a narrow stretch held the old railway line from Oban.

The Sea Life Centre is a major stopping off point for many visitors in the area. Opened in 1979 it was the first of what is now a successful chain of centres around the United Kingdom coast line and now in Europe. It differs from the old image of an aquarium having huge tanks recreating natural environments, which can be viewed from different angles and enabling big fish and other sea creatures to be seen and in some cases touched. A remarkable experience for anyone who has not yet had the pleasure of gently patting a stingray on the head. The Sea Life Centre's philosophy is very much one of education through improving understanding and behind the displays a great deal of conservation work is carried out and a sort of RSPCA shelter for fish and marine mammals is in operation. The Oban centre concentrates particularly on seals and rescues numerous abandoned pups each year, brought there from all over Scotland. Visitors are also able to see this work going on and talks are given on all aspects of the centre's work.

A south-westerly (right) turning on to the B845 leads through Glen Salach and the Barcaldine Forest to Loch Etive. A road then runs along the north shore of Etive to meet the A828 again at a stretch of Loch Etive near its entry to the sea where the loch is only 656ft (200m) wide and it is bridged. This narrow stretch contains the United Kingdom's only sea water waterfall, the Falls of Lora, which reverse their direction with the tide.

On the Loch Etive road at **Ardchattan** is Ardchattan House Gardens and Priory. The house is the second oldest inhabited house in Scotland and the gardens which slope down to the loch are open to the public. The thirteenth-century chapel ruins adjoin the garden. It was here that Robert the Bruce convened the last ever Gaelic speaking parliament in 1308.

Three miles (5km) north of Oban stand the substantial remains of **Dunstaffnage Castle,** built in the thirteenth century on a rock with great curtain walls and round towers. Flora MacDonald was imprisoned here briefly after she helped Bonnie Prince Charlie in his escape from defeat at Culloden. It ceased to be occupied around 1900 having

The humpback Bridge over the Atlantic separates Seil Island from the mainland

been taken from the McDougalls and given to the Campbells by Robert the Bruce, given back to the McDougalls, then finally to the Stewart Dukes of Argyll (then Campbell Earls). Before the present castle was built a stronghold existed in Viking times when this was Dalriada, the ancient capital of the original Kingdom of the Scots. It was here that the Stone of Destiny was kept until AD843 after the first King of Scotland was crowned.

Oban has been a touring centre for the West Highlands since tourism began, and is also the main ferry terminal for Caledonian MacBrayne services to many of the Inner Hebrides. Steamer services first came to the town in the nineteenth century and they have become the lifeline for island communities as well as an easy way for tourists to take their cars to the isles. Indeed it was one David MacBrayne who introduced the service, eventually combining with the Caledonian Steam Packet Company to form CalMac.

The name 'Ob' comes from the Viking word for shelter and Oban means 'Sheltered Bay', protected mainly by the Isle of Kerrara, separated from the mainland by a very narrow strait of the same name and sheltering Oban from the seas beyond.

Oban's main seafront street is the Esplanade where shops of all sorts from chain stores to craft outlets can be found, as well as the Victorian frontages of long established hotels, with the harbour just across the street. The town is dominated by McCaig's Tower and was

Suilven, one of the ancient mountains of Scotland (Chapter 10)

The wild countryside surrounding Achiltibuie (Chapter 10)

From the top of Inverary's church tower the views over Loch Fyne are breathtaking (Chapter 11)

Scenic beauty in Glen Etive, north-east of Oban (Chapter 11)

Boat trips operate between Easdale village and Easdale Island

actually built in 1897 by a local banker, John Stuart McCaig who was humanitarian enough to want to create employment in the town while at the same time creating a family monument. Unfortunately his funds for the project ran out before it was completed and the interior has now been landscaped.

Oban's other visitor attractions are mostly recent. The Oban Experience is an audio-visual exhibition of the town's past. There is also a gallery of nineteenth- and twentieth-century Scottish painters, a popular glassworks, a nearby rare-breeds farm, the inevitable local distillery visitor centre and an exhibition of miniaturisation of rooms, furniture and so on.

A small road following the coast north of the town leads past **Dunolie Castle**, a former stronghold of the MacDougalls of Lorn. The ruined tower house dates from the thirteenth century but there has been a fortified building here since at least AD600. Earlier buildings are recorded as having been burnt by Irish raiders in AD698. King Somerled, a MacDougall chief, lived there in 1130. The lands were forfeited after the McDougalls opposed Robert the Bruce but later restored. The same thing happened when Cromwell's troops occupied it and moved on and then again after the 1615 Uprising. The McDougalls finally left the castle in 1746, moving to nearby Dunollie House which remains the clan chief's residence to this day (and is private). The coast road goes on to Ganavan Sands, Oban's best beach.

Gylen Castle, on the **Isle of Kerrera**, is a 3 mile (5km) walk from the ferry landing. This was another MacDougall stronghold, in this case dating from the sixteenth century. It was destroyed by Cromwellian troops in 1647.

The road south from Oban to Lochgilphead (and ultimately Tarbert and the Kintyre peninsular) is the A816. A short day trip from Oban along this road is **Seil Island** and **Easdale Island**. To reach these you must turn off on to the B844 (right) after about 6 miles (10km), by a village called **Kilninver**, where there is a salmon fishing visitor centre and restaurant. Seil is officially an island, but is only separated from the mainland by a trickle of a stream in summer months and the humpback bridge crossing this by Clachan is known as the Bridge over the Atlantic.

This narrow road continues through rural scenery then over a hill with magnificent west coast views from its summit, and eventually down to the little village of **Easdale**. This is an idyllic archetypal west coast fishing village beloved of TV drama series producers and is linked by a free boat trip (5 minutes) to Easdale Island. The folk museum in the village tells the tale of the quarrying industry that used to operate in the area. This has now been replaced by craft shops.

MULL

It is a very short and easy crossing from Oban to Mull on Caledonian MacBrayne ferries. On arrival at **Craignure** many people walk up the road to Craignure Station to catch one of the steam or diesel trains that runs on the 10¼ gauge track of the grandly titled Mull and West Highland Narrow Gauge Railway to **Torosay Castle**. The trains are timed to coincide with ferries and the trip is well worth taking. The railway was conceived in the mid-1970s and opened in 1983. Since then it has gone from strength to strength. On clear days there are views of Ben Nevis, the Glencoe Hills and the island of Lismore. The route also passes through a wildlife area where primroses and rhododendrons can be seen in full glory during spring and early summer. The miniature trains are generally based on 'full-size' engines, the latest modelled on the *Puffing Billy* railway steam engines from Australia.

The train ride offers excellent views of reconstructed **Duart Castle**, the prominently positioned thirteenth-century home of the Clan MacLean chiefs. The keep dates from this period but the MacLean's,

A train pulls out of Torosay station on the Mull and West Highland Narrow Gauge Railway

who had had formidable seaborne power, had supported the Jacobite cause in the eighteenth century and thus lost their lands and the castle went to ruin after 1750. Restoration carried out by Sir Fitzroy MacLean began in 1912 and today tours are arranged. There is also a tea room for visitors and exhibitions of clan and family memorabilia.

Torosay Castle was designed by David Bryce in 1858 and remains a family home today. The interior is in Victorian/Edwardian style and the frontage is of neo-Gothic design. Exhibitions contained therein are not just local interest but also detail explorations of Antarctica, Loch Ness monster hunts and wartime escapes. The Isle of Mull Weavers are also located here and loomside demonstrations are given. The 12 acre (5 hectare) castle gardens has a wide selection of rare and interesting plants set in various concept gardens, including Japanese, Eucalyptus walk, Italian statue walk and water gardens.

The A849 runs south through woodland and then becomes single track and crosses the 40 mile (64km) length of Mull. The desolate mountain scenery of Glenmore is quite surprising after the shelter of the island's east coast and the greenery of the mainland around Oban. It is more reminiscent of land from Glencoe to the north. In fact the landscape is in keeping with the Morvern, Ardnamurchan and Moidart peninsulas west of Fort William and only separated from Mull's north-east coast by a narrow strait, but hundreds of miles distant by mainland roads. Minor roads lead from the A849 to the south coast from Strathcoil (dramatic route around Loch Spelve) and shortly before **Pennycross** down to **Carsaig**, where a path leads to the Carsaig Arches, carved by the sea in to the basalt rock.

Further along the main road at **Bunessan** the Isle of Mull Wine Company is in operation, producing dry, medium and sweet wines. The medium is mixed with vodka to create the Mull Riveter. Tours and tastings are arranged and nearby a second attraction is an Angora Rabbit Farm. These are quiet friendly animals used to being handled and there are other animals on the farm as well as a nature trail. The A849 ultimately reaches **Fionnphort** where there is a shop and tea room and from where it is a short hop over to Iona.

The main road around the northern two thirds of Mull is the B8035 and then the B8073. Stretches of this route which cut in to the sheer cliffs on the edge of Ben More (3,169ft/966m) are not for the nervous driver, but the rewards in coastal scenery and views to Staffa, Tiree and Coll as well as smaller islands are splendid.

The roads join at the head of Loch Na Keal, at the entrance of which lies the 5,000 acre (2,000 hectare) **Isle of Ulva**, opened to the public by the Howard family who own it. This is 2 minutes away by ferry and there is a visitor centre here with displays on the island's past and present. This was historically the seat of the Clan MacQuarrie and there is a small display of Clan memorabilia. Five waymarked trails have been laid out. Other places of interest are the ruins of the home owned by explorer David Livingstone's parents and a Thomas Telford designed church.

Lachlan MacQuarrie, a Governor of New South Wales and known as the 'Father of Australia' was born at **Ulva Ferry** in 1761. He died in 1824 and his mausoleum on the Gruline Estate (which he owned) here is now the property of the National Trust of Australia.

In the north-west corner of the island the area around **Burg**, which includes many high cliffs and a 50 million year-old 'fossil tree' is owned by the National Trust. There is no vehicle access beyond **Tiroran** and a 5 mile (8km) walk is involved. One of the best beaches on the west coast is at **Calgary** (the Canadian city of the same name was settled by emigrants from this part of Mull).

Round the coast to the north and at **Dervaig** the Mull Little Theatre, the United Kingdom's smallest professional company, play throughout the summer months. There is also a Heritage Centre in the village offering an 'audio-visual' tour of Mull.

Tobermory, Mull's only real town is a familiar picture postcard sight with colourful houses around the large sheltered harbour, some dating from the eighteenth century. Sunk somewhere in the harbour mud is the wreck of a Spanish galleon from 1588. Apparently it held the treasure chest of the *Armada*, but this has not been recovered. Some of the crew were held in Duart Castle for a time. There are a number of craft and community shops in the town to meander through, and the Tobermory Chocolate Factory should not be missed, the fresh truffles are out of this world.

The picture postcard town of Tobermory, Isle of Mull

There is also a distillery at the south end of the town where guided tours are arranged. It was founded in 1798 and the present buildings date to that first period of operation up to 1826. Following that there were long periods of shut down and it was last revived in the 1970s. However it has not distilled whisky, at the time of writing, since 1981.

IONA

Iona, 'the jewel in the ocean', is the cradle of Scottish Christianity where St Columba landed in AD563 to bring Celtic learning, art and Christian teaching to Scotland. He died here in AD597. The peaceful and beautiful island became a place of pilgrimage but was pillaged by Vikings for two centuries until the 1100s, although the kings of Scotland (from Fergus MacErc to Macbeth) were also buried here during that period. A Benedictine Order was established in the early thirteenth century under the protection of the Lord of The Isles, the self ruling Donald Clan chief. The last abbot died in 1499.

The abbey has been restored in the twentieth century and is run by the ecumenical Iona community. The cathedral is open to visitors, indeed it is possible to stay for a week and join in community life. There is a hotel, restaurant, teashop, abbey gift shop and Heritage Centre on the island. The centre includes displays on past life in Iona and is housed in the old Church of Scotland manse built by the omnipresent Thomas Telford in 1828. There are numerous other religious features to the island, some from ancient history, some more recent and a good deal from the present day. John Smith, leader of the Labour Party, was buried here in May 1994.

STAFFA

Uninhabited Staffa lies 7 miles (11km) west of Mull and is about 1 mile (2km) long, by ¼ mile (½km) wide. It is famous for its basalt rock formations, the best of which is to be found in cathedral like **Fingal's Cave**. This in turn was made more famous by Mendelsohn's *Hebrides* overture. The island was given to the National Trust in 1986 by a Mr John Elliot of New York as a birthday present to his wife. She remains 'steward for life' of the island. Access to the island depends on weather conditions. Visitors follow in the footsteps of Queen Victoria, Sir Walter Scott, Keats, Tennyson, Turner and Wordsworth.

LISMORE

Tradition has it that St Columba had preferred Lismore to Iona as first choice for his religious settlement, but St Moluag beat him to it. Moluag named the island Lios Mor meaning in Gaelic 'Enclosure' or 'Sanctuary' according to some sources and 'Great Garden' according to others. The cathedral church named after him stands on the site of his missionary teaching centre. The Bishopric of Argyll was transferred here in 1236. Lismore is a low lying and fertile island, the highest point is Barr Mor at 416ft (127m). However it is still a good vantage point from which to view the mountains on the mainland and Mull. It takes 50 minutes to reach here from Oban by CalMac ferry. The boat arrives at **Achnacroish** which is a short walk from the island's impressive Iron Age broch at Tirefuir.

COLL

Coll with Tiree are the two outer most Inner Hebrides and are separated from each other by a 2 mile (3km) strait so notorious for currents and roughness that the regular Caledonian MacBrayne ferries take a longer trip to **Arinagour** on Coll from Scarinish on Tiree, a 20 mile (32km)/1 hour trip.

The impressive entrance of Fingal's Cave, Isle of Staffa

Most of the population of Coll live close to the ferry port, but both islands are fertile and low lying and are famous for their deep bays with fabulous beaches. Both islands also contain a wealth of ancient monuments, especially prehistoric fortresses. Breacachadh Castle at the southern end of the island is a recently restored fifteenth-century tower house standing at the head of Loch Breacacha. This is a private house but visits are occasionally allowed.

TIREE

Tiree's Gaelic nickname means, 'land beneath the wave tops', a reference to its flatness, the highest point being 400ft (122m) above sea level. The name 'Tiree' itself however means 'Land of Corn'. The island has been famous for its corn production. This agricultural success may be partly put down to the fact that Tiree has no rabbits. Another claim to fame is that the island gets the most sunshine of anywhere in the country, but also some of the strongest winds, due to its flatness and lack of tree cover.

The Hebridean Trust run a museum at the Old Signal Tower at **Hynish**. This tells the story of the construction of the Skerryvore Lighthouse which can be seen 11 miles (18km) south-west of Tiree through a telescope.

Further Information
— South of Fort William —

Places to Visit

Appin
Kinlochlaich House Garden Centre
☎ 063173 342
Open: all year, Monday to Saturday,
9.30am-5.30pm, April to
October Sunday from 10.30am.

Ardchattan
Ardchattan Garden
Ardchaattan Priory
By Connel
Open: daily, Easter to October.

Bunessan
Angora Rabbit Farm
Bremenvoir
Ardtun
Bunessan
☎ 06817 429

Isle of Mull Wine Company
☎ 06817 403
Tours: Monday to Saturday, 10.30am
and 11.30am. Afternoon tours Monday
to Friday at 3.30pm and 4.30pm

Coll
Breacachadh Castle
Isle of Coll
☎ 08793 444 or 353
Private house, occasional visits
arranged, telephone to enquire.

Craignure
Duart Castle
☎ 06802 309
Open: May to September, daily,
10.30am-6pm.

*Mull & West Highland Narrow Gauge
   Railway Company Limited*
☎ 06802 494 0r 421
Open: April to October, generally runs
30 minutes after ferry arrival.
Tickets available from station or from
Caledonian MacBrayne office at Oban
Pier.
Trains may run at other times and by
arrangement with groups.

*Torosay Castle & Gardens and Isle of Mull
   Weavers*
☎ 06802 421

Castle
Open: April to mid-October, daily,
10.30am-5.30pm
Gardens open: summer 9am-7pm;
winter, daylight hours.

Dervaig
Old Byre Heritage Centre
☎ 06884 229
Open: Easter to October, daily,
10.30am-6.30pm

Glencoe
Glencoe Chairlift
☎ 08556 226

National Trust Visitor Centre
☎ 08552 307
Open: April to October, daily, core
hours 10am, 5.30pm.
Open longer in summer.

Iona
Heritage and Visitor Centre
Open: Monday 9.30am-4.30pm,
Tuesday to Saturday 9.30am-4.30pm.
Closed Sunday.

Kilninver
Highland Salmon Centre
☎ 08526 263

Kinlochleven
The Aluminium Story
Kinlochleven Visitor Centre
Linnhe Road
Argyll
PA40 4RU
☎ 08554 663
Open: April to October, Monday to

Friday, 10am-5pm, weekends, 12noon-
4.30pm. October to April Tuesday and
Thursday, 10am-noon and 1pm-5pm
Wednesday, Friday and Saturday
10am-noon and 1pm-3pm.

Oban
Argyll Pottery
Dalrannoch
Barcaldine
☎ 0631 72503

Oban Distillery Visitor Centre
Stafford Street
☎ 0631 64262
Open: all year, Monday to Friday,
9.30am-4.15pm. Open
Saturdays Easter to October.

The Oban Experience
Heritage Wharf
Railway Pier
Open: Monday to Saturday from 9am.
Open Sunday from June to September.

Oban Glassworks (Caithness Glass)
Lochavullin Industrial Estate
☎ 0631 63386
Open: all year, Monday to Friday, 9am-
5pm and Saturday 9am-1pm (May to
September).

Oban Rare Breeds Farm Park
New Barran
☎ 03177 608 or 604

Sea Life Centre
Barcaldine
Argyll
PA37 1SE
☎ 063 172 386
Open: February to December, daily,
9am-6pm (7pm in summer holidays).
Open weekends only at other times.

World in Miniature
North Pier
Oban
☎ 0631 66300
Open: daily 10am-5.30pm, except
Sunday, opens 2pm.

Taynuilt
Cruachan Power Station
☎ 08662 673

Tiree
The Old Signal Tower Museum
The Hebridean Trust
13 Rawlinson Road
Oxford
☎ 0865 514494
Open: all year.

Tobermory
Tobermory Distillers
☎ 0688 2119
Open: Monday to Friday, June to
September, 10am-4pm (other times by
appointment).

Ulva
The Boathouse Visitor Centre
☎ 06885 264
Open: daylight hours.

Travel
West Highland Way
Countryside Ranger Service
Highland Regional Council
Glen Nevis
By Fort William
☎ 0397 705922

Caledonian MacBrayne
Head Office
Ferry Terminal
Gourock
PA19 1 QP
☎ 0475 33755 Fax: 0475 37607
Oban Office: ☎ 0631 62285
Fax: 0631 66588
Tobermory Office: ☎ 0688 2017

Explore Mull
Shepherds Cottage
Dervaig
Isle of Mull
☎ 06884 209
Tours and guided walks

**Isle of Mull Landrover Wildlife
   Expeditions**
Ulva House Hotel
Tobermory
Isle of Mull
☎ 0688 2044

**Mull & West Highland Narrow
   Gauge Railway**
Staffa Trips
Seaview Cottage
Isle of Iona
☎ 068884 242

Turus Maraa
Penmore Mill
Dervaig
Isle of Mull
☎ 06884 242
Tours to Staffa and Treshnish Isles.

Tourist Information Offices
Oban
West Highland & Islands of Argyll
Tourist Board Information Centre
Albany Street
Argyll
PA34 4AR
☎ 0631 63122
Fax: 0631 64273

Ballachulish
☎ -8552 296
Summer only.

Craignure
☎ 06802 377
Fax: 06802 497
Open: April to October.

Fort William
Cameron Centre
☎ 0397 703781

Tobermory
☎ 0688 2182
Fax: 0688 2145

Tyndrum
☎ 083384 246
Summer only.

12 • The Western Isles

Remote, desolate, beautiful; the Western Isles or Outer Hebrides have to be one of the most interesting communities in the United Kingdom. The curiosity stems from a richness of unusual character-istics which for some are contradictory, for others perfectly logical. The variety of landscapes combined with large areas of inland water have given the islands international importance for their natural heritage. There are four national nature reserves here and many other designated sites. Ornithologists and botanists alike will find much to interest them, as will all lovers of huge clean empty sandy beaches.

The islands themselves number in their hundreds and stretch for 130 miles (209km) from the Butt of Lewis in the north, to Barra Head in the south. They are located between 30 and 40 miles (48 and 64km) off Scotland's north-west coast and differ from one another in many geographical, historical and cultural respects. Probably because of these differences, despite their proximity, there is little neighbourli-ness or general inclination for inhabitants of one island to travel to the next. There are, of course, various ways of 'island hopping' but each main island is also linked separately to the mainland by Caledonian MacBrayne's ferries, and communications with the mainland are better than between the islands themselves.

There is only one community big enough to warrant the name 'town' in all the isles and this is Stornoway on Lewis, where about a third of the islands' population live, the rest being scattered in small communities around the whole area. The major islands are Lewis, Harris, the Uists, made up of North Uist, Benbecula and South Uist, linked by causeways, and Barra. Seven other islands are inhabited — Bernera, Scalpay, Berneray, Baleshare, Grimsay, Eriksay and Vatersay. Human habitation dates back at least 6,000 years, originally mega-lithic people who were superseded by the Celts from Ireland. The islands have only been part of Scotland for the last 700 or so years. They were handed over in 1280 when the Norsemen, who invaded,

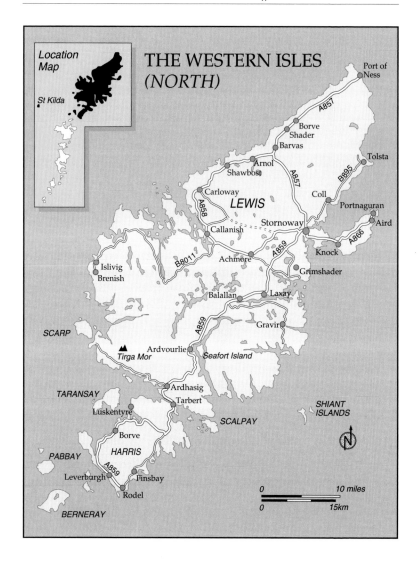

and eventually settled here, from the ninth century onwards, signed the Treaty of Perth after losing the Battle of Largs in 1266. The Norse influence remains clear in many of the place names. The title of Lord of The Isles was created by the Norse shortly before they lost control of the Hebrides and this title was maintained after the Scots established clan rule.

One big difference between the individual islands is in religious belief. The majority of the population on Lewis and Harris and North

Uist are staunchly Protestant (Free Church), while the people in Benbecula, South Uist and Barra are almost exclusively Catholic. The Hebrideans' zealous adherence to the Sabbath is legendary and testimony to their continued isolation from the declining power of the church in most of the United Kingdom. Even before Christianity, the Western Islanders were fervently religious, understandable in the midst of such beauty, and being so much at the mercy of super-human forces. There are many prehistoric remains here, including the Callanish stones, ranked second to Stonehenge (Salisbury Plain, Wiltshire, England) but considered by many people to be even more impressive.

Where the two current faiths come together is in their desire to maintain their heritage, affecting the visitor particularly in the predominance of the Gaelic language. In recent years there have been strong attempts to half, even reverse, the decline of Gaelic, thanks partly to the modern world's belated attempt to cling to its local heritage in the wake of globalisation. This attitude contrasts with that of previous centuries when the language, like the kilt, was banned by Scotland's English rulers.

Most people do speak English to bilingual standard, but one result of the new mood is that road signs have been changed from English, or even anglicised Gaelic, to the 'definitive' version of the language. Except around the major population centres (such as Stornoway) the signs are in **Gaelic only**. This can cause problems for visitors with maps in English, or even in an English version of Gaelic with the Gaelic word written out in English phonetics. The result is that it looks like Gaelic, sounds to the untrained ear like Gaelic, but it is not what it says on the road sign. Even those who are aware of the different languages may be confused by whether they have the English or Gaelic name in front of them. For example Borve and Borgh or Liceasto and Lickisto — some publications list in one order, some another, apparently taking for granted that the uninitiated will guess which is which.

We have endeavoured to give place names in their correct Gaelic spelling in brackets after the English version when each place is first mentioned, and also in the index at the end of this book. We apologise to any Gaelic speakers offended by the order, which merely reflects the likelihood that the majority of readers of this book will speak English as their first tongue, and also for any inadvertent errors. The tourist board produces a list of all place names and road signs as well as leaflets with information on the basics of Gaelic pronunciation and language. The list of place names on Lewis and Harris are divided into districts which may be unfamiliar to the visitor. Fortunately, there being so few roads on the islands, it is usually relatively straight forward to guess where you are especially as the pronunciation of place names in either language normally works out with pretty much the same word.

Religious feeling is strong on the Western Isles, particularly in Lewis and Harris. The major practical upshot of the strong faith of the islanders is that virtually all shops, filling stations, pubs and many accommodations are closed on the Sabbath. There are also no flights or ferries into Harris or Lewis on Sundays, although some links are open to the outside world from the Uists and Barra.

They have an old saying here: 'When God made time, he made plenty of it' and that sums up the islands and their people best. There really is no rush here, and even in the more remote areas of the Highlands the Western Islanders are famed for their relaxed hospitality and their liking for conversation. The only way that business is done here is with patience and good humour on both sides. Add to this the space, the beauty and the peace, and there can be few places in Britain, if not the world, where it is easier to relax.

LEWIS (Eilean Leodhais)

Lewis is the largest of the Western Isles and where most of the population live. It is mainly flat, (compared to most of the islands at least) apart from where it nears Harris, and is almost entirely covered in peatland, averaging about 6ft (2m) in depth. The only town, **Stornoway** (Steornabhagh), is on the east coast of the island. The biggest building in all of the Western Isles is nearby. This is **Lews Castle**, built by James Matheson, remembered as probably the most popular owner of Lewis, who purchased the island in 1844. His arrival marked the welcome ending of a period of particularly brutal oppression, exploitation and clearance through several generations of rule by a branch of the Mackenzie family. They had gained possession in 1610 from the MacLeods; the latter remains the commonest Western Isle surname to this day. The Lewis MacLeods had a castle stronghold located where the harbour now stands.

Matheson was brought up in Lairg where he had witnessed the clearances carried out by order of the Countess of Sutherland when he was a 12-year-old in 1808. He was later involved in the Far East china trade, where he made a fortune, which he then proceeded to spend, during the remaining 34 years of his life, on Lewis. His works included the construction of more than 200 miles (322km) of road, with required bridges, and the establishment of a successful steam ship link. He also founded seventeen schools and the island's first industrial venture, a peat extraction plant, linked to the kilns by a tramway across the bog.

His largest expenditure was on the construction of the mock Tudor Lews Castle to replace the old Seaforth Lodge. The surrounding moorlands were drained and a parkland created which included many imported trees. The park is now known as Lady Lever Park after the wife of a later owner. Today the castle is a public college where demonstrations of crofting skills such as shearing, Harris tweed weaving and sheep dog handling take place in the summer. Stornoway itself is not a particularly picturesque town but is lively and friendly with many pleasant areas. Points of interest include a lampstand on the harbour front which has a plaque commemorating the various Royal visits to the islands. Martin's Memorial (1885) on Francis Street, stands on the site of the house where explorer Sir Alexander MacKenzie was born. The great Canadian river is named after him.

The old Town Hall was damaged by fire in 1928 but has since been restored and now houses a museum and the Lantern Art Gallery (Museum nan Eilean Steornabhagh agus An Lanntair). The gallery maintains a lively programme of events and exhibitions with a strong emphasis on Gaelic culture and artistic influence. The museum contains displays illustrating the history of Lewis and the daily life of the inhabitants over the years.

The local churches include St Peter's Episcopal Church (1839) which contains an ancient sandstone font brought from the hermit's chapel on the remote Flannan Isles, off the west coast of Lewis. The bell (1631) was once Stornoway's town bell and David Livingstone's Bible is kept in the vestry.

Some years after Matheson's death Stornoway and indeed all of Lewis and Harris were purchased by Viscount Leverhulme, born William Lever, the founding father of the company that bears his name and manufactures virtually all the well known washing up liquids, washing powders and soaps other than those made by Proctor & Gamble. He bought Lewis in 1917 and added Harris in 1919 and had a genuine interest in helping the Western Islanders to greater prosperity with regenerative schemes to help the crofting, farming and tweed industries. He built roads, a fish canning factory, modern housing and industrial units. When knighted he added to his title the suffix 'Of The Western Isles'. His short-lived plans included the development of Leverburgh (An T-ob/Tob), a fishing village in Harris.

The Port of Ness on Lewis

Leverhulme was not welcomed with open arms by all of the islanders however, since he arrived just as they were being given the opportunity to own and work as free men on their crofts, and they much preferred that to becoming employees again, even well-paid ones. The memories of the clearances were still fresh and the few landlords in the past who had begun good works had tended to die or depart suddenly leaving no long-term help for the islanders. Therefore there was considerable resistance to Leverhulme's good intentions to raise prosperity by collective employment and general modernisation.

Leverhulme left Lewis in 1923 after a relatively short period of possession with estimated losses of £1.5 million in the islands. After his death a few years later his trustees quickly departed so his plans finally died with him. Obviously not embittered by the islanders' reaction to his plans, he gave them Stornoway and his nearby castle of Lews with 600 acres (240 hectares) of land. They decided to accept the offer.

The Eye Peninsula (An Rubha) juts out to the sea east of Stornoway, affording some shelter to the boats in the bay. It is almost an island with its access road protected by a sea wall when the Minch gets rough. Two miles (3km) east of the town at **Aiginis** (Aignish) there is the ruined church of St Columba at 'Ui', containing some finely carved tombs of the MacLeod family. Down a minor road south are sheer cliffs at **Swordale** (Suardail), home to colonies of seabirds. The peninsula also contains a craft shop at **Shulishader** (Sulaisiadar) and a tea-room at the point. The lighthouse at **Tiumpan Head** (Rubha an Tiumpain) offers excellent views across the Minch to the mainland; sometimes whales and basking sharks can be seen.

The B895 that follows the coast north-east from Stornoway, past the airport, is one of Leverhulme's unfinished works, ending at **Tolsta** (Tolastadh). There are lovely beaches along here and a bridge that leads nowhere as the road, intended to reach Ness (Nis), has not yet made it. The road passes through **Coll** where there is an active pottery and tea-room. At **Gress** (Griais) there are the remains of an eighteenth-century mill.

The A857 road to the lighthouse and cliffs at Butt of Lewis runs north-west from Stornoway through desolate boggy lowland to reach the Atlantic Coast, which runs north-easterly towards Port of Ness (Port Nis). Shortly after passing the junction with the A858 which follows the coast south-westerly, there are three sites of historical significance near to the road. These include one of the few battle sites known to exist on the islands: this is at **Balanthrushal** (Baile an Truisiel), sometimes spelt Ballanthrushal, where the last fight between the Macaulays of Uig and the Morrisons of Ness took place. Nearby are the **Shader** (Siadar) standing stones and old village site. On the coastal side of the road at **Ballantrushal** is the Clach an Trushal monolith, the largest single monolith in northern Scotland standing 18ft (5m) high.

The people of **Ness** (Nis) are famous seafarers and the local harbour here was begun in 1883 with funding from the widow of James Matheson and the Fisheries Board. There is a weavers shop, which offers demonstrations in Ness itself, as well as a tea-room. The local historical society maintain a display of the area's history.

The most northerly village on the Isle of Lewis is **Europie** (Eoropaidh) where a small church can be reached along a footpath across private croft-land. Dedicated to St Molua, its origins are shrouded in mystery and myth. It has Norse, Irish and possibly pagan connections, and was long a place of pilgrimage for those suffering from ailments as diverse as insanity and sores.

Following the Atlantic Coast south-west and turning on to the A858 at **Barvas** (Barabhas) the village of **Arnol** soon appears where there is a famous black house, preserved in its original state as an invaluable stop for those wishing to experience the former lifestyle of the inhabitants of the Western Isles. The house was shared by both residents and their cattle and was built without cement, with a

The Black House, preserved in its original state at Arnol, Lewis

thatched roof and central peat fire in the kitchen. In the preceding settlement of **Bru** (Brue) there is a permanent exhibition of Hebridean landscapes (Solas nan Eilean), including St Kilda.

The next settlement, **Bragar**, contains a whalebone arch made from the huge jawbone of a blue whale that came ashore in 1920. The harpoon which killed it was still attached to the body and forms part of the arch. The next few settlements of **Shawbost** (Siabost) and **Carloway** (Carlabhagh) contain a folk museum, craftshop, weavers and the remains of an old black house village.

Before turning to follow Loch Roag, the road passes **Dun Carloway**, one of Scotland's best preserved brochs, 2,000 years old and of standard design. Hearth areas unearthed in a 1971 excavation are thought to indicate that part of the building was used to fire pottery. The highest part of the surviving wall still stands some 70ft (21m) high.

The 4,000-year-old **Callanish** (Calanais) Standing Stones are eerily beautiful, as well as being of great archaeological importance. They are tall slender pillars of local gneiss, interpreted by various interested parties along similar lines to Stonehenge — a druid temple, a megalithic calendar, a parking space for passing space ships or just a few of the local folk turned to stone by a wizard back in the mists of time. The stones are more visible now than they had been for several millennia as 5ft (1½m) of peat was dug away from the base of them in the nineteenth century by Sir James Matheson, to use for fuel.

Apart from the main circle there are several smaller circles in the vicinity known as Callanish II, III and IV. Local people used to gather at the stones on midsummer morning, up to the nineteenth century, and await the procession of a spirit down the main avenue, preceded by the song of a cuckoo.

The A858 now goes back eastwards towards Stornoway, passing a stone circle at **Achmore** (Acha Mor), 5 miles (8km) from Callanish but the B8011 and B8059 follow the west coast further towards the Harris Border, affording some beautiful views of west coast islands in one of the few hilly areas of Lewis.

The main Harris road from Stornoway is the A859 which runs down the east coast through a desolate and mostly uninhabited landscape towards the top of Loch Seaforth (Shiophoirt). Before reaching this point however the road follows Loch Erisort and a minor road then turns off east to follow the other side of that loch.

Standing Stones of Callanish

This road passes by the remains of St Columb's Church and another ruined dun. It eventually reaches **Lemreway** (Leumrabhagh) from where there is a good view out across the Sound of Shiant to the uninhabited Shiant Isles. These straits are the legendary home of the 'Blue Men' who spend their time stirring up storms and challenging mariners to recite Gaelic verse better than they can, or perish beneath the waves. A little further along the A859 a second minor road to the east follows the top of Loch Seaforth, and passes an ancient stone circle and the remains of the former seat of the Lairds of Seaforth.

HARRIS (Eilean Hearadh)

Few maps show where Lewis ends and Harris begins. It is not, as many think, at the island's capital, Tarbert, where east and west coasts almost meet, but a good way north where a line is drawn from the eastern end of Loch Resort, over the peak of Stuklaval to **Ardvourlie** (Aird A Mhulaidh) Castle, on the edge of Loch Seaforth, opposite Seaforth Island. This small, steep sided island is half in Lewis and half in Harris.

Famed for its tweed and renowned for the tenacity of its fishermen, the island's prosperity has always moved in fits and jerks against the underlying constancy of the traditional industries. Fish farming, seaweed farming and coastal super-quarrying are current income earners. Harris has little fertile ground with much of the rare areas of the flat lands covered by 5ft (1½m) of peat. Birdlife is stunning with everything from puffins to golden eagles to be seen. Herds of red deer are maintained for the North Harris porting estate and there is excellent trout and salmon fishing. Also to be seen, on occasions, are basking sharks in the Minch and a unique strain of bumble-bee, *bombus jonellus var. hebredenis*.

This is the most mountainous area of the Western Isles, and indeed much of Harris is made up of steep hills and mountains, a contrast to the sometimes dreary peat moors of Lewis. The 'island' is divided in to north and south, but both halves remained under MacLeod ownership until 1868 when the Earl of Dunmore, who had bought the island in 1834, sold the north part to Sir Edward Scott for £155,000. Lord Leverhulme picked up both parts again for a 6 year period around the 1920s for about a third of the price paid more than 50 years earlier. Today North Harris (excluding Scalpay and Scotasay) remain under one ownership while South Harris has been broken up into a number of smaller estates.

Ardvourlie Castle, in reality a Victorian hunting lodge, is a good place to start. It is now restored as a guest house with many period features, serving traditional recipes, using local ingredients, to residents and visitors alike. The A859 continues along the side of the 18 mile (29km) long fjord-like Loch Seaforth towards Tarbert (An Tairbeart), capital of Harris and the main port for Caledonian MacBrayne connections to the Uists and Uig on Skye. The road winds through the mountainous north of Harris, popular with hill walkers and climbers; the highest peak, Clisham (2,622ft/799m) is to the west of the road.

Before the road turns away from the coast to cut through to West Loch Tarbert however, a very new road from Maaruig (Maruig), not marked on many maps, continues south to **Rhenigidale** (Reiningeadal) which, until the road was built, was famous for not having a road link! The views from here are so beautiful that people made the effort to walk to see them.

When the A859 does reach West Loch Tarbert at **Bunavoneadar** (Bun Abhainn Eadarra), the remains of an old whaling station, established by the eternally whale-friendly Norwegians before World War I, can be seen. Many local men were once employed in this industry. Lord Leverhulme bought the station along with most other places and, ingenious as ever, intended to use the oil extract to make soap at Port Sunlight and make the remaining meat in to sausages to sell to African natives. Six thousand tons of whale meat were landed but apparently the Africans were not hungry for it.

The B887 follows a very scenic route along the Atlantic Coast north-westerly to the coast at **Hushinish Bay** (Huisinis). This has a lovely beach and nearby there are views across to the island of **Scarp** which had its own school until as recently as the 1980s. One of the island's claims to fame is that it was the site of an unsuccessful attempt to deliver mail by rocket in the 1930s. Inventor Herr Zucker made one attempt, complete with special 'Rocket Mail' postage stamp and trial firing date frank, but although the rocket made it across it exploded on impact, destroying most of the mail. The experiment was not repeated, thus creating a small sensation for philatelists.

The road passes **Abhainn Suidhe Castle** (Amhhuinnsuidhe), the traditional home of the proprietor of the North Harris Estate and closed to the public (car parking nearby is not popular with the owners either). It was built in 1868 by the Earl of Dunmore, and Sir James Barrie began work on his novel *Mary Rose* within the house. Nearby Loch Leosaidh reaches the sea through a series of small waterfalls where you may see salmon jumping in June and July.

The huge Seilebost sandy beach near Luskentyre, Harris

Tarbert (An Tairbeart) is perched between West Loch Tarbert and East Loch Tarbert. This is the main metropolis of Harris with ferry port, garage, tourist information office, hotel, two churches and about a dozen shops. These include the Islands Book and Craft Shop which sells original water-colours and books of island interest. There are sometimes exhibitions in the Old Hostel arranged by the Local History Society.

The A859 follows East Loch Tarbert for a few miles before skirting between the mountains to reach the Atlantic Coast and the Sound of Taransay (Taransaigh). A circular route is possible here as a minor road follows the Minch coast to the south and east of South Harris. The two coasts contrast dramatically with huge sandy beaches in the north and small bays and miniature fjords to the south. The latter contains numerous small fishing communities, cleared to the rocky areas from the more fertile land on the opposite coast. Two of these are neighbouring **Drinishader** (Drinisiadar) and **Scadabay** (Scadabhagh) where there are about half a dozen different Harris Tweed workers giving displays and selling goods. The villages are reached by an unlisted road south. There are sometimes local exhibitions here too.

Just as the A859 reaches the coast an unlisted road turns off to the right at **Luskentyre** (Losganitir) and the huge sandy inlet below it share the village's name. The area is famed for its birdlife (waders, wild fowl and migrants), fishing, fauna, and there are even some trees. A headland opposite the isle of **Taransay** (Tarasaigh) contains the Clach Mhicleoid Standing Stone or 'MacLeods Stone', a single monolith. Taransay island was named after St Tarran and contains the remains of his chapel and that of St Keith. Traditionally men were buried at St Keiths and women at St Tarrans, those buried in the wrong churchyard were disinterred over night.

At **Scarista** (Sgarasta) by **Borve** (Na Buirgh) there is a 9 hole golf-course, a craft shop and a standing stone. Borve Lodge was Lord Leverhulme's home after he left Lewis; he built the circular walled garden. Scarista House, originally the principal Church of Scotland Manse for Harris and one of the few listed buildings in the Western Isles is located nearby. This is now run as a guest house.

Slightly further on another magnificent bay begins, rounded off by the Toe Head (Goban Tobha) peninsula jutting out at the west corner of Harris. The hill rises to just over 1,000ft (305m) and on a clear day it is possible to see St Kilda from the top. Easier to spot is the small island of Coppay, 2 miles (3km) to the west, which is a favoured breeding site for seals. Near to **Northton** (An Taobh Tuath) at the foot of the head is a neolithic site of considerable local importance, discovered in the 1960s by a Professor from Aberdeen University. There is a genealogical research service at Northton and sometimes exhibitions covering all of the Western Isles.

Leverburgh (Obbe/An t-Ob) was renamed by Lord Leverhulme who had big plans for the village in 1923 when he spent £250,000 building piers, jetties, roads and houses. There were huge catches of fish in 1924 but all was abandoned in 1925 when Leverhulme died and all the buildings were sold off to a demolition company for £5,000. They removed almost everything. Several managers' houses remain, still some of the best homes on the island. Hulme Hall is now a school.

A 7 mile (11km) circular walk from Leverburgh starts at An Clachan, 328ft (100m) from the local school where cars can be parked off the road. Detailed directions are available from the tourist office but the route can take in the Obbe Hill (338ft/103m) from which there are excellent views of the Sound of Harris and the Minch. In good weather St Kilda, Skye and North Uist can all be seen. The route then passes the southernmost tip of the Harris mainland at Renish Point (Rubha Reanais).

At **Rodel** (Roghadal) a visit to St Clements Church is a must, this is one of the major architectural attractions of the Western Isles. The church is located on an old religious settlement but the current

St Clements Church at Rodel, one of the major architectural attractions of the Western Isles, Harris

buildings date from around 1520, and are the work of Alexander VII of Harris (Alasdair Crotach). His tomb, and that of his son, within the church walls, are two of the most impressive in the Western Isles. The hunting scene on one of the panels within the grave is thought to depict Crotach himself. There are also many graves from the MacLeod family, whose badge, the bull's head, is much on display. Traditionally each time a family member died his body was laid out in the stone coffin which had an iron grate about 12 inches down inside the coffin. When the next member passed away, the remains of the previous occupant were 'shaken down' through the grate in to the bottom of the coffin, and the new resident lain to rest upon the grate.

There are many interesting and unusual pictures and carvings throughout the church, including one of the earliest known of a man in a kilt. There are also several rather 'colourful' depictions which probably pre-date the church itself, possibly pagan fertility symbols acceptable to early Christians, as similar examples are to be found in the nunnery of Iona and are fairly common in Irish churches from this era. A rare bat, the Pipistrelle, is found in the locality.

SCALPAY (SCALPAIGH)

This is a thriving community at the end of Loch Tarbert, separated from Harris by a narrow strip of water. The population has remained constant in recent years during a general decline elsewhere. The main industry is, once again, fishing and there is a knitwear factory to visit. At **Eilean Glas** on the eastern tip of the island is one of four lighthouses originally constructed in 1789, the 'new' tower dates from 1824 and is now automated.

Bonnie Prince Charlie landed here in 1746 a fortnight after his defeat at Culloden and was sheltered by one Donald Campbell while his supporters tried to buy a boat in Stornoway. The suspicions of a local minister were aroused and he arranged an invasion of Scalpay to try to capture Charles and collect the £30,000 reward. Donald Campbell repulsed the invasion and Charles escaped.

ST KILDA

The spectacular and stunning beauty of St Kilda

This group of islands of spectacular and stunning beauty is the byword among Scottish islanders for all that is wrong with the attitude of distant, apparently indifferent, mainland government towards them. In 1930 the remaining thirty-six inhabitants were evacuated from the main island of **Hirta** at their own request and the landlord, Sir Reginald MacLeod, turned down requests by 400 more people to settle there. Instead the island passed to the National Trust For Scotland in 1957 who leased it to the Nature Conservancy

Council, now Scottish National Heritage. Permission was given for a military base to watch the missiles sent up from Benbecula. Ironically, the main reason for the islanders request for evacuation, a lack of modern facilities, was reversed by the military who brought in the generators, tractors, helicopter link and medical facilities which might have sustained the population. The military has hosted weddings on Hirta in the early 1990s.

National Trust volunteer working parties visit the island each year to work on the gradual restoration of the village buildings which stood round Village Bay. The local people had existed through crofting and 'fowling' among the great colonies of sea birds (eating puffin and gannet meat and using fulmar oil). Some of the United Kingdom's greatest cliffs are to be found here, with amazing birdlife to match. Unique to the islands are a species of mouse, a St Kilda wren and now even a wild Soay sheep! In 1987 the island was named as Scotland's first World Heritage Site by UNESCO.

BERNERAY (BEARNARAIGH)

The best known of the islands around the Hebrides which are each called Berneray is located in the Sound of Harris (another previously described lies off Lewis and a third being at the southern tip of the Western Isles). This is a favoured retreat of Prince Charles. The population are as familiar as any non-royal can be with His Royal Highness, who enjoys helping with manual work on the crofts and joining in social events. His visits have occasionally been documented by invited TV crews. To the north of Berneray is the fertile Isle of **Pabbay**, cleared of its 300 inhabitants in the early nineteenth century. It is still farmed and now supports a herd of red deer.

NORTH UIST (UIBHIST A TUATH)

The isles of North and South Uist, with Benbecula (Beinn na Faoghla) in between, run almost due south from the Sound of Harris down to the Sound of Barra. North Uist seems to be more loch than land and the islands' only real road (A865) does a circuit (with the A867) of the top of the island then follows the west coast with its almost continuous sandy beach right down to the south. All three isles are dotted with ancient monuments and nature reserves and are generally made up of wild lands and high hills in the east, numerous trout filled lochs between the hills, and more fertile plains and magnificent beaches on the Atlantic Coast. The three are linked by causeways, but

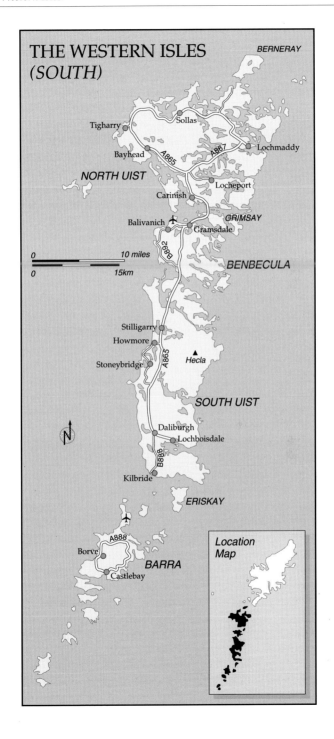

THE WESTERN ISLES
(SOUTH)

BERNERAY

Tigharry

Sollas

NORTH UIST

Bayhead

A865

A867

Lochmaddy

Locheport

Carinish

GRIMSAY

Balivanich

Gramsdale

B892

BENBECULA

0   10 miles
0   15km

Stilligarry

Howmore

A865

Hecla ▲

Stoneybridge

SOUTH UIST

N

Daliburgh

Lochboisdale

B888

Kilbride

ERISKAY

A888

Borve

BARRA

Castlebay

Location
Map

historically there is a dividing line between North Uist and Benbecula. The latter is linked with South Uist and Barra as Catholic islands under a different ownership to North Uist. **Lochmaddy** (Loch Na Madadh) is the main village in North Uist. It has the Caledonian MacBrayne ferry point for Harris and Skye and there is a tourist information office here and a few shops. The A865 round the coast soon reaches the **Balranald Nature Reserve** (Baile Raghaill), 3 miles (5km) north of Bayhead (Ceann A Bhaigh). This is a typical Hebridean marshland and shore area, important for plants and nesting birds. The reserve is near Hosta where the island's Highland Games and cattle show are held each July. Also nearby is the only folly in the Western Isles, Scolpaig Tower, constructed in the nineteenth century on the remains of a dun. One of the best ruined duns in the area is Dun Torcuill, located on a partly man-made island in the tidal Loch an Duin near Lochmaddy. It is not far from Dun Sticcer, also constructed on an island, near the ferry departure point for Berneray.

Heading west from Lochmaddy on the A867 a number of significant ancient monuments are to be found about 1 mile (2km) before the road reaches its junction with the A865 south. Most significant of these is the passage grave known as Barpa Langass which was excavated in 1911 to reveal neolithic and Bronze Age artifacts, but it is not safe to enter this 5000-year-old cairn. Next to this are the oval standing stones known as Finn's People (Pobull Fhinn).

At **Carinish** (Cairinis) the Trinity Temple (Teampull Na Trionaid) was a significant place of learning in medieval times, believed to have been established in the thirteenth century by Beatrice (Beathag), daughter of Somerled. Duns Scotus studied here, a Franciscan who lived between 1266 and 1308 and was a leading divine and one of the greatest Scottish medieval philosophers. However after criticism of his thinking after his death the word 'dunce' appeared in the English language. Near to the temple is Teampull Clann A'Phiocair, chapel of the McVicars who taught at the temple. The 'Field of Blood', site of a clan battle between the MacDonalds of Uist and the MacLeods of Harris, is adjacent to the remains.

BENBECULA (BEINN NA FAOGHLA)

Benbecula is smallest of the Uists and consists mainly of low level fertile land and innumerable small lochs. The island enjoyed increased prosperity when the military arrived to launch rockets from Balivanish. A swimming pool and squash court were among the luxuries they brought with them, as well as employment and a 45 per cent increase in the local population. The Uists' airport is also located here. The island is now linked to North Uist by the North Ford Causeway, opened by the Queen Mother in 1960. This link takes in the Isle of Grioimsay (Griomsaigh) which has an active fishing community.

In Benbecula there is a wealth of ruined cairns, standing stones and duns. The island originally belonged, with South Uist, to the MacDonalds, and was quite a prized asset until the collapse of the kelp boom in the early nineteenth century. The islands were sold in 1827 to a more oppressive regime which attempted to teach Protestantism, in English, to Gaelic-speaking Catholic children. Matters were improved somewhat, in South Uist at least, by an English Catholic teacher whom the islanders brought in themselves in 1890 when the Crofters Act protected them from eviction for doing so. He spoke no Gaelic on arrival but the language barrier was overcome, helped by the fact that he spoke 'plain English'. The teacher's notes refer to children arriving without shoes and socks in mid-winter, sitting in wet clothes all day and having nothing to eat.

Apart from the scenery, birdlife, fishing and surfing, the island's attractions include Culla Bay at Nunton (Baile nan Cailleach), one of the best beaches in the Western Isles. The Museum Sgoil Lionacleit has been established 4 miles (6km) south of the main village Balivanich (Baile a' Mhanaich) on the B892 at Linaclete (Lionacleeit). The school, cafeteria, library and sports facilities are also here and ceilidhs are staged throughout the summer. Exhibitions are organised along with events to illustrate the history of the Uists and Barra. The ruins of Borve Castle, built around 1350 as the principal residence of the Clan Ranald, testify to the power of that family in years gone by.

SOUTH UIST (UIBHIST A DEAS)

South Uist has the Uists' only substantial hills, which make up about half of its area and are located on the east side. The highest of these are Beinn Mhor and neighbouring Hecla, both at around 2,000ft (610m). As with Benbecula much of the west coast is fringed by a continuous long sandy beach and there are many more ancient monuments. One of the initially surprising sights to be seen after entering North Uist on the South Ford Causeway (dating from 1983, replacing an older structure from 1943) is the huge statue of the Madonna and Child, 'Our Lady Of The Isles', standing 30ft (9m) high on the Ben Rueval (Hill of Miracles). This was erected in 1957 by the

One of several ruined chapels at Howmore, South Uist

local community with assistance from people all over the world and is the work of Hew Lorimer. It may seem ironic or appropriate that the military range control building is located on the hill above, according to your point of view.

Before the statue, however, the road passes a turning for **Lochdar** where there is a unique Hebridean jeweller creating Celtic and wildlife designs. At neighbouring **Eochar** (Ant-Iochdar) there is a small black house museum. Back on the A865 another causeway crosses Loch Bee where a variety of wildfowl can normally be seen, before nearing Our Lady of the Isles.

Soon after the statue, a turning east on to the B890 to Loch Skipport (Sgioport) on the coast, passes alongside Loch Druidibeg which forms a part of a large nature reserve. This is an important breeding site for greylag geese and sanctuary to many other birds. At **Howmore** (Tobha Mor) there are several ruined chapels dating from the twelfth or thirteenth centuries. This has long been an important ecclesiastic site, the chiefs of the Clan Ranald are buried here. The current Church of Scotland is one of only two retaining a central communion pew. The village also has some thatched cottages surviving.

An unmarked road some 7 miles (11km) south of the statue on the A865 leads to **Ormaclete House** (Ormacleit) and castle which took 7 years to build by 1708 for the ill fated chief of the Clan Ranald. Seven was clearly not the chief's lucky number, as 7 years later the house was burnt down, apparently accidentally, the day before the Battle of Sherriffmuir when he himself was killed. Nearby is the Bornish (Bornais) standing stone, a single monolith overlooking the Atlantic. A few miles further south is the South Uist War Memorial and then at **Milton** (Gearraidh Bhailteas) a cairn erected in the ruins of the house where Flora McDonald was born in 1722, she being the best known of Bonnie Prince Charlie's helpers.

At **Askernish** (Aisgernis), 3 miles (5km) further on, the Uist's only golf course is to be found, along with access to the wonderful beach. From here the A685 veers westwards to **Lochboisdale** (Loch Baghasdail), the Caledonian MacBrayne ferry port for Oban and Barra. There is a craft shop, tea-room, hotel and garage service here. Where the A865 turns west a road (B888) continues to the southern tip of the Uists, passing a prehistoric circular dwelling on dunes near **Kilpheder** (Cille Pheadair) and then **Pollachar** (Pol a Charra), where there is another standing stone.

ERISKAY (Eiriosgaigh)

Eriskay in the Sound of Barra, just off the South Uist coast, can be reached by car ferry from Ludag. The island's main claim to fame in the twentieth century is that a ship called *The Politician* went aground just off the island in 1941. The crew were all rescued and the 24,000 cases of whisky in the hold were not entirely ignored. The island's first pub was opened in 1988 and some of the rescued bottles are on display there. Look out for the entirely coincidentally named 'Politician' public house when you visit. Perhaps of slightly greater historical significance is the fact that Bonnie Prince Charlie first landed on Scottish soil here in 1745 at the start of his ill-fated attempt to regain the British Crown from the Stuarts.

BARRA (Barraigh)

Barra is most southerly of the major Outer Hebridean islands and one of the most varied within its small area, being almost a microcosm for all the Hebrideans, within its 12 mile (19km) circumference. Most visitors arrive on the Caledonian MacBrayne ferry from Oban on the mainland or Lochboisdale, South Uist. The crossing from Oban takes some 5 hours on the comfortable ferry which arrives at **Castlebay** (Bagh A Chaisteil), the main settlement on the island.

The first building to greet the visitor is Barra's main piece of architecture, **Kisimul Castle**. This impressive fortress was built on an island in the bay by the MacNeills in the fifteenth century, although its main tower dates back to 1120. In those days, when clan chiefs sported names like Ruari the Turbulent, the MacNeills had something of a reputation as fearless raiders, unafraid of capturing passing ships. Kisimul Castle is considered the best surviving example of Hebridean defences in all the Western Isles. It was destroyed by fire in 1795 and lay derelict until 1938 when a distant member of the MacNeill family and fourty-fifth Clan Leader, an American architect, returned to his ancestral home and renovations began. Work was completed in 1970 and Kisimul remains under MacNeill ownership, but is usually open to the public twice weekly (by boat crossing). MacNeill is a familiar name on the island.

The Isle of Barra Pottery is also located at **Northbay** (Bagh a Tuath) near Castlebay where handthrown stoneware is made and sold. Nearby is Victoria Rock, next to the dam which, when viewed from the Northbay side, is said to resemble Queen Victoria's profile. There is a statue of the Virgin and Child, Our Lady Of the Seas, on the isle's highest hill, Heaval, which rises to 1,000ft (305m) behind Castlebay.

The church of St Barr near the airstrip at the north end of the island dates from the twelfth century. One of the ruined buildings has been restored and contains the replica of a grave stone containing a Celtic cross one side and Norse runes on the other. The original has been taken to Edinburgh. Sir Compton Mackenzie is buried here. The church was constructed as 'Cashels', almost a mini monastery, with church and living accommodation for the clergy contained within a walled area.

There are in excess of 1,000 species of wildflower surviving in Barra. These may have been one of the features that attracted Sir Compton Mackenzie, author of the story version of *Whisky Galore*, to live on the island. The popular film of the book of the event at Eriskay was also made here in 1948.

A causeway has quite recently been constructed to link Barra to the small Isle of **Vatersay** (Bhatarsaigh), to the south. A granite memorial here is testimony to much of the sad history of the whole of the Western Isles in the nineteenth century, when many of the local population were turned out of their homes by land owners in the notorious clearances. The only option for most was emigration to North America, Australia or New Zealand. The Vatersay memorial is to a ship called the *Annis Jane* which was lost off the island, along with more than 350 souls aboard, many from the Hebrides; all cleared from their homes and en route to America.

Further Information
— The Western Isles —

Places of Interest

Due to the nature of tourism and travel on the Western Isles, most of the craft workers studios and shops (Potters, Harris Tweed Weavers etc.) maintain an 'open-door' to visitors at most reasonable daylight hours Monday to Saturday. Generally 9am to 6pm or 8pm. It may often be worth telephoning ahead. Current day-by-day advice should be available from the tourist office. Most historical relics are open to anyone at any time, so there are few places where there are regular set opening hours.

Arnol
Lewis Black House
Isle of Lewis
Arnol
☎ 031 244 3101
Open: all year except on Sundays.

Benbecula (Beinn Na Faoghla)
Museum Sgoil Lionacleit
Open: all year, hours vary.
☎ 0870 2211 ext 137

Castlebay (Bagh A Chaisteil)
Kisimul Castle
Isle of Barra
☎ 08714 336
Open: May to September, Wednesday and Saturday afternoons, by boat trip.

Stornoway (Steornabhagh)
Lantern Art Gallery
Isle of Lewis
Town Hall
South Beach Street
Stornoway
☎ 0851 3307
Open: all year, Monday to Saturday, 10am-6pm. Admission free.

Museum Nan Eilean Steornabhagh
Town Hall
South Beach Street
Stornoway
☎ 0851 3773

Open: June to August, Tuesday to Saturday, 10am-12.30pm and 2-5.30pm. September to May, Tuesday to Saturday, 2-5pm. Admission free.

Tourist Information Offices

Borgh
Outer Hebrides Crafts Association
Borgh Pottery
Fivepenny House
Isle of Lewis
☎ 0851 850345

Castlebay (Bagh A Chaisteil)
Main Street
Barra
☎ 0871 810336
Open: Easter to October.

Lochmaddy (Loch Na Madadh)
Pier Road
North Uist
☎ 0876 500321
Open: Easter to October.

Lochboisdale (Loch Baghasdail)
Pier Road
South Uist
☎ 0878 700286
Open: Easter to October.

Stornoway (Steornabhagh)
Western Isles Tourist Board
(Bord Turasachd Nan Eilean)
26 Cromwell Street (26 Sraid Chrombail)
Isle of Lewis (Elean Leodhais)
PA87 2DD
☎ 0851 703088
Fax: 0851 705244
Open: all year.

Tarbert (An Tairbeart)
Pier Road
Harris
☎ 0859 2011
Open: Easter to October.

13 • Orkney Isles

It is not quite the 'Land of the Midnight Sun' but at midnight in midsummer you can still see the rays of the sun away in the north (provided it is not raining). There are more than seventy islands making up Orkney, and countless 'islets' too small to make island status; about a third are populated. The total area covered by the islands is 376sq miles (975sq km).

Much of Orkney is flat and rural; something of a shock for those arriving from the desolate and mountainous Highland landscape. The Scandinavian influence remains omnipresent from the days of the Vikings and the ancient historical remains of inhabitants up to 6,000 years ago are still clearly visible. While other islands off the Scottish west coast have unique identities, there is still a feeling of Scottishness; Orkney's seems to look east more than west. Geologically, however, Orkney is another part of the same old red sandstone which lies beneath Caithness.

The present population is just over 20,000 and, although the original inhabitants can be traced back much further, the first written reference to the islands dates from 330BC. This was a recording made by Greek explorer Pytheas who circumnavigated the islands around them and claimed to have sighted the edge of the world. Most likely this was Foula off the Shetland Islands . The Roman fleets made treaties with or suppressed the Orcadians in the first century AD and there is then a jump in recorded literature to the twelfth century when the Norse sagas of the Vikings' arrival were first created.

Orkney Mainland and Copinsay

The Orkney mainland is divided into two sectors on a line between Kirkwall and Scapa Bay. They are simply east and west, the east being the flatter and smaller of the two halves, only about a quarter the size of the west.

Kirkwall is a very attractive and rather cosmopolitan town. Its

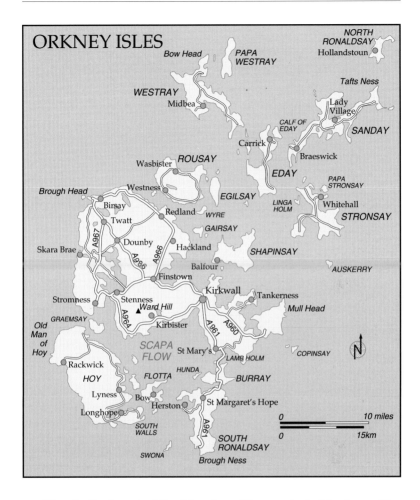

position in the heart of the islands, with a protected harbour (the 'Peerie Sea') made it a natural cross-roads and thus trade and administration grew up here. The original area name of Papdale means 'Priests Valley', and is believed to originate from settlement in the early eighth century by missionaries of the Roman Church sent from the Pictish heartland. Kirkwall comes from the Old Norse 'Kirkjuvagr' meaning 'Church Bay' and is mentioned in the Viking's *Orkneyinga Saga*. This was soon after St Olaf's Church had been completed and dedicated to King Olaf the Holy of Norway.

In the early twelfth century Orkney was divided in to by two Earldoms, one of which was ruled by more respected Earl Magnus Erlendsson who was murdered by his jealous cousin Earl Hakon. Magnus tomb was soon after said to have divine powers and became

*Shopping
in Kirkwall*

a shrine for pilgrims. He was canonised in 1135 and shortly afterwards Magnus nephew Rognvald Kolsson vowed to build a magnificent stone minster and in 1137 work on St Magnus Cathedral
began. It was completed in 1152, along with the adjacent Bishop's
Palace.

In 1263 King Haakon the Old of Norway used Kirkwall as a base
in his attempt to maintain control of the Western Isles, but after
defeat at the Battle of Largs he fell ill and died in the Bishop's Palace.
It is thought that Robert the Bruce may also have spent a winter in the
Bishop's Palace during a low point in his fortunes before returning
to win the Scottish Crown.

Kirkwall Castle was completed in 1383 by which time the town
was divided into two, with the Burgh under the Earl's control and the
'Laverock' belonging to the church. A rugby-like game, the ba',
played between the 'Uppies' (Bishop's Men) and 'Doonies' (Earl's
Men) each Christmas and New Year survives to this day.

From the twelfth to fifteenth centuries the Scots moved into the area and when a daughter of Danish King Christian I married James III in 1468, Orkney was pledged to Scotland in lieu of her dowry. Later attempts to pay off this debt by the Danes were apparently misplaced by the new owners! In 1486 Kirkwall was given the status of Royal Burgh which allowed for twice weekly markets, controlled trades, the imposition of local law and order. A period of tyranny followed in the late sixteenth and early seventeenth centuries when a branch of the Stewart family resided in Kirkwall Castle, forcing the Orcadians to work for them or face torture and imprisonment. In 1650 Oliver Cromwell sent armies to quell Royalist support in the islands, with the result that many of his men became friendly with the locals and stayed, bringing in new techniques in horticulture and other areas.

A period of stability followed until the early nineteenth century as the centre of island growth shifted to Stromness. In 1809 work began on two small iron piers built to Thomas Telford's design. The west pier remains largely unchanged to this day, but the east has been much extended and encased in concrete, although the small cast-iron lighthouse remains. There are many places of historic interest, all dominated by the magnificent cathedral which took 300 years to reach its 'final' version and today shows Romanesque, Traditional and Gothic influences. Outside stands a replica of the Mercat Cross dated from 1621, a copy of the original which once stood at the bottom of the Strynd but is now within the cathedral. It has always played an important part in Kirkwall's history being the place where proclamations were made.

The Bishop's Palace was rebuilt in the late fifteenth century and renovated in the mid-sixteenth by Bishop Robert Reid, Orkney's last great medieval Bishop and the founder of Edinburgh University. The Bishop also restored St Olaf's Kirk, built in 1035, possibly of wood. It was burnt down by English marauders in 1557 after which it was used as a poorhouse and carpenter's shop before becoming ruinous about 250 years ago.

The Earl's Palace was built in 1600 by Earl Patrick Stewart but never completed as he ran out of money, was jailed and eventually executed for treason. The slate roof was sold in 1745 and the palace has been roofless ever since. The thirty-two trees in the grounds, mostly sycamore, were probably planted around 1840. The Strynd is an old passage way named after a stream that used to run through the area. The small garden adjoining it was the town's botanical garden in the eighteenth century and contains trees such as beech, lime and Irish ivy, unusual at this latitude. Tankerness House was originally two manses for cathedral clergy but it was extended in 1574 by the first Protestant priest, former archdeacon Gilbert Fulzie. It is now a museum of Orkney life.

Shopping in Kirkwall is a very rewarding experience as it combines a unique mix of designer jewellery and woollens shops, with normal high street stores and traditional general stores and merchants selling a range and variety of products no longer available, now that most high streets have been chopped up by the chain stores. Names to look out for include jewellers Ola Gorie and Ortak and Judith Glue knitwear.

One of Kirkwall's major attractions is the Highland Park Distillery (1798), Scotland's most northerly, which has excellent visitor facilities including an audio visual and video display, half-hourly tours, a shop and a collection of over 2,000 historic postcards from Orkney. Visitors also receive a free dram of the 12-year-old malt, widely respected by connoisseurs as one of the world's best. Michael Jackson's authoritative *Malt Whisky Companion* gives the distillery a rare maximum five stars and the whisky a high scoring 87 out of 100, describing it as 'The greatest all rounder in the world of malt whisky'.

Leaving Kirkwall on the A960 and heading south-easterly towards Kirkwall Airport, the landscape is largely flat and rural. Kirkwall Airport was originally known as Grimsetter and nearby is Wideford Farm from where Captain Fresson flew on 30 May 1934 to establish the first internal airmail service in the United Kingdom.

Soon afterwards a left turning leads towards **Rerwick Head** where the remains of a World War II Coastal Defence still stand. On the road there, to the right, is Bossack Quarry from which much of the material required for the building of the Churchill barriers was obtained and on the left the twin lochs of Weethick, unique to Orkney in that each is contained within a double ayre or shingle bar. Evidence of use as a harbour in Viking times has been found and 'nousts', where boats were hauled up when not in use, can be seen.

The road then nears the coast at Mill Sand, famous for shellfish and birdlife, as is the inland Loch of Tankerness at this point. Species to be seen include curlew, lapwing, oyster catcher, redshank, turnstone, shelduck and the bar-tailed godwit.

The Hall of **Tankerness** nearby is on the site of a twelfth-century Norse chieftain's drinking hall. From 1630 until the turn of the century it was the home of the Baikies of Tankerness, whose Kirkwall townhouse is now the Tankerness House Museum.

Back on the A960 the road passes the Bay of Suckquoy at the end of Deer Sound before crossing the sandy isthmus at Dingieshowe which connects Deerness to the mainland. On one side, set into the shore at intervals, rows of 'dragons' teeth' wartime concrete anti-tank landing defences can be seen. An older defensive structure, a broch mound, is strategically placed among sand dunes on the south side.

Deerness has numerous coastal features of natural and man-made importance. These include The Gloup, named from the old Norse 'Gluppa' or cavern, a collapsed sea cave separated from the sea by a land bridge. At the Brough of Deerness the remains of an early Christian church can be found, accessible only by a narrow and dangerous cliff track and virtually cut off at high tide. There is also a rock stack with a cap of sediment known as Muckle Castle at the south side of the island. At the north end, not far from Mull Head, stands the Covenanters Memorial erected in 1888 to mark the area where 200 Covenanters, made prisoner at the Battle of Bothwell Bridge, were ship-wrecked on the 'Crown' in 1697. The Covenanters had refused to accept the introduction of the English Common Book of Prayer in 1638 and were being transported to the American colonies.

To the south-east of Deerness lies the high wedge-shaped island of **Copinsay**, with a lighthouse first lit in 1915 perched on 300ft (91m) high cliffs. On the north side there are the remains of an Iron Age fort and a small area of grass which is said to be enough to 'fatten one sheep, feed two or starve three'. The island is now the James Fisher Memorial Reserve of the RSPB and is the nesting site of 40,000 pairs of guillemots and kittiwakes.

Returning from Deerness on the A960 it is possible to reach the south coast and the causeways to Burray and South Ronaldsay by turning left on to the B9052. This takes you to the A961 leading north to Kirkwall. Near the large village of **St Mary's** is a nineteenth-century laird's mansion called Graemshall. This is home to a private collection of valuable antiques on display three afternoons a week. The collection was assembled from scratch, with a minimal budget, during the lifetime of Norrie Wood and now numbers nearly 1,000 items. The modern Commodore Motel at St Mary's also has a fascinating private display, in this case photographs of the construction of the Churchill Barriers. Leaving Kirkwall and heading west there is a choice of routes to the south or north of the mainland. The A965 is the main route over to Stromness while the A964 takes a more leisurely southerly route. Shortly before Houton, a main ferry point for travel to Flotta and **Lynness on Hoy** there are the remains of Scotland's only circular medieval church, which dates from the twelfth century. Nearby is the 'Earl's Bu', the remains of a Viking

The famous 3,000-year-old Stone Age village of Skara Brae

drinking hall. The last major pitched battle fought on Orkney soil took place a few miles inland from here when the army of King James V, led by the Earl of Caithness, was sent to crush a revolt against taxes and feudalism by the islanders. The Orcadians won the day.

Finstown, on the northern coast, is a pleasant village which grew up early in the nineteenth century when a public house was opened on the site of the present Pomona Inn. The village name seems to have come from an Irish soldier called Phin who retired to open the bar here after the Napoleonic Wars. Binscarth Wood, just west of the village, is large by Orcadian standards (9 acres/4 hectares); the trees were planted 300 years ago and support a wealth of wildlife.

The area inland from here is the parish of **Harray**, the only Orkney parish not to have a coastline. The large local loch is one of the best for fishing in the islands however (and like many Orkney lochs no permits are required). Unlike most other parishes the people here actually owned their land and Harray was known as the parish of a hundred lairds.

The A966 and then A967 follows the coast around Orkney's largest land area, where hills have the opportunity to rise up quite quickly from sea level. Much of this hill area is RSPB reserve where protected birdlife includes red-throated divers, hen harriers and short-eared owls. Peat underlies most of the heather here and it is cut around May time from peat banks clearly visible from the road.

There is an opportunity to take a minor road running parallel but slightly west of the main road from Finstown. This passes **Langalour** after about 2 miles (3km), a nineteenth-century Orkney farm complete with neuk beds which was originally a longhouse shared by both the farmer's family and their animals.

A few more miles along this road, a T-junction gives the option of travelling west to Loch of Harray or east to the coast. The west road will take you near towards **Corrigall** Farm Museum created in a restored nineteenth-century farm. The east road leads to Rendall where the Doocot is a fine example of a dovecot.

Across Eynhallow Sound from Rousay, in the parish of Evie, is the **Broch of Gurness**, one of the best preserved brochs in Orkney, dating from the first century. A road leads inland from here across the Birsay Moors towards **Dounby**, where there are basic facilities (hotel, fuel). Nearby there is also the popular Fursbreck Pottery which runs a mail order service as well as a small garden centre within an old Victorian manse, specialising in Orkney-grown alpines. The road passes the Click Mill, a horizontal waterwheel-driven mill no longer in use but still in tact.

Staying on the coast road (A966) **Burgar Hill** now appears, the site of three experimental wind generators first erected in 1983. The A966 now becomes A967 as it heads down the west coast, a little inland; there are minor roads closer to the coastline which many may prefer. The west coast is bounded by the Atlantic and has some spectacular and accessible cliff scenery with associated coves and stacks.

The Brough of Birsay is cut off by the tide and opening times vary accordingly. The attractions are the remains of early Norse and Christian settlements. It was one of the most important Viking sites in the British Isles where Thorfinn the Mighty once had a palace. After a pilgrimage to Rome in 1050 he also built a church here, although there is some debate locally as to where it stood.

The stark remains of the Earl's Palace by Birsay Bay date from the late sixteenth century, built by the unpopular Earl Robert Stewart. Nearby is Boardhouse Mill which is water powered, still operational and open to visitors. It produces 'Bere-meal' from the traditional four-rowed barley and it is in the right place as Birsay has been described as 'the garden of Orkney' being highly regarded for its cereal crop. At **Kirbuster**, east of Loch Boardhouse, there is another farm museum in a restored nineteenth-century farmhouse containing stone neuk beds and a central fireplace. South of the Birsay Bay is **Marwick Head** on which stands a memorial to Lord Kitchener who drowned in 1916 when *HMS Hampshire* sank off the headland with the loss of all but twelve of the crew.

The Ring of Brodgar stone circle at Stenness

At Sandwick the coastal B9056 road nears **Skara Brae**, the famous 3,000-year-old Stone Age village, which is in a remarkable state of preservation providing a clear glimpse of life in neolithic times. It was uncovered by a storm in 1850 and has since been excavated. The houses contain stone furnishings, fire places and drainage.

The B9056 becomes the B9055 as it approaches **Stenness**, east of Stromness and passes two important prehistoric sites. The Ring of Brodgar stone circle once contained 60 stones, of which 36 now remain upright or as broken stumps. It is about 5,000 years old, as is Maes Howe, Western Europe's finest chambered tomb. It was raided by the Vikings in the twelfth century. The collection of runic inscriptions found within is the largest at one site in the world. Neighbouring Tormiston Mill contains an exhibition centre with shop and refreshments.

Stromness is Orkney's second largest settlement and has been popular throughout history thanks largely to its sheltered natural deep water harbour. A castle at Cairston is recorded in the *Orkneyinga Saga*, which reports that in September 1152 Harald Maddadson took refuge from cousin Erlend there. The first village began to develop in the 1620s when the Bishop of Orkney issued feus on the steep west side of the harbour. Land measuring 240ft (73m) of land was available at a feu of 24 chickens. By 1627 the church at Cairston had a recorded 480 communicants.

Stromness boomed throughout the eighteenth century as it was located on a major passageway west while the English Channel was unsafe due to European Wars between 1688 and 1815. That being said there was strong danger from pirates via this northern route. Most infamous was John Gow, a resident of Stromness and the inspiration of Sir Walter Scott's book, *The Pirate*. Also at that time the Hudson Bay Company recruited in the area and the whaling industry grew rapidly. Captain Cook's boats *Discovery* and *Resolution* called at Stromness en route back from the South Seas in 1780 where the captain had been killed.

By 1821 Stromness had a population nearing 3,000 and a main street that narrowed to only 4ft (1m) wide at Porteous Brae, which led to a complaint from Sir Walter Scott on a visit in 1814 that he could not get a cart through the street. St Peter's Church was built the same year to accommodate a congregation of 1,200; today this is a community hall.

The population peaked at 3,200 shortly before World War I with the herring boom coming to an end. The temperance movement gained support and the town was declared 'dry' from 1920 to 1947 by local referendum. Current prosperity continues to rely on the sea, with a roll-on roll-off ferry terminal and fishing fleet. There are numerous points of interest, too many to list here, but a leaflet is available from the tourist office. They include The Whitehouse, built in 1680 and so named because it was the first house in the then village to be built of lime mortar rather than clay. Captain Bligh dined here when Captain Cook's ships called in 1780, befriending George Stewart who lived there and served on *HMS Bounty* during the 1789 mutiny. Stewart was later immortalised in Byron's poem *Torquil*.

The Pier Arts Centre was formerly owned by Edward Clouston, The Hudson Bay Company's recruitment agent in 1836. They were renovated in 1987 and now house a collection of twentieth-century British art. Inland from here is the spot where Bessie Miller sold 'fair winds' to sailors 200 years ago. She was immortalised as 'Norna of the Fitful Head' by Sir Walter Scott in *The Pirate*.

Hoy, Graemsay, Flotta and South Walls

The dramatic summits of Ward Hill and the Cuilags of Hoy are in contrast to most of low flat Orkney and can be seen from many places on the mainland. Indeed the name **Hoy** means 'High Island'. It is the second largest island in Orkney and contains some of the most dramatic scenery. The sandstone that makes up much of the island is joined horizontally and vertically which has resulted in some spectacular coastal features, culminating in the famous 449ft (137m) high Old Man of Hoy and the 1,135ft (346m) vertical cliffs at St John's Head, some of the highest in Britain. Some of the other stacks still contain the remains of old hermit dwellings on their summits.

Taking the ferry to the north of Hoy from Stromness on the mainland, you are likely to stop briefly at **Graemsay** which lies between the sounds of Clestrain and Burra in the western entry of Scapa Flow. Two of the most interesting features of the island are its lighthouses completed in 1851, works of art rather than utilitarian, Alan Stevenson's design at Hoy High is a white 108ft (33m) tower tapering to a balcony supported by Gothic arches. The light room under the lantern has brass ventilators adorned with the heads of Wind Gods and the keepers' houses at the foot of the tower are built in a style similar to Assyrian temples!

The B9047 runs down the sheltered east coast of Hoy, starting near the Moaness Pier where the ferry will arrive. **Ward Hill** which towers above this point is the highest hill in Orkney (1,571ft/479m) and from here every island in Orkney can be seen, and sometimes even Fair Isle 60 miles (97km) away, but not Rysa Little which is the closest one.

A road leads a short way to the north of the island and the Broch of **Braebister**, an Iron Age fort built some 2,000 years ago. Mounds 6 to 9tf (1 to 3m) high still stand there.

Heading southwards there is a turning right to the south of Ward Hill which is the only road across to the west coast of Hoy and the settlement at **Rackwick**, thought by many to be one of the most beautiful spots on Orkney. Otters may be seen here. It is a 90 minute walk (steep in places) from Rackwick to the **Old Man of Hoy** on a marked footpath. This 450ft (137m) high stack was first climbed in 1966 by a team led by Chris Bonnington. Further north on the coast is St John's Head, one of Britain's highest cliffs at 1,135ft (346m).

Soon after turning on to the Rackwick road you will pass a large block of sandstone standing out from the landscape. This is the **Dwarfie Stane**, to the south of the road. This is the only example of a rock cut tomb in Britain (there is another in the Wicklow Mountains, south of Dublin) and is some 3,000 years old. The entrance leads to a short passage with two chambers off.

The Dwarfie Stane is well known in Norse mythology and its name refers to the belief that dwarves tunnelled into rock. The stone was made famous in Sir Walter Scott's *The Pirate* where it is described as the favoured residence of Trolld, a dwarf mentioned in the *Northern Sagas*.

Between Rackwick and the Dwarfie Stane on the north side of the road, **Berriedale Wood** is the most northerly natural woodland in Britain. Orkney's only hazel trees are here along with rowan, birch and aspen. It is likely that woodland of this type was prevalent across Orkney 5,000 years ago.

Back on the east coast and driving south on the B9047 you pass the lonely grave of Betty Corrigall, a young girl left pregnant and deserted by a visiting sailor in the nineteenth century. She took her own life, and therefore had to be buried on the parish boundary rather than in the graveyard. The grave is across the road from Scad Head viewpoint where there is an excellent panorama of Scapa Flow.

Lyness contains the famous but now abandoned naval base and cemetery. There is much here for anyone interested in naval history, warfare and in particular Scapa Flow. The cemetery contains some of the dead from the Battle of Jutland, others from several of the major wartime sinkings (*HMS Hampshire, HMS Vanguard, HMS Royal Oak*) and two of the first three German airmen shot down in World War II. In the deserted base itself the pump house has been converted into an interpretation centre where the history of Lyness can be relived. Today the view includes Elf's huge oil terminal and usually oil tankers of all nationalities.

The road now does a loop around North Bay to **South Walls**, passing the Martello Towers and Longhope Battery built on each side of Longhope Bay. These were constructed between 1813 and 1815 to protect Baltic convoys from the American Navy and priva-teers. Each tower contained foundations for twenty-four pounder cannons, as well as gunners quarters. They were renovated in 1866 and operational in World War I.

The bay on the east coast of South Walls is **Osmondwall**, leading in to Kirk Hope. This was Asmundavagr, a favourite shelter for Viking ships. It is famous for being the location of the forcible baptism of Jarl Sigurd the Stout in AD955 by King Olaf Tryggvason. Although seen by many to be an important event in Orkney's early Christian history, it is unlikely that Jarl Sigurd could be considered a true convert as he only went through with the ceremony after being given the choice of that or decapitation by King Olaf, and he contin-ued to display raven symbols of the Norse god Odin long afterwards.

Nearby is the Longhope Lifeboat Memorial to the eight man crew of the *T.G.B.* boat, lost with all eight crew in 1969 while trying to rescue the crew of a Liberian vessel in the Pentland Firth. The lifeboat station, situated at Brims in South Walls, was established in 1834 and has saved over 500 lives.

Lamb Holm, Glimps Holm, Burray, Hunda, Swona and South Ronaldsay

The southernmost point of **South Ronaldsay**, **Brough Ness**, also the southernmost point of the Orkney Islands, is only 5 miles (8km) from the mainland at Duncansby Head. A passenger ferry links the island to John O'Groats in the summer months. At the northern end causeways link South Ronaldsay to the Orkney mainland via Burray, Glimps Holm and Lamb Holm.

The causeway links between the islands are known as the Churchill Barriers, and they were constructed by hundreds of Italian prisoners of war, imprisoned at Camp 60 on **Lamb Holm** and others during World War II. They were properly paid and allowed radios and bicycles after Italy's capitulation in 1943. One of the camp's sixty prisoners, Domenico Chiocchetti, created what is now known as the Italian Chapel on the island, turning a Nissen hut into a church, the result is absolutely incredible, especially considering Chiocchetti's circumstances and resources. He returned to repair the building, using public donations, in 1960.

The causeways blocked the eastern entrance to world famous Scapa Flow, and the wrecks of 'block ships' sunk as temporary barriers prior to the construction of the causeways can still be seen. Their 4 year, £2.5 million construction involved over a million cubic metres of rock, topped with more than 50,000 concrete blocks. Construction required specially built power stations, railways and even an overhead cableway brought back from Iraq, where it had been used to construct a bridge over the Tigris. Construction had been first mooted in World War I, but was eventually given the go ahead after the sinking of *HMS Royal Oak* in 1939 by a U-boat, causing the loss of 833 crew. Now an official war grave, memorial services are held annually by the navy above the wreck.

The main settlement on **Burray**, **Burray Village**, was a small herring station in the late nineteenth century, but the name derives from the Old Norse 'Brochs-isle' suggesting that its history is as old as the rest of Orkney. Echnaloch and Echnaloch Bay are rich with wildfowl and there is a wonderful sandy bay. The isle of **Hunda** is popular with those animals and birds that do well in areas of minimal human habitation, in this case otters, seals and Arctic terns.

South Ronaldsay's main settlement is in the north of the island at **St Margaret's Hope**, an attractive village with houses dating from the seventeenth and eighteenth centuries. The pier was originally built in the seventeenth century for lobster fishing. The village gets its name from the unfortunate Margaret, Maid of Norway, who was

The interior of the Italian Chapel on Lamb Holm

en route to marry Prince Edward, later King Edward II of England, when she died here in November 1290. She had been proclaimed Queen on the death of her grandfather, Alexander III of Scotland when she was only 7 years old. Her death was a major factor in the Wars of Independence at that time. The 'Hope' of the village's name does not reflect any aspirations of poor Margaret however, but is from the Old Norse *Hjop* meaning Bay. On the third Saturday in August each year a little festival takes place when a parade of brightly dressed girls and boys is followed by the Boy's Ploughing Match using miniature ploughs. There are also two museums in the village, one the Orkney Wireless Museum, the other an Old Smiddy Museum.

To the west lies sheltered Widewall Bay and the Sands O'Right beach. At the north end is a ruined broch, burial site of Earl Thorfinn Skull Splitter in AD963. The headland nearby is Hoxa Head which contains a lighthouse and some impressive defences from both World Wars.

Churchill Barriers blocked the eastern entrance to the world famous Scapa Flow

Block ships were deliberately sunk as temporary barriers to the entrance of Scapa Flow in wartime

Oban's picturesque harbour (Chapter 11)

St Oran's Chapel is the oldest surviving building on Iona, dating from the twelfth century. In the background is the main abbey (Chapter 11)

Easdale Island (Chapter 11)

Following the west coast south of Widewall Bay, Harrabrough Head is a good site for puffin spotters. At **Castle of Burwick** near the south of the isle, 2,000 year old fortifications can still be seen. Nearby St Mary's Church contains the site of one of the earliest chapels on Orkney and an interesting stone with two footprints carved on it. You may also see a disused Victorian school constructed at the bequest of William Tomlinson (1739-1829) who made a fortune working for the Hudson's Bay Company. On the east coast the Tomb of The Eagles is a fine stalled chambered tomb dating back to around 3000BC. The name comes from the claws of many sea eagles found there in excavations. Windwick Bay is popular with the seals once again, who may have pups there in the autumn.

The abandoned island of **Swona**, off the south-west corner of South Ronaldsay, is inhabited by a herd of now wild cattle. There is an interesting difference in the flora and fauna as a result, with rich pastures and wild flowers in the summer, compared to the close nibbled land left by the more common flocks of sheep. There are automatic light beacons at each end of the island.

Shapinsay, Thieves Holm and Helliar Holm

Shapinsay is a low island lying a few miles north of Kirkwall across a stretch of deep water called The String. The ferry journey takes 25 minutes and passes the small island of **Thieves Holm** (to the west) which used to house thieves and witches, but today only ornithologists are incarcerated there. The ferry reaches Shapinsay through Elwick Bay, where Viking King Hakon sheltered 100 of his ships in 1263 before setting off for the battle of Largs in Ayrshire and the final defeat of the Vikings in Scotland.

The major feature of Shapinsay, and indeed one of Orkney's major architectural achievements, is **Balfour Castle**. This is generally identified as a Victorian building but is in fact a Victorian extension of an eighteenth-century house. The previous building on the site, Cliffdale, had been burnt down by the Hanoverians in 1746 after the then owner had supported the Jacobite cause. Much of the Balfour Estates, which cover most of Shapinsay, had been gifted to the Balfour family (who originated in Fife) by the Bishop of Orkney in 1560. In 1796 half of the island was bought by John Balfour from money he made in India, for £1,200. The other half was bought by David Balfour in 1847 for £14,000. He had architect David Bryce enlarge the house to its current size. The Balfour Estate was sold to the Zawadski family earlier in the twentieth century, and they purchased the house in

1961 when the last of the Balfour family died without heirs (despite having had four wives). There are twice weekly tours of the castle organised from Kirkwall and the castle now accepts paying guests who can will enjoy the wonderful variety of fruit and vegetables grown in the castle gardens.

Balfour village, once called Shoreside, dates originally from the seventeenth century but grew with the estate which employed the residents as estate workers and suppliers. The look of the island was completely changed by David Balfour between 1848 and 1874, as he increased cultivated farm land from 700 to 6,000 acres, mainly divided up into square 10 acre (4 hectare) fields. Over 1,500 cattle and 2,000 sheep, including many prize winners, are exported from the island annually. Away from the agriculture and around the coasts however, plenty of wildlife continues to thrive.

Elsewhere on Shapinsay there is an excellent old water mill, and a mid-eighteenth-century gas works, both now disused, as are the World War II gun emplacements at Salt Ness on the west coast. There are also examples of 'ayres', strips of sea water totally cut off from the sea by narrow necks of land. The father of Washington Irving, the first internationally famous American writer, was born in the north of the island at Quholme; he emigrated to New York in 1763. The farm at East Lairo contains prize winning goats who will allow you to bottle feed their kids and sample their cheese. The uninhabited island of **Helliar Holm**, south of Shapinsay, contains broch, chapel site and cairn as well as an automatic lighthouse.

Rousay, Egilsay and Wyre

Rousay's hills, purple in summer, are easy to see from the mainland. Once again many bird species make the island their permanent or migratory home. Man too, has been here for thousands of years and there are over 100 archaeological sites, many well preserved.

The most famous is the **Midhowe** chambered cairn or 'Great Ship of Death', excavated in the 1930s after which a building was constructed around it. The skeletons of twenty-five people as well as sheep, cattle and deer were found here. Close by are more substantial remains, this time of Midhowe broch, built in a prominent position above Eynhallow sound. South of Midhowe is **Westness Bay** where a famous brooch was found, now spirited away for display at the Royal Museum in Edinburgh.

Rousay's history in more recent years has not been a happy one as it fell victim to the infamous clearances in the nineteenth century. Deserted houses at **Westness** bear testimony to the misery of that time.

The most famous archaeological site on Rousay is the Midhowe chambered tomb

Westness House was the mansion of the Traill family, Lairds of Orkney. The original house was destroyed by Hanoverian forces in 1745 following their Jacobite support, but the laird was later cleared of having Jacobite sympathies and it was rebuilt. The Traills then built Trumland House in 1873 and moved in. The Westness Walk is a unique woodland walk, free to visitors, and is also part of an RSPB reserve. Rousay's attraction to birds of all kinds makes it a magnet for ornithologists also. **Hellia Spur** at the north-west corner is one of Europe's most important seabird colonies, home to puffins, gulls guillemots and razorbills. On the heather slopes inland hen harriers and peregrine falcons may be seen.

The island of **Egilsay**, east of Rousay, contains the church of St Magnus, built about 150 years after his death. The church is unique in that it has a circular tower, now 49ft (15m) high, but probably originally 66ft (20m) with a conical roof. The design shows Irish influence and there were at least two others on Orkney in the past (at Deerness and Stenness). This is the same St Magnus to whom the famous cathedral in Kirkwall is dedicated. Magnus met his cousin Hakon here on 16 April 1115, having previously agreed that each arrive with two ships full of their men. Hakon was rather naughty in arriving with eight ships, Magnus refused his men's offer to fight to defend him anyway and told Hakon that he would either go to Rome, go to prison in Scotland or be maimed and imprisoned locally. Hakon accepted the last offer but the blood thirsty chiefs demanded Magnus' head. His tomb soom became a place of miracles and pilrimages. A cenotaph was erected in 1937.

On **Wyre** (the name means Arrowhead), a small isle off the southeast of Rousay, there are the remains of the oldest stone castle in Scotland, which has the rather friendly name of 'Cubbie Roos' Castle and dates from the twelfth century. It was probably built by Kolbein Hruga. Nearby is St Mary's Chapel from the same century also thought to have been founded by Kolbein or by his son Bishop Bjarni Kolbeinson.

Stronsay, Papa Stronsay, Auskerry and Linga Holm

Low lying **Stronsay** is about 8 miles (13km) long at maximum, but has been carved up by large bays leaving several peninsulas joined together to make up the isle. The resulting landscape has several beautiful sandy bays and some dramatic cliff coast to the east. A major geological feature in that area is the dramatic cliff opening known as Vat O'Kirbister, which has Orkney's finest natural arch above it. Nearby are three stacks with the remains of religious hermitage sites on top of each.

Stronsay's history is similar to that of many of the Orkney isles, having an eighteenth-century kelp boom which saw the island's population reach 3,000. James Fea of Whitehall on Stronsay was the first man in Orkney to produce kelp in 1722 and a particularly well preserved kelp kiln can be visited on Papa Stronsay, a short boat trip from Whitehall.

Papa Stronsay contains two medieval chapel sites and at the height of the herring fishing boom could be reached on a Sunday by walking across the decks of ships harboured between it and Whitehall on Stronsay. Norse Earl Rognvald Brusison was killed here in 1046, while he was fetching malt to celebrate Yueltide.

Whitehall was also a major herring fishing port during that industry's boom period in the 1900s, having 300 boats tied up at peak periods. The village takes its name from a house built there in the 1670s by Patrick Fea in Charles II's reign.

Stronsay is rich in bird life, flora and archaeological relics. The latter include brochs at Lamb Ness, Burgh Head and Hilloch of Baywest. Some particularly interesting flora is to be found growing by the Pow, a track which leads to the Bay of Houseby at the south of the island. These include some white thistles, a naturalised plant belonging to Southern Chile and Patagonia.

The small island of **Auskerry** 3 miles (5km) south of Stronsay is a breeding site for many seabirds including puffins, arctic terns and a large number of storm petrels. There are a large number of archaeological remains here. The island of **Linga Holm** to the west is popular with common seals, and with grey seals in October and November. It is now a reserve for the rare North Ronaldsay sheep.

Eday and Calf of Eday

Eday, 14 miles (23km) north of Kirkwall, is centrally situated within the six largest isles north of the Orkney mainland. Its name in Old Norse is 'Eid-e' meaning 'Land of the Isthmus'. It differs in landscape from the others in that it is hilly, especially at its southern end, which is largely peat and heather covered. The inhabitants live mostly in the fertile coastal plain. Otherwise there are many similarities to the rest of the isles as one would expect. There is the same richness of birdlife and achaeological remains, most notably the Stone of Setter, probably the finest of its type in Orkney.

It is likely that Eday was much more extensively farmed and was more arable in prehistoric time; ancient stone walls have been found beneath the peat. The island's rock has long been in high regard in the islands too, with much of the stone used to construct St Magnus' Cathedral coming from here.

The major house on the island is at **Carrick**. The famous Orcadian pirate John Gow reached the end of his working life when he set out to raid the house in February 1725. His ship ran ashore en route and when he sought help he was overpowered and ended up being executed in London a few years later. The house probably dates from 1633, the date on the courtyard gateway.

The small **Calf of Eday** contains numerous ancient remains including a stalled cairn, Iron Age houses and chambered tombs. There is also one of the United Kingdom's best surviving seventeenth-century saltworks. It is thought that they began operating in the eighteenth century. The Faray Isles, west of Eday, are uninhabited except by sheep, grey seals and storm petrels.

Westray and Papa Westray

The 2 minute flight between Westray and Papa Westray is believed to be the world's shortest scheduled air service. About 700 people live on the larger isle making it the largest populated of the northern Orkney islands. This success in population retention stems largely from the modernisation of traditional farming and fishing, which has enabled the islanders to produce some of the best livestock you will find anywhere, and Orkney's largest white-fishing fleet.

Once again there are numerous ancient sites to visit, and a major find was made in one as recently as 1981 when the richly carved 'Westray Stone' was found, dating to 3000BC. This has now been moved for permanent display in Tankerness House Museum, Kirkwall. Westray families supported the invasion of a second generation of Vikings in 1137. Other visitors from far away who settled here were survivors from the Spanish *Armada* when, in 1588, a damaged boat sought refuge in Pietowall Harbour.

Other ancient remains include those of more small monastic communities on the precipitous rock stack of Castle of Burrian. More recent is Noltland Castle, erected by Gilbert Balfour who held high office under Mary Queen of Scots. According to tradition the castle is linked by underground passage to the Gentleman's Cave on the west side of the island.

Westray is another paradise for hikers and bird watchers with a particularly popular walk from Noup Head lighthouse. The RSPB reserve contains the largest nesting site for guillemots known anywhere.

Off the north-east corner of Westray lies **Papa Westray** or Papay, only 4 miles (6km) long and 1 mile (2km) wide. But limited size does not mean limited in features, as 6,000 pairs of nesting Arctic terns, the largest concentration in Europe, will testify! Nor does it mean a lack of historical remains. The Knapp of Howar has been certified the oldest surviving domestic structure in north-west Europe and the chambered cairn at Holm of Papay is older than the better known Maes Howe on Orkney mainland. There are two chapels on the island, dedicated to St Boniface and St Tredwell. It is possible that the Roman missionary St Boniface, whom historians believe came in to conflict with the Celtic clergy, may have fled the Pictish Court and come to live on Papay.

Sanday

Sanday has many of the attractions of the other northern Orkney islands and, like Stronsay, is made up of a number of interlinking peninsulars with some beautiful beaches within the bays. Sixteen miles (26km) long and with a population of 550 this is one of the largest of the northern isles, it is also one of the richest in archaeological remains. The neolithic chambered tomb at **Quoyness**, dating from 2000BC, is regarded as one of Orkneys finest. A group of over 300 prehistoric burial mounds at **Tafts Ness** may be some of the most important in the United Kingdom. A find of a Viking burial ship in the early 1990s was regarded as the archaeological discovery of the decade by some experts. The ninth-century occupants were complete with rare items to take with them en route to Valhalla, the Norse afterlife. The find was uncovered and soon afterwards destroyed by winter storms.

Sanday had an early attraction for the Vikings who liked the sheltered sandy bays to beach their longboats. They made the island in to the granary of Orkney at that time, even exporting grain to Shetland. Today the farming is for beef, there is also a small fishing fleet and 140 home based knitters have formed a co-operative producing Fair Isle designs. The work is centred at the Wool Hall in **Lady Village** where visitors are welcome by prior arrangement. Again this is an island for ornithologists, among the rare sitings here was a North African trumpeter finch in 1981, only the third to be recorded in the United Kingdom.

North Ronaldsay

North Ronaldsay is the most northerly and most remote Orkney isle and maintains traditions more than any other. The island is only 4 miles (6km) long by 2 miles (3km) wide, but is an important stopping off point for migrating birds including many rare varieties. North Ronaldsay is totally surrounded by a 13 mile (21km) stone dyke. The sheep are kept on the shoreline and live on seaweed, except at lambing time. The collective farming of them is one of the last remaining parts of communal farming in Orkney. Seaweed, washed ashore by strong tides, has played a valuable part in the islands history. At the height of the kelp boom in the eighteenth century the population was five times what it is today. There was also a good indigenous fishing fleet, now largely defeated by commercial trawlers.

The only concentration of trees on the island is in the gardens of Holland House, originally built by the Traill family who bought the island in 1727. Three cannons, rescued from the wreck of the *Crown Prince* in 1744 stand on permanent guard. This is one of many wrecks around the island, which has submerged skerries to the north and a reef to the south. The Traill family's direct descendants still reside in

Holland House and it was the Traill Laird in 1907 who built the windmill which is believed to be among the last working windmills in Scotland. The previous mill fell in to disuse after the grinding stone split and killed the miller.

There are several ancient remains on the island including a 13ft (4m) high standing stone, unusual in that it has a hole through its upper part. There is also the remains of a broch at Burrian which was occupied by the Picts at least until the ninth century AD. The Burrian Cross, an early Christian symbol, was found carved in to a stone here.

Further Information
— Orkney Isles —

Places to Visit

Birsay
Brough of Birsay
Details as for Maes Howe, Stenness.

Kirbuster Farm Museum
Open: May to September, Monday to Saturday.

Harray
Corrigall Farm and Folk Museum
Open: March to September, 10.30am-1pm and 2-5pm. Sundays 2-7pm.

Fursbreck Pottery
☎ 0856 77419
Open: Monday to Friday 10am-6pm, 2-6pm Sundays.
Occasionally closed for lunch on Mondays and Wednesdays only from 12.30-1.30pm.

Old Manse Garden Centre
Open: Tuesday to Sunday, 2-6pm.

Holm
Norwood Antiques
Open: May to September, Sunday, Wednesday and Thursday afternoons.

Kirkwall
Bishop's Palace
Details as for Meas Howe, Stenness, except Palace closed October to March.

Earl's Palace
Details as for Meas Howe, Stenness, below, except Palace closed October to March.

Highland Park Distillery
Holm Road
☎ 0856 874619 Fax 0856 876091
Open: all year. Monday to Fridays, 10.20am-4pm. Tours every 30 minutes except November to Easter when tour at 2.30pm only. Open Saturdays in July and August.

Tankerness House Museum
Broad Street
Kirkwall
Open: all year, Monday to Saturday, 10.30am-12.30pm and 1.30-5pm. Open Sundays, May to September, 2-5pm.

Sanday
Wool Hall
Lady
☎ (Sanday) 08575 367 to arrange visit.

Shapinsay
Balfour Castle
☎ 0856 71 282
Open: Sunday and Wednesday afternoons.

East Lairo Goat Farm
☎ 0856 71 341
Open: Friday to Wednesday, 2-4pm.

Shapinsay Community Enterprises
☎ 0856 71 283
Open: every day during summer.

South Ronaldsay
Orkney Wireless Museum
St Margaret's Hope
☎ 0856 83462
Open: April to September daily 10am-7pm.

Skara Brae
Details as for Maes Howe, Stenness.

Stenness
Maes Howe and Tormiston Mill
☎ 031 244 3101 (Historic Scotland, Edinburgh)
Open: April to September, Monday to Saturday, 9.30am-6.30pm, Sunday 2-6.30pm.
October to March, as above but close 4pm. Last ticket sold 30 minutes before close.

Stromness
Stromness Museum
52 Alfred Street
Open: Monday to Saturday, 10.30am-1pm and 2-5pm.

Tourist Information Offices
Kirkwall
Orkney Tourist Board
Broad Street
☎ 0856 872856
Fax: 0856 875056

Stromness
Orkney Tourist Board
Ferry Terminal Building
☎ 0856 850716
Fax: 0856 850777

Travel
British Airways Express
☎ 0856 872494
Tourist multi-trip tickets to numerous islands are normally available.
Additional British Airways Services from mainland UK.

Kirkwall
Orkney Islands Shipping Company Limited
4 Ayre Road
Orkney
KW15 1QX
☎ 0856 872044
Fax: 0856 872921
Services between all the major islands, mini cruises also arranged. Also P&O Services from Aberdeen.

John G Shearer & Sons Car Hire
Ayre service Station
Burnmouth Road
Orkney
KW15 1QY
☎ 0856 872950
Fax: 0856 875460

St Ola
Go Orkney
South Cannigall
☎ 0856 874260

14 • Shetland

Due to its geographical position Shetland is frequently associated first with Orkney, and then with Scotland. While it is fair to say Shetlanders have a shared Viking heritage with Orkney, as well as parts of north-east Scotland and indeed isles away to the north such as the Faroes and Iceland, the similarities do not run much deeper. The Shetland landscape is much more reminiscent of the northern Scottish Highlands, peat covered and treeless, than fertile Orkney. The people of Shetland themselves differ in many ways from the 'clannish' Scots. It is therefore a common misconception to think of the Shetlands as Scottish island; which they have never really been. Indeed, as the first Scottish rulers treated Shetland very badly, there is sometimes some resentment of the islands' southern 'owners'.

Shetland measures 95 miles (153km) from north to south, and nearly 50 miles (80 1/2km) from east to west. That being said, you can never be more than 3 miles (5km) from the sea anywhere in Shetland. Even the widest bits of land are cut into by long narrow 'voes', what would be called fjords in Scandinavia. The voes, cliffs, stacks and reefs that surround the islands make them a nightmare for shipping and there are known to be over 1,500 wrecks lying in the waters offshore. This, combined with largely clear and unpolluted sea, makes Shetland a heavenly place for divers with clear visibility in up to 66ft (20m) depth. Another common error is to refer to the islands as the 'Shetlands'. Although there are about one hundred islands (of which fifteen are inhabited), this is either 'Shetland', or the 'Shetland Islands'. The name probably derives from the Norse 'Haltyeland' meaning 'Land of Retreat'.

Shetland was part of the Scandinavian empire for nearly 700 years. That rule came to an end when the islands were pawned to Scotland by Christian I, King of Denmark and Norway, to pay the dowry for his daughter Margaret's wedding to King James III of Scotland. They were never actually sold to Scotland so may still be considered 'in hock' from Scandinavia! Indeed although the events

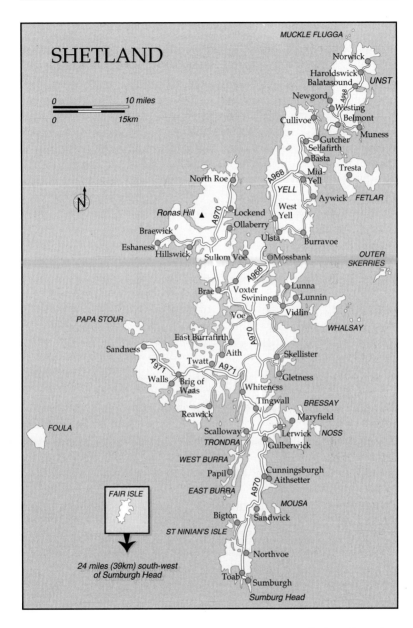

SHETLAND

0   10 miles

0   15km

MUCKLE FLUGGA

Norwick

Haroldswick
Balatasound   UNST

Newgord

Westing

Cullivoe   Belmont

Muness

Gutcher
Sellafirth

Basta   Tresta

North Roe   A968   Mid-
             YELL   Yell

West   Aywick   FETLAR
Yell

Ronas Hill ▲ Lockend

Braewick   Ollaberry

Ulsta

Eshaness   Burravoe

Hillswick   Sullom Voe   OUTER
                 Mossbank   SKERRIES

A968

Brae   Voxter   Lunna
    Swining   Lunnin

Voe   Vidlin

PAPA STOUR   WHALSAY

East Burrafirth

Sandness   Aith   Skellister

A971   Twatt   A971

Walls   Brig of   Gletness
     Waas   Whiteness

Tingwall   BRESSAY

Reawick   Maryfield

FOULA

Scalloway   Lerwick   NOSS
TRONDRA   Gulberwick

WEST BURRA

Papil   Cunningsburgh
        Aithsetter

EAST BURRA   A970

MOUSA

Bigton   Sandwick

ST NINIAN'S ISLE

FAIR ISLE

Northvoe

24 miles (39km) south-west
of Sumburgh Head

Toab   Sumburgh

Sumburg Head

took place in 1469, Shetland probably retains more of a Scandinavian feel than a Scottish one. There is little tartan to be seen or the other badges of 'Scottishness' paraded in Scotland. Most of Shetland's 50,000 place names are Norse, and although the Shetland dialect is

The famous
Shetland pony

basically lowland Scots, about 10,000 words of Scandinavian origin remain. The islands were inhabited for several thousand years before the Norsemen arrived, but virtually all place names and language still dates from this period. The Romans actually sailed up to the islands 2,000 years ago, decided that they were the end of the world and thus named them 'Ultima Thule' meaning 'The Final Frontier'.

Shetland is arguably the most friendly place in Britain, with some of the most open minded people. Perhaps living daily with the realities (and wonders) of nature, including the extremes of weather, and being surrounded by unfriendly seas, has led the islanders to see beyond petty prejudices. One tourist magazine sums up the usual attitude to visitors with the words, 'Welcome to Shetland, it is good of you to visit us and we are pleased to have you share our home for a while.' Few tourist brochures elsewhere are so honest, straight-forward and friendly!

The islands' location does have an upside, with nearly 19 hours of sunshine in late June (and a comparable amount of darkness in mid-winter). The months around the longest day are the driest and the islands do benefit to some extent from the Gulf Stream, being a little warmer on the whole than they might be otherwise considering their 60 degree latitude. Shetland is 200 miles (322km) from Aberdeen, or Bergen in Norway or the Faroes; it is as far away from London as are Bilbao in Spain, Milan in Italy or Nice in the south of France. It is also as easy to reach as these places from, London with direct flights and no customs formalities!

Traditionally the islanders survived on knitting, fishing and crofting but had a big boost in the early 1970s with the advent of the North Sea Oil Industry. The knitting industry is perhaps most characteristic of Shetland. It developed from the production of coarse cloth from the wool of sheep brought in by the Norse settlers and used as part payment of land tax to the Norwegian king. By the seventeenth century this was a cottage industry, particularly noted for producing stockings (it is recorded that 50,000 pairs valued at 6d each were exported in 1790). This was a time when thousands of Dutch fishermen descended each year on the islands as a base for herring fishing and they, together with other European nationals, formed a ready market. Today it is the Fair Isle designs that are most famous.

Another famous Shetland feature is the Shetland pony. Although there are no records of when the ponies arrived and where they came from, a pre-Viking Pictish stone depicting a horse with rider is seen as evidence that they were roaming the hills long before the arrival of the Vikings. While the eighteenth and nineteenth century saw sheep replacing people in Scotland a law of 1847 saw Shetland ponies replacing children as workers in the coal mines. Many descended into the darkness never to see the light of day again. The Marquis of Londonderry was one man with mining interests who started a stud on the islands to supply the pits with Shetland ponies.

Most of the ponies on the United Kingdom mainland are descended from these pit ponies and are black in colour, the ponies who are still on the islands are likely to be lighter coloured and slightly lighter build. Historically the ponies roamed the hills on common grazing land. This is still the case on some of the outlying islands but many crofters have now fenced in their sections of the common grazings. With Shetland's extremes of weather the beasts had to be hardy and, like the sheep, are able to generate high nutrient value from scant vegetation. They may also drink sea water to gain more minerals.

The Mainland

The main town, in fact really the only town in Shetland, is **Lerwick**, and it is here that the P&O ferries arrive from Aberdeen (flights arrive at Sumburgh, about 25 miles/40km south, and mostly depart to the islands off Shetland mainland from Tingwall, 5 miles/8km east.

The name Lerwick is inevitably of Norse origin, *leirvik* has the rather unflattering translation of 'muddy inlet'. The Norse name was presumably given while the Norsemen ruled, although the town did not exist until 1590, years after the islands were pawned. The Norse based language did survive in the remoter parts of Shetland until the late eighteenth century however. In any case there is certainly not much mud to be seen there now. Instead the town centre is huddled along a semi-pedestrianised main thoroughfare (Commercial Street), with a main road following the harbour side. This is the original and most scenic part of the town. Beneath it there are many old tunnels leading to the harbour and used by smugglers in former centuries. Newer suburbs stretch out for a few miles on several sides of the town. Lerwick's harbour is very impressive, often filled with a wide variety of boats from passenger liners and bulk carriers to ocean-going yachts. All take refuge from the Atlantic in the peaceful bay, sheltered by the isle of Bressay.

There are many places of interest around the town, most easily reached on foot. These include the substantial remains of a 2,000-year-old Pictish broch at the south end of Clickimin Loch (looking rather odd with the modern housing estate so close). The broch was originally sited on an islet in the loch, but the level of the loch was lowered in the nineteenth century and the islet became part of the shore. Settlement there dates back to 700BC and unusual features include two entrances rather than one. More recent and more central to Lerwick is the Town Hall, built in 1982 and still used by the council. In the hall upstairs there are several stained glass windows, one of which commemorates the marriage of King James III to Norwegian Princess Margaret in 1468. There is also a good view of Lerwick and beyond from the roof!

Across the road is the Shetland Library and Museum, which contains exhibits tracing the islands' history from the beginning. Other exhibitions are to be found in the summer months in the Isleburgh Community Centre on King Harald Street, which contains old photographs of the town. Shetland's various fiddler bands tend to practice here as well, and visitors are normally welcome. The Galley Shed houses an exhibition of the Up-Helly-A' Viking festival still maintained annually in Shetland. This 'fire festival' involves 900 disguised men carrying flaming torches behind a replica Viking longship and attracts visitors and Shetland exiles from all over the world. Trips on a replica longship are also possible. The Scottish Women's Rural Institute (SWRI) regularly demonstrate the Shetlander's famous hand knitting skills in St Olaf's hall.

The town's major fortification is Fort Charlotte, designed and constructed by John Mylne for King Charles II in 1665. It was burnt down by the Dutch in 1673 and rebuilt in 1782. The fort once housed twenty cannon and is now the local Territorial Army headquarters; it is also open to the public. Finally the Bod of Gremista is the restored eighteenth-century fishing booth of Arthur Anderson. He was co-founder of the P&O shipping company.

The Shetland mainland can be divided into four approximate parts from Lerwick: the south, west, north-east and north-west. The south route is generally along the more sheltered east side on the main A970 road to Sumburgh Head. However, by taking the A970 north or the B9073 south, you will quickly reach **Scalloway**, the second settlement of Shetland, on the west coast. Indeed this was once the islands' capital. The castle that dominates the village is that of Earl Patrick Stewart and does not have a happy history. Its construction perhaps marks the low point of Scottish oppression of the Shetlanders when it was built in 1598. The Earl was executed in 1615 and the castle fell into disrepair soon afterwards: he had used the islanders as virtual slave labour in its construction, the story of which is told in an exhibition.

Scalloway prospered in the nineteenth century as a result of cod fishing, the success of which financed the building of many of the village's old houses. In World War II this was also the departure point of British and Norwegian agents for German occupied Norway and there is another exhibition of this operation, known as the Shetland Bus. Modern attractions include a Shetland Woollen Company outlet next to the castle and a Shetland glass factory where glass blowing demonstrations are given. The village is protected from the worst of the weather by Gallow Hill, a former place of execution. The last such act was in 1732 when a mother and daughter, both witches apparently, were burnt at the stake.

South of Scalloway the B9074 crosses two bridges, first on to the isle of Trondra and then to Burra, which have led to population growth. **Burra** is divided by long narrow voes into east and western halves and has several good beaches as well as the usual bird filled cliffs and sea stacks. The famous Papil Pictish stones were found here, the ruined church there dates from the early nineteenth century but was itself built on a monastic settlement. The twelfth-century church of St Lawrence was also built on an earlier site, this time an eighth-century Celtic church. Weaving courses are organised on **Hamnavoe**, the main settlement on West Burra while there is a working croft, open to visitors, on **Trondra**.

Back on the A970 south along the eastern coast of the mainland (a good 10 minute drive away, at a stretch) is **Fladdabister** now a peaceful little hamlet and once a busy village centred on a limestone quarry industry. Two circular kilns remain on a rocky outcrop and there is some prominent grassland that actually originates from grasses brought back from the Falklands by Shetland seafarers long ago. The road then passes the Aithwick Headland, cut into from the south by a voe which provides one of the few safe anchorages on this stretch of the east coast. A Norwegian earl was ship-wrecked nearby in 1143 on a short lived pilgrimage to the Holy Land.

A minor road descends some miles further south along to the A970 to Sandwick. The road south from Cunningsburgh passes an ancient soapstone quarry where kitchenware, fishing weights and similar were produced between Bronze Age and Viking times. Conical mounds in the area are the old spoil heaps from this industry. **Sandwick** is a peaceful fishing village containing Sandlodge, a baronial mansion of the local landowners dating from the eighteenth century (not open to the public). The family formerly ran a copper mine next door for about 200 years until earlier in the twentieth century.

It is from Sandwick that boat trips are organised over to the isle of **Mousa** which contains the best preserved of all brochs, surviving to a height of over 43ft (13m). This longevity may be due to the lack of other settlement in the area — many brochs lost their stone to new buildings nearby and there has been speculation that many if not all brochs were once towers like Mousa. The structure includes a wheelhouse from the third and fourth centuries. The last time it was occupied however is related in the *Orkneyinga Saga*, when Earl Harald sailed from Caithness in 1153 with the object of murdering Erlend the Young who wanted to marry Harald's mother Margaret. Erlend had actually abducted Margaret when Harald had said no to match and had kept her in the broch at Mousa. When Harald arrived he was forced to besiege the broch, it being considered too difficult to attack, and eventually all ended peacefully with Harald accepting the marriage on the understanding that Erlend supported him in his attempt to gain control of the Earldom. *Egil's Saga*, also mentions the broch, as the place sought for shelter by a ship-wrecked couple in AD900.

Gaada Stack, off Foula (Chapter 14)

The Shetland Islands
are home of the
diminutive Shetland
pony (Chapter 14)

On Shetland there is a
richness of birdlife
(Chapter 14)

The peaceful fishing village of Sandwick, Shetland's mainland

Boat trips are organised to the broch, passing seabird and seal colonies and sometimes otters. There is another broch, guarding the other side of the sound's entrance, located at Burraland about 1 mile (2km) south of Sandlodge. The walls of this remain 12ft (4m) high. There are also the remains of a dun in the area, standing 5ft (1½m) high on an islet in Brindister Loch. At nearby Cumliewick Ness there is a blow hole through which the sea makes some very strange noises! Further south at **Hoswick** there is a new exhibition of weaving machines and other Shetland industry with a small tea room and shop, while at **Levenwick** there is a working tweed, rug and scarf maker.

The southern part of Shetland's mainland is one of its most densely populated areas (although 'densely populated' gives the wrong impression of any part of Shetland apart from the seabird colonies on the cliffs). Just south of Channerwick the B9122 makes a loop on to the west coast, only a few miles away, and reaches the remarkable **St Ninian's Isle**, remarkable because it is joined to the land by a unique sandy tombola created by the tide washing around each side of the island. It is very odd to walk along a stretch of sand and have open sea lapping away on each side of you with the waves breaking about 50yd apart. Tombolas are a feature of Shetland's coast, rare in most other parts of the world. St Ninian's Holy Well and Chapel date from the twelfth century although there are also Iron

The great broch on the isle of Mousa

Age and Bronze Age remains. A school boy discovered silver bowls, brochs and other items inscribed with Pictish symbols under a cross engraved slab here in 1958. These are now held at the Royal Museum in Edinburgh, but there are replicas at the Shetland Museum in Lerwick.

The south is reached at **Sumburgh Head** surrealistic place with one of Europe's greatest archaeological sites, a very modern airport and a beautiful beach with turquoise-blue seas all within about 100yd of one another. Add to this the fierce tidal forces south of the head which led the Norsemen to name it 'Dynraustrrnes' or 'Headland of the Roaring Tide' and you have an amazing mix of natural and man-made features.

Jarlshof was much admired by Sir Walter Scott and is remarkable in that there is clear evidence of continual habitation for over 3,000 years in its well preserved shell. These include remnants from settlements in neolithic, Bronze Age, Iron Age, Viking and even seventeenth-century times. There is an interpretation centre adjoining the site. The wonderful sandy beaches of **Quendale Bay** lie along side the site and on a warm day you can paddle in the sea, look up into the blue skies and watch the endless flow of huge helicopters flying out to the oil rigs offshore from Sumburgh. It is possible to explore the area by pony too, with a trekking centre at nearby **Dunrossness**. There are several other ancient sites in the area including brochs at Brough Head, Clumie Loch and Dalsetter near Boddam. **Boddam** also has a museum, contained within a restored nineteenth-century croft house with memorabilia from that period. There is a Norse derived horizontal water mill at the site, these were known as click mills because of the sound they made. North of Lerwick the A970 takes a wide sweep around the valley before beginning its trek northwards towards Sullum Voe or Yell and passing through desolate valleys similar to parts of the north Scottish Highlands.

It passes a side road to **Tingwall** and the west after a few miles (the A971). Tingwall is the location of the main inter-island air strip, 5 miles (8km) from Lerwick. It is named after the original Shetland parliament (in Norse this is 'Ting') and Law Tingholm here at the north end of Tingwall Loch. A standing stone nearby denotes the site where seven men were killed when a session of the parliament became rather violent in 1389. There is also an agricultural museum at nearby **Veensgarth** located in buildings dating from the eighteenth century.

The Loch of Strom is Shetland's largest brackish loch and the ruined castle on it was built by the Sinclairs in the sixteenth century. Nearby is **Hjaltasteyn** where jewellery is hand crafted and includes Shetland gem stones. The A971 now rounds the top of sea loch Weisdale Voe. A road leaves from here for Sandwater and the three storey **Weisdale** Mill, which has been converted into a museum.

The western mainland is covered in small lochs. The coastal village of **Walls** contains one of Shetland's many remarkable old general stores where islanders can buy pretty well anything. They make up orders of groceries for the residents of Foula, carried over twice or more each week by the mail boat which departs from here to the island. There are numerous ancient sites in the area once again, including burnt mounds and many cairns. The village also has its own gold and silver jewellery designers and one of northern Scotland's best vegetarian restaurants. **Sandness** at the end of the A971 has a small industrial estate where Shetland's only woollen spinning mill is located. A ferry can be taken from here to Papa Stour on certain days. The B9071 follows the north-west coast via Aith to Voe. This passes the sheltered sea area of **Swarbacks Minn** where the entire British fleet once anchored in World War I. The island of **Vementry** contains World War II gun emplacements and Shetland's best heel-shaped cairn.

Back on the east coast the A970, a beneficiary of the oil boom, skirts **Loch of Girlsta**, Shetland's largest and deepest and named after Geirhilda the daughter of a Viking, who drowned in it. She is said to be buried on an island at the south end of the loch. The loch contains Arctic char along with other fish species. At the north end of the loch a B road turns eastwards to follow the coast (B9075). This has many war time connections with World War I sea planes landing on Cat Firth and Norwegian refuge boats arriving in the area. This road meets the Aith road described earlier and rejoins the A970 at **Voe**, a village with painted wooden buildings, often described as Scandinavian in style. Its location once made it an important trading post and later a centre of the Norwegian-run whaling industry.

Look out for otters crossing at Sullom Voe, Shetland's mainland

The A970 runs north-west from Voe towards the great oil terminal, and the A968 cuts north-easterly for the Yell ferry terminal.

It is worthwhile going back on to the east coast minor road (B9071) further north and heading on to the remarkable and historic 5 mile (8km) long peninsular of **Lunna Ness** however. The church here dates from 1753, probably the oldest still operational in Shetland, and containing a leper's hole. Lunna House, a former land owners mansion, was the headquarters of the Norwegian resistance and the 'Shetland Bus' operation, and there are many burnt mounds in the area. The Hunter's Monument is a lookout tower built by the owners to keep an eye on tenant fishermen.

The north-west coast of the mainland is a virtual island in itself, tenuously linked at the end of **Sullom Voe**, a long sea inlet as well as the name of Europe's largest oil terminal. The A970 is still going strong at this point, and it is a minor detour for those who wish to go and gape at the huge oil refinery. Not many huge petrochemical plants can claim to have a 'Warning, Otters Crossing' sign by the road in front of the main gates!

The small settlement of **Hillswick** contains some of Shetland's best restaurants, accommodation and a good craft shop. The island's oldest pub, The Booth, which dates from 1698 is also here down by the sea. The Hillswick Wildlife Centre is located here, where ill or injured seals and otters are cared for, including victims of the Braer oil spill in the early 1990s.

The B9078 continues westerly from here and the coastal scenery becomes more spectacular with stacks and cliffs of increasing height. To the north across Ronas Voe is steep sided **Ronas Hill**, the highest point in Shetland at (450m/1,476ft). The road reaches it's end at Stennes and the Eshaness lighthouse. A memorial here recalls an eighteenth-century man who developed a local smallpox vaccine.

Back on the A970 northwards the road passes the end of Ronas Voe and a monument to Dutch sailors who died in a battle in the voe in 1674. The cliff scenery is as stunning as ever while the interior is littered with small lochs which attract birdlife and anglers alike.

Bressay

Bressay is clearly visible from Lerwick and is the easiest off-shore island to reach from the mainland, only a 5 minute boat trip away across Bressay Sound. Its proximity to Lerwick has not affected the island's tranquillity, particularly at the top of the Ward of Bressay, from where you can see the four furthest points of Shetland, on a good day. Most of the island's population live on the west coast, looking across to Lerwick. The best beaches are generally at the north of the island, with sea cliffs at the south.

Noss

The isle of Noss, a National Nature Reserve, lies just off the east coast of Bressay. The island has impressive seabird colonies located on cliffs of about 600ft (183m). However bird watching is not the main occupation here. Noss is actually managed as a sheep farm, having fine grazing for about 400 Shetland ewes. Over 80,000 seabirds live on the island, along with a few wardens who spend the summer months at Gungstie on the south coast. This building dates from the seventeenth-century and includes a corn-drying kiln.

Whalsay

Whalsay has an economy mainly based on a successful and modern fishing fleet. It is easily reached by ferry from Laxo. The associations with sea are recorded in the restored Hanseatic Booth in **Symbister** which now houses an island museum. As everywhere in Shetland there is a richness of bird life, with waders on the lower lying parts of the island, which rise to cliffs on the east coast. It is here that the rare sea aster is found and it is the only place where the plant grows in Shetland so please do not pick. Again, as with all of Shetland, there is a richness of ancient monuments including a particularly rare double group of Bronze Age cup marks at **Brough**. There are also the remains of a black house fort on an islet on the south shore of Huxter Loch — wear your wellies.

Outer Skerries

With a small population on a little group of islands only 2sq miles (5sq km) the Outer Skerries could be considered one of Shetland's most successful communities. The success is doubly remarkable considering the fact that these are particularly spartan islands, a good way off the east coast of the mainland, with little fertile land. The mainstay of the local economy has been fishing, and the islanders now have their own salmon farm and fish processing plant. The two inhabited isles are Housay and Bruray, which are linked by a bridge. Success in the late twentieth century may be measured by the new school and community centre, and regular links to the mainland by Loganair flights from Tingwall and a small ferry.

Yell

Yell is the largest Shetland isle apart from the mainland. It lies sandwiched between the north-east coast of the mainland, the west coast of Fetlar, and the south-west coast of Unst, and is easily reached by a regular ferry from Brough on the mainland. The main road on to Unst goes first up the west coast of Yell as far as **Harkland**. On the coast north of here there are the remains of a monastic settlement made up of two rows of small dwellings and facing a similar settlement at Kame of Ibister, across Yell Sound. The road then crosses to Yell's east coast through an interior of moorland.

Midway across the island the road passes the end of **Whale Firth**, which has impressively steep sides and is best viewed from **Grimister**, reached by taking a minor road north. Plants growing wild here including juniper and honeysuckle. Whale Firth is one of the two inlets that penetrate right into the heart of Yell from the sea. The other is **Basta Voe** which the main road must go right round to reach the east coast. Passing the ferry terminal the road goes on to the north coast of the island and a fine beach at **Gloup Ness**. The memorial at Gloup Voe is to fifty-eight fishermen, drowned in a storm in 1881.

Minor roads such as the B9081 follow the south-eastern coast of the island, departing from **Mid Yell**, one of the main settlements and site of a modern leisure centre funded by the oil industry. This is also the route to take for more antiquities including an Iron Age fort near Aywick (where there is also a local knitwear centre) and a ruined broch at Goosabrough. The latter is near to one of Yell's few beaches and just north of **Burravoe** where Shetland's only independent museum, at the Old Haa, is located. This building dates from 1672 and the museum is run by volunteers.

Fetlar

Considering its size of 15sq miles (39sq km), its comparatively fertile land, and its easy accessibility from the northern Yell ferry, it's a little surprising that Fetlar's population is less than 100. Three possible clues are that the island has little peat, little natural protection from the elements and no sheltered harbours. The road and most of the homesteads are on the south side of the island, including the disused ancestral home of the Nicholson family, local land owners. A lack of people generally leads to lots of wildlife, and the island is one of the favourites of Shetland's most famous naturalist Bobby Tulloch. It was also to Fetlar that snowy owls first came in 1967. Parts of it are designated sites of special scientific interest while Vord Hill contains a 1,700 acre (680 hectare) RSPB reserve. Most of Britain's population of red-necked phalaropes nest around Loch of Funzie. There is a chambered cairn and a ring of thirty-eight stones, probably the remains of a Bronze Age cairn, by the reserve.

There are several other ancient remains dotted around the island, together with more recent remains of a former fishing station. The cliffs support vast colonies of seabirds, and there is perhaps Shetland's biggest colony of grey seals at the foot of them. Fetlar's version of the Shetland pony was once much in demand and they still roam the hillsides, although their numbers have declined.

Making good use of an old boat, North Unst

Unst

Unst is the most northerly inhabited isle in Britain. There are week-day flights from both Tingwall and Sumburgh on Loganair, or a short car ferry crossing from Yell, passengers having crossed to Yell on a previous ferry from the mainland. The main road through the centre of the island is a good one, wider than most and built by crofters in the nineteenth century in exchange for payment in food. There are some areas of fertile farmland that quickly give way to steep hills. The hills end with spectacular cliffs in places such as **Tonga Head**, with fine sandy beaches all around the islands in the valleys between (notably at Sand Wick and Outer Shaw). Some of the beaches yield semi-precious stones such as garnets. There are more than twenty-five sites of historical significance on Unst, ranging from Britain's most northerly Viking house on the edge of the beach at **Skaw**, through Iron and Bronze Age brochs at **Underhoul** and **Tivla** respectively, to Shetland's largest standing stone at **Boardastubble** and late sixteenth-century **Muness** Castle in the south-east corner.

The northern part of Unst is covered by a 2,450 acre (980 hectare) National Nature Reserve administered by the Nature Conservancy Council. About 100,000 birds breed here; more than half of these are puffins, but otherwise there is everything from the Shetland wren to

Muckle Flugga, the most northerly point in Britain

the fierce great skua or 'bonxie'. Access is unrestricted but dogs are not allowed. The spectacular coastal scenery includes cliffs of up to nearly 600ft (183m) in height and the skerries of Muckle Flugga and Out Stack, the most northerly point in Britain.

Papa Stour

Although only 2 miles (3km) long, this 'Priest's Isle' has 21 miles (34km) of coastline! This gives some idea of the number of inlets, cliffs, stacks and sea caves to be found here, regarded by some of Europe's best. At the turn of the nineteenth century over 300 people lived on Papa Stour (the remains of about twenty-five water mills can be found). This dropped to twenty-four in the early 1970s but has now recovered somewhat to stand at about thirty-five. A ferry goes out three mornings a week from Reawick on the mainland while there is a once weekly flight from Tingwall airstrip. The island has the predictable stunning richness of birdlife and ancient remains, one of the more interesting being the site of an eighteenth-century leper colony. Most settlement today is on the sheltered east side (as it always has been).

Foula

There can be little doubt amongst those who have visited Foula in good weather that it is one of the best places on earth. It is difficult to

Cottage industries have long supported the livelihood of many Shetland families

justify such a sweeping statement unless you have spent a little time on the island, but it has probably got a lot to do with the remoteness from the rest of the world. On top of that, there are the extremes of the place — the amazing sheer cliffs along the west coast rising to 1,300ft (396m), and the winds, which once gusted to a United Kingdom record of 198mph (319kph) in a winter storm (summer tourists bewitched by the place should remember the realities of winter life for the islanders). Then there are the birds. The place has had many names, the current one means 'Bird Island'. Most omni-present are the threatening skuas, the Arctic variety masters of dive bombing while the huge great skuas, Lancaster bombers of the bird world, sail in to smack you on the head should you inadvertently wander near their young. There are an estimated 125,000 pairs of birds on the island, which measures 3 miles (5km) by 4 miles (6km). That is twice as many as on Fair Isle.

The hi-tec know-how is already there, along with the animal husbandry experts. While Foula's population would not describe themselves as 'thriving' the community is certainly healthy. The islanders have seen costly redevelopment of the harbour (cam-paigned for through several generations since the late nineteenth century), and a unique wind/water hydro power plant which pumps water up to a hillside loch when there is abundant wind and lets it run down again to power the turbines when there is not. There is also a primary school and community hall. Fax machines and computers have arrived on the island and the inhabitants bring in work for themselves from the outside world, be it weather reports, weaving skills courses or tourist accommodation. The weaving skills are taught in a beautiful sunny studio. They also export their expertise in island life through Highland Forum and the Islands Council.

If flights at Tingwall can not depart all assistance is offered, a B&B found and booked, a lift back into Lerwick (no charge) arranged and collection next morning (no charge) and a promise to call should the weather change. They are long experienced at letting people down gradually and in helping visitors to control the frustration of never being sure just when a landing on the cliff-top grass air-strip will be possible, wind and sheep permitting.

You could of course get the ferry, which is cheaper than the flight and slightly less likely to be stopped by the weather. The crossing is 20 miles (32km) of open Atlantic from Walls in a little boat.

Foula time has always been different to the rest of the world. The islanders are famed for still celebrating Old Yule, rather than Christmas, a week into January. In the summer months the near 24 hour daylight, combined with an absence of the usual wake up noises of traffic and other people, means time can lose its relevance.

The island's unique identity has always had a place in folklore, its inaccessibility has probably been the prime factor in saving it from the common fate of those islands close enough to the mainland to be able to see the arrival of electricity and good roads, so that they can not ignore the fact that they are 'missing out'. Foula's communal electricity supply went on line in the late 1980s, a unique mix of water and wind power. It was perhaps the last island to become part of the current United Kingdom and when the Northern Isles were pawned to Scotland in the fifteenth century by the rulers of what is now Denmark and Norway, Foula retained the Old Norse dialect until the late eighteenth century, while the Scottish Lairds' oppression of Shetland mirrored the English Lords' abuses in Scotland. At one point the island even had its own 'Queen', said to be the most beautiful woman on the west coast of Shetland. Other island legends, include the existence of a bottomless pit, the Lum O'Ljorafjeld. This was wisely covered over and the entrance is now lost, probably good news if the rumours that trolls live at the bottom are true.

One of the landing points for boats on Fair Isle

Fair Isle

Fair Isle is described by The National Trust For Scotland, who now own it, as the most isolated inhabited island in Britain. Those bothered by such status claims might argue that Foula is marginally more difficult to reach by boat or plane, but this is certainly a very isolated isle almost exactly midway between Orkney and Shetland.

Fair Isle is probably most famous for two things — its bird life and its jumpers. More than 300 different species of bird have been recorded here. That is sixty more different types than there are varieties of wild flowers in the colourful meadows between the hills and sheer sandstone cliffs that make up the island's 3½ miles (6km) length by 1½ mile (2km) width. The high point on the island is Ward Hill 712ft (217m) from the top of which Fair Isle farmers lit bonfires in Norse times (according to the *Sagas*) and in later years a watch was kept for privateers, press gangs and enemy submarines. There is a small local museum on the island, and a windmill which generates electricity for the islanders.

The development of Fair Isle knitwear can possibly be traced to one crucial event in 1588 when the flagship of the supply squadron of the Spanish *Armada* was wrecked on the island, although many dispute the whole tale. In any event the ship in question was actually a German vessel, chartered by the Spaniards, and the 300 survivors

The breathtaking cliffs of northern Fair Isle

of the wreck who spent 6 weeks on the island probably imparted their knowledge of natural dye production. This resulted in the first Fair Isle designs which would have only two colours in any one row and bands of octagons and crosses in various designs, known as 'oxo' patterns, with smaller patterns in rows between.

Initially the designs had little more than curiosity value but by the early nineteenth century their fame had spread to the extent that much travelled Sir Walter Scott paid a shopping visit in 1814. In the early twentieth century demand for plain knitwear fell away and patterned knitwear became all the rage and in 1922 the Prince of Wales wore a Fair Isle jumper as captain of the Royal and Ancient Golf Club at St Andrews. By this time the designs were in production across Shetland and the Prince was aware he was promoting the island's products. This was the start of the colourful twenties and soon Fair Isle designs were gracing high fashion magazines, golf clubs and the new ski resorts. Today, despite the necessity to move to machine knitting to meet demand, the hand-knitting tradition is still going strong. The island is reached by a small post boat (2½ hour crossing, often with porpoises along side) or by British Airways Express aeroplane from Tingwall airstrip (20 minutes).

Further Information
— Shetland —

Places to Visit

Boddam
Croft House Museum
Open: May to September, daily, 10am-
1pm and 2-5pm.

Burra
Beth abba Studio (spinning tuition)
Setter
Hamnavoe
☎ Hamnavoe 688
Open: Wednesdays.

Dunrossness
Dunrossness Ponies Riding and Trekking
☎ 0950 60556

Fair Isle
Bird Observatory
☎ 03512 258
Open: April to October.

Foula
Frank & Penny Millsopp (Weaving Courses)
Broadfoot
Foula
Shetland ZE2 9PN
☎ 03933 3239

Hillswick
The Booth Pub and Hillswick Wildlife Centre
☎ 9123 348

Hoswick
Da Warp & Weft Tea Room and Exhibition Centre
Open: May to September, daily,
10.30am-5pm.

Lerwick
Bod of Gremista
Open: June to September.

Clickimin Broch
Open: Monday to Saturday, 9.30am-
7pm, Sunday 2-7pm.

Isleburgh Exhibition
Isleburgh Community Centre
Open: June to August, Wednesdays
and Fridays from 7.30-9.30pm and
Thursdays from 2.30-4.30pm. (Shetland
Fidlers' Society practice here from 8pm
on Wednesday nights and the junior
fiddlers on Fridays from 7.30pm).

St Olaf's Hall SWRI Exhibition
Open: June to August, Tuesdays,
10.30am-12noon and 2.30-4pm.

Up-Helly-A' Exhibition
Galley Shed
St Sunniva Street
Open: May to September, Tuesday 2-
4pm and 7-9pm, Friday, 7-9pm and
Saturday 2-4pm.

Levenwick
Mouat's Cottage Weavers
Nethertown
Levenwick
☎ 09502 222

Mousa
Mousa Ferry
☎ Sandwick 367

Sandness
Jamieson's Spinning Shetland Limited
Sandness Industrial Estate
Sandness
Shetland ZE22 9PL
☎ 0595 87 285
Open: Monday to Friday, 8am-5pm and
at other times by prior arrangement.

Scalloway
Shetland Glass
Unit 1
Blydoit Industrial Estate
Scalloway
☎ 059588 432

Shetland Woollen Company
Castle Street
☎ 059588 243
Open: Monday to Friday, 9am-5pm,
and same hours on Saturdays from
May to September.

Trondra
Croft Trail
Burland
☎ Scalloway 430
Open: Monday to Saturday, 11am-6pm.

Veensgarth
Veensgarth Agricultural Museum
☎ Gott 344
Open: June to August, no fixed
opening hours.

Walls
Edmund Wishart Silver & Gold Jewellery
Stapness
Wall
☎ 059571 310

Weisdale
Weisdale Mill
☎ 0595 2941

Whalsay
Hanseatic Booth Museum
Symbister
Open: all year. Monday to Saturday
9am-1pm and 2-5pm. Sunday 2-4pm.

Yell
Old Haa Museum
Burravoe
Yell
☎ 095782 239
Open: April to September, Tuesday to
Saturday (excluding Friday), 10am-
4pm. Also open 2-5pm Sundays (closed
Mondays also).

Bobby Tulloch Boat Trips
☎ 0957 2226

*Norman Tulloch (knitwear, grocery, fuel,
  accommodation)*
Aywick
☎ Mid Yell 2077

Useful Addresses
Scottish Sub-Aqua Club (Shetland Branch)
Lerwick ☎ 0595 3327
Sullum Voe ☎ 9918 297

Nature Conservancy Council
73 Commercial Street
Lerwick

Shetland Anglers' Association
3 Gladstone Terrace
Lerwick
☎ 0595 3729
Publishes free leaflet detailing seventy-
five recommended lochs for primarily
trout fishing, available from tourist
office.

The Shetland Knitwear Traders Association
175a Commercial Street
Lerwick
Shetland ZE1 0JL
☎ 0595 5631 or 5081

Zetland Diving Club
Sandwick
☎ 95 228

Travel
AIR
British Airways Express
Internal Shetland flights, flights to
Shetland, and to smaller
Shetland islands and Fair Isle.
Glasgow Head Office:
Information: 041 887 1111
Reservations: 041 889 3181
Tingwall (Shetland) Office: 0595 84246

CAR HIRE
Lerwick
Star Rent-a-Car
22 Commercial Road
Shetland ZE1 0LX
☎ 0595 2075

Tourist Information Office
Shetland Islands Tourism
Market Cross
Lerwick
Shetland ZE1 0LU
☎ 0595 3434
Fax: 0595 5807
Publishes leaflets on knitwear, ponies,
fishing, shopping birdlife and archae-
ology on the isles and has huge mail
order stock of relevant publications.

Fact File: Scotland

ACCOMMODATION

ACCOMMODATION EN ROUTE
It is a long drive/train journey from southern or central England to most of northern Scotland and the isles described in this book so an en route stop will normally be essential. Equally those arriving from North America may wish to recuperate from the flight and the loss of hours by spending a night or two in one of Scotland's big cities, before travelling onward. Recommended hotels are:

Edinburgh
Sheraton Grand ✳✳/✳✳✳
1 Festival Square
Edinburgh
EH3 9SR
☎ 031 229 9131
Fax: 031 229 6254
Telex: 72398

Loch Lomond
Balloch Hotel ✳/✳✳
Balloch
Dunbartonshire
G83 8LQ
☎ 0389 52579
Fax: 0389 55604

Glasgow
Glasgow Marriott ✳✳/✳✳✳
500 Argyle Street
Glasgow G3 8RR
☎ 041 226 5577
Fax: 041 221 9202
Telex: 776355

ACCOMMODATION GRADING
Beyond the usual AA and RAC star gradings, the Scottish Tourist Board grade all their members' accommodation (over 4,000 properties), from campsites to country house hotels. They rate facilities with a 'Crown' award, on a 1-5 crown grading scheme which has slightly

different meaning depending on whether it is for self-catering or catered accommodation. The Crowns refer to facilities and in addition a 'quality' guide is given on four levels, 'Approved', 'Commended', 'Highly Commended' and 'Deluxe'. So an establishent that has a little blue oval plaque on the door with five crowns and the word 'deluxe' is likely to come out top.

As a guide to facilities they are pretty accurate, and usually the commendation is accurate too. The grading scheme is a good guide to modern hotel facilities, but perhaps is not always the best way to judge the kind of atmosphere that might put your holiday in Scotland in to a different league.

ACCOMMODATION AGENCIES

Beyond the recommended establishments in the individual sections of this book, there are several agencies offering properties of all kinds throughout Scotland.

Holiday Cottages (Scotland)
   Limited
Lilliesleaf
Melrose
Roxburghshire
RD6 9JD
☎ 08357 481

The Landmark Trust
Shottesbrooke
Maidenhead
Berkshire
SL6 3SW
☎ 062 882 5925

Scottish Country Cottages
Suite 2d
Churchill Way
Bishopbriggs
Glasgow
G64 2RH
☎ 041 772 5920

Scottish Farmhouse Holidays
Drumtenant
Ladybank
Fife
KY7 7UG
☎ 0337 30451

Scotland's Heritage Hotels
2d Churchhill Way
Bishopbriggs
Glasgow
G64 2RH
☎ 041 772 6911

Scottish Tourist Board
23 Ravelston Terrace
Edinburgh
EH4 3EU
☎ 031 332 2433

Scottish Youth Hostel Association
7 Glebe Crescent
Stirling
FK8 2JA
☎ 0786 51181

BANKING & MONEY

Many visitors from England to Scotland are surprised when they do not find the 'Big Four' high street banks on every street corner in every town. In fact Lloyds, Barclays, Nat West and Midland have reciprocal agreements with Scottish banks and if it is envisaged banking services will be required for an English resident who banks with one of these four, it would be worthwhile checking before you come to Scotland which Scottish bank is likely to be of most help. In some cases the reciprocal agreement may mean you do not pay a charge for cashing a cheque, for example, which you might otherwise. Cash machines in Scottish bank walls are generally linked to United Kingdom, European and worldwide networks such as Visa and Link and it is likely an English bank card will work in one or more Scottish bank's machine, again it saves time once you arrive in Scotland if you check which one it is before you go. Three banks that operate throughout the United Kingdom are The Royal Bank of Scotland, Abbey National and the TSB. Most of the high street building societies are represented across Scotland.

The currency in the United Kingdom is the stirling which is based upon 100 units or pennies. Coins in circulation are 1p, 2p, 5p, 10p, 20p, 50p, and £1 coin (equal value to a Scottish £1 note). Notes in circulation are £1.00 (Scottish banks only) £5, £10, £20, £50. There are two other banks that mostly operate in Scotland, The Clydesdale and the Bank of Scotland (not to be confused with The Royal Bank of Scotland). These two (along with The Royal Bank of Scotland), issue their own bank notes and you are likely to receive this 'Scottish money' wherever you go. Apart from the fact that there are three different types of each denomination of note, they correspond largely with English paper money. English money is accepted everywhere in Scotland and Scottish money is legal tender anywhere in England.

Banking hours are generally the same as the rest of the United Kingdom, except in small villages where the local branch may arrive in the back of a van, or only be open a few mornings a week as a mobile force switches between three or four different community banks during the week.

CLIMATE

Scotland's weather is the subject of many a postcard, both the picture side and the writer's comments. While Great Britain as a whole has a reputation for rain, Scotland just has a reputation for bad weather. The first frosts can come in September, along with snow on the hill tops, and can continue through until June. Rain can be torrential and fog or 'Scotch mist' may hang around for days. But then you get the one clear blue day and it makes up for all the rest. You just have to hope that one day is when you are visiting, and ideally a few together.

One thing for sure is that there is no guaranteed time for good weather. You can only be sure it will be warmer in August than January. But you might get those beautiful days in mid-winter and long periods of rain or cloud through the summer months. Another thing to consider is the daylight hours, which are shorter in winter than much of England with the sun only appearing from 10am until 3pm in the far north around December and January. The positive side is that in June and July it hardly sets and on a good day you can still see quite clearly at midnight. For that reason, and the fact that the midges and the mass of fellow tourists have not really begun to arrive, May and June are often particularly good months to see Scotland. Late September and October are equally attractive for the same reasons (the midges and mass of tourists have died off); the days may be shorter but the autumn colours are stunning.

Scotland's mountains, valleys and proximity to the North Sea, the Atlantic and the Gulf Stream make weather conditions very difficult to predict. There may also be wild differences in weather conditions within a few miles of land. It is quite common to watch rain cloud bring gloom and damp up one valley as you stand in the next one bathed in sunshine.

DISABLED TOURISTS

Scottish Tourist Boards give advice on access to attractions. For more information contact:

Scottish Information Service For The Disabled
18 Claremont Crescent
Edinburgh
☎ 031 229 8632

FESTIVALS

Many Scottish towns and villages still have a traditional 'Gala Week' in the summer, which usually encompasses a variety of festivities, shows, contests and so on. A lot of coloured bunting decorating a remote village for no obvious reason normally denotes 'Gala Week'. Gala Weeks can include Highland Games.

In larger towns there are other festivals organised annually. Scotland hosts a number of popular folk festivals, notably in Inverness and Orkney and there may also be military musical tattoos. Many large agricultural shows also thrive and survive. Gaelic culture is promoted and enjoyed in other festivals, in particular the annual Mod, a sort of Gaelic Arts Olympics held in a different town each year for over a century now.

HIGHLAND GAMES
Highland Games take place across Scotland through the summer months, often even in small villages. Traditional events include caber tossing, hammer throwing and tug o'war. There may also be athletics events such as sprints, long jumping as well as equine challenges. Most games include a musical and dance element with contests in traditional skills of Highland dance and piping. Today it is likely that there will also be modern features such as fun fairs and bouncy castles.

The Highland Games is a good place in which to see local people wearing 'real' kilts and behaving like real Highlanders as most take the events and their tradition seriously, not as a tourist spectacle. The kilts are usually family owned, not the sort of shiny formal garb rented for wedding attire and business functions.

HISTORIC BUILDINGS

Scottish Explorer Tickets are sold by:
Historic Scotland
20 Brandon Street
Edinburgh EH3 5RA
☎ 031 2444 3101/3170

The National Trust For Scotland
5 Charlotte Square
Edinburgh EH2 4DU
☎ 031 226 5922

LANGUAGE

Language in Scotland varies tremendously and is strongly affected by dialect. Gaelic was spoken widely in all but south-western Scotland until after the Norman Conquest of England, after which the language was pushed northwards in to the Highlands as variations on English became the norm. But it is vastly more complex than that!

The Vikings brought old norse to northern and coastal Scotland and words and phrases and corruptions of Norse remain strong in the Northern Isles today. People on the remote island of Foula off Shetland were still speaking a version of Old Norse a few centuries ago. Then there was the fact that remote communities developed different forms of Gaelic, words were spelt differently and then the English speaking arrivals just wrote down words as they sounded and incorporated them in to the English language. Other influences (amongst many), include Old Scots, Middle English and French (the first language of Mary, Queen of Scots). Today dialects such as Glaswegian have such natural strengths that they are virtually languages in their own right and, when combined with a strong accent, may be incomprehensible even to other Scots.

Some areas of Scotland on the north-west coast and in the Hebrides still have Gaelic as the first language, and this language is now being promoted by Regional Councils and national government who are investing money in Gaelic teaching in schools, play-groups and television programmes.

Scottish	English
Alba	Scotland
Brae	Steep Hill
Bridie	Pie originating in Forfar
Burn	Stream
Caledonia	Scotland
Ecosse	Scotland
Firth	Estuary
Haggis	Barley with sheep's stomach
Kirk	Church
Laich	Low, bottom (used especially in Moray district)
Laird	Lord
Loch	Lake
Neeps	Turnip
Sassenach	English
Smokie	Smoked fish originating near Arbroath

LICENSING HOURS

Scotland generally has had much less strict licensing laws than England for many years, but there are wide variations. In fishing towns and villages pubs may open early in the morning to accommodate fishermen. In many places Friday night drinking hours extend to 1am on Saturday morning in a normal pub; but because of the stronger belief in the Sabbath pubs and even night clubs usually stop serving alcohol at 11.45pm on a Saturday night. However pubs are open on Sundays but alchohol is not for sale in shops on a Sunday.

PUBLIC HOLIDAYS

Public holidays differ sometimes in Scotland to England. Most notably Scotland is still on holiday on 2 January and does not celebrate the late August Bank Holiday. Instead the first Monday in August is a Bank Holiday in Scotland. However a lot of the time Scotland tends to close down, on English Bank Holidays too, as many businesses have their head offices in England. Other Bank Holiday's include Good Friday, Easter Monday, the first Monday in May and December 25 and 26. In addition there are 'local holidays' in many towns and districts, particularly in the north. These are usually on Mondays and can occur almost monthly and today affect about half of businesses and shops which will stop trading. There can be confusion for visitors as a holiday in one town one Monday can be followed by a further local holiday in a neighbouring town the next. In practice, apart from the big holidays at Christmas and New Year therefore, Bank Holidays in Scotland are only 50 percent effective.

Scottish school holidays differ from the English ones too. Scottish school children tend to break up in late June or early July and return mid-August, having autumn half term, often for a fortnight, in early October, before the English one. Christmas holidays often extend later in to January than in England but there is rarely a half term break in spring or summer.

RESTAURANTS

While it is true that some traditional Scottish pies such as bridies are quite stodgy, and that the Scots are connoisseurs of the humble 'tattie' (potato), the reality is that traditional fayre is generally fish or cereal based. In terms of food quality in restaurants there are many similarities with the rest of the United Kingdom at all levels. However Scotland is the home of salmon, fresh sea fish, Aberdeen angus and most of the United Kingdom's soft fruit.

Scottish cuisine and the establishments that produce it are promoted by:

Taste of Scotland
33 Melville Street
Edinburgh EH3 7JF
☎ 031 2220 1900

Vegetarian restaurants in northern Scotland are listed in: *The Vegetarian Guide to the Scottish Highlands & Islands* Janey Clarke (available from the author at 2 Burnfarm Cottages, Avoch, Ross-shire, IV9 8RG)

SPORT

Sports popular in Scotland include fishing, golf, rugby, football, shooting, running, cycling, climbing, skiing, mountain-biking and riding. A sport called shinty is played in many northern areas. It is similar to the Irish game of hurling and internationals are played between the two nations. There are vague similarities to hockey, in that the stick used is roughly the same, but there are many differences between the two games and it would be wrong to assimilate them too closely.

Useful addresses are:
The Scottish Sports Council
Caledonia House
South Gyle
Edinburgh EH12 9DQ

Mountaineering Council For Scotland
4E Battery Terrace
Oban
Argyll PA34 5DN

GOLF
A leaflet and map showing all the golf courses in the Highlands is published by:

Highlands & Islands Enterprise
Bridge House
20 Bridge Street
Inverness IV1 1QR
☎ 0463 234171

The Scottish Tourist Board (details in Accommodation section page 2) produce a map showing Scotland's 400 courses.

'Freedom of the Fairways Passport' sold for fifteen courses in the Borders by the Scottish Borders Tourist Board (See Tourist Information Offices section page 13), can be bought in advance or from outlets for 3 or 5 day durations.

TELEPHONE SERVICES

Many rural areas of Scotland have had lines and exchanges up-graded in recent years by British Telecom and it is highly likely that during the later half of the 1990s virtually all 3 and 4 figure numbers will be replaced. Where numbers listed in this book therefore become out of date, a recorded telephone message will normally advise you to redial and give you the new code and number prefix.

The international telephone code from USA and Canada is 011 44. From Australia 0011 44. When telephoning internationally, delete the area code first digit (0).

TIPPING

If you are happy with the service you have received in a tea room café, or restaurant you may consider it worth leaving 50p/£1 for the staff.

TOURIST INFORMATION OFFICES

Outside the United Kingdom Scotland is represented by the British Tourist Authority. Main offices are:

Australia
British Tourist Authority
210 Clarence Street
Sydney NSW 2000
☎ (61 2) 267 4555

Canada
British Tourist Authority
111 Avenue Road, Suite 450
Toronto
Ontario M5R 3J8
☎ (416) 961 8124, 925 6326

UK
British Tourist Authority
12 Regent Street
Piccadilly Circus
London SW1Y 4PQ
☎ (081) 846 9000

USA
British Tourist Authority
551 Fifth Avenue
Suite 701
New York
NY 10176
☎ 212 986 2200

British Tourist Authority
World Trade Center
350 South Figueroa Street
Suite 45
Los Angeles
CA 90071
☎ 213 628 3525

REGIONAL
Scottish Tourist Board
23 Ravelston Terrace
Edinburgh
EH4 3EU
☎ 031 332 2433

Scottish Tourist Board
19 Cockspur Street
London SW1Y 5BL
☎ 071 930 8661

City of Aberdeen Tourist Board
St Nicholas House
Broad Street
Aberdeen AB9 1DE
☎ 0224 632727
Fax: 0224 644822

Angus Tourist Board
Market Place
Arbroath Anguis DD11 1HR
☎ 02241 722609 or 76680
Fax: 0241 78550

Isle of Arran Tourist Board
Information Centre
Brodick Isle of Arran KA27 8AU
☎ 0770 2401 or 2140
Fax: 0770 2395

Aviemore & Spey Valley Tourist
 Board
Aviemore
Inverness-shire PH22 1PP
☎ 0479 810363
Fax: 0479 8111063

Ayrshire Tourist Board
Suite 1005
Prestwick Airport
Prestwick KA9 2PL
☎ 0292 79000
Fax: 0292 78874

Banff & Buchan Tourist Board
Collie Lodge
Banff AB45 1AU
☎ 0261 812419
Fax: 0261 815807

Scottish Borders Tourist Board
70 High Street
Selkirk TD7 4DD
☎ 0835 63435 or 63688
Fax: 0750 21886

Bute & Cowal Tourist Board
 Information Centre
7 Alexandra Parade
Dunoon
Argyll PA23 8AB
☎ 0369 3785 or 3755
Fax: 0369 6085

Caithness Tourist Board
Whitechapel Road
Wick
Caithness KW1 4EA
☎ 0955 2596
Fax: 0955 4940

Clyde Valley Tourist Board
Horsemarket
Ladyacre Road
Lanark ML11 7LQ
☎ 0555 662544 or 665709
Fax: 0555 666143

Dumfries & Galloway
Tourist Board
Campbell House
Bankend Road
Dumfries DG1 4TH
☎ 0387 50434
Fax: 0387 50462

Dunoon & Cowal Tourist Board
Information Centre
7 Alexandra Parade Dunoon
Argyll PA23 8AB
☎ 0369 37555
Fax: 0369 6085

East Lothian Tourist Board
Brunton Hall
Musselburgh EH21 6AE
☎ 0368 63353
Fax: 031 665 7495

Edinburgh Marketing
Waverley Market
3 Princes Street
Edinburgh EH2 2QP
☎ 031 557 1700
Fax: 031 557 5118
Telex 727143

Forth Valley Tourist Board
Annet House
High Street
Linlithgow
West Lothian EH49 7EJ
☎ 0506 844600
Fax: 0506 670427

Fort William & Lochaber Tourist
  Board
Cameron Centre
Cameron Square
Fort William
Inverness-shire PH33 6AJ
☎ 0397 703781
Fax: 0397 705184

Gordon District Tourist Board
St Nicholas House
Broad street
Aberdeen AB9 1DE
☎ 0224 276276
Fax: 0224 644822

Greater Glasgow Tourist Board
39 St Vincent Place
Glasgow G1 22ER
☎ 041 204 4400
Fax: 041 204 4772

Inverness, Loch Ness and Nairn
  Tourist Board
23 Church street
Inverness IV1 1EZ
☎ 0463 234353
Fax: 0463 7106609
Telex 75114

Isle of Skye And South West Ross
  Tourist Board Tourist Informa-
  tion Centre
Portree
Isle of Skye IV51 9BZ
☎ 0478 2137
Fax: 0478 2141

Kincardine & Deeside Tourist
  Board
45 Station Road
Banchory
Kincardineshire AB3 3XX
☎ 03302 2066
Fax: 03302 5126

Kirkcaldy District Council Infor-
  mation Centre
South Street
Leven
Fife KY8 4PF
☎ 0333 29464
Fax: 0333 22150

Loch Lomond, Stirling and the
  Trossachs Tourist Board
41 Dumbarton Road
Stirling, FK8 2LQ
☎ 0786 75019
Fax: 0786 71301

Mid Argyll, Kintyre and Islay
  Tourist Board
The Pier Campbeltown
Argyll PA28 6EF
☎ 0586 52056
Fax: 0586 53291

Midlothian District Council
7 Station Road
Roslin
Midlothian EH25 9PF
☎ 031 440 2210

Moray District Council
117 High Street
Elgin
Moray IV30 1EG
☎ 0343 543388
Fax: 0343 540183

Oban
Mull & District Tourist Board
Albany Street
Oban
Argyll PA34 4AR
☎ 0631 63122
Fax: 0631 64273

Orkney Tourist Board
6 Broad Street
Kirkwall KW15 1NX
☎ 0856 872856
Fax: 0856 875056

Perthshire Tourist Board
45 High Street
Perth PH1 5TJ
☎ 0738 38353
Fax: 0738 30416

Ross & Cromarty Tourist Board
Information Centre
North Kessock
Inverness IV1 1XB
☎ 046373 505
Fax: 046373 701

Shetland Islands Tourism
Market Cross
Lerwick
Shetland ZE1 0LU
☎ 0595 3434
Fax: 0595 5807

St Andrews and North East Fife
Tourist Board
2 Queenss Gardens
St Andrews
Fife KY16 9TE
☎ 0334 72021
Fax: 0334 78422

Sutherland Tourist Board
The Square Dornoch
Sutherland IV25 3SD
☎ 0862 810400
Fax: 0862 810644

Western Isles Tourist Board
4 South Beach Street
Stornoway
Isle of Lewis PA87 2XY
☎ 0851 703088
Fax: 0851 705244

West Highland & Islands of Argyll
Tourist Board Information
Centre
Albany Street
Oban
Argyll PA34 4AR
☎ 0631 63122
Fax: 0631 64273

TOURIST TRAILS

'Tourist Trails' and 'Heritage Trails' are created by local and regional tourist offices, usually supported by free literature available from tourist information centres. Such routes are definitely a good idea for those wanting a 'direction' to their holiday as they often try to include places bye-passed by much of the tourist trade and which the tourist board wants to promote. Existing Tourist Trails include: Borders Woollen Trail, Burns Trail, Solway Coast, Heritage Trail, Whisky Trail (Speyside). For further information see also: Chapter 1 The Borders; Chapter 2 The South-West (Dumfries and Galloway); Chapter 6 The Spey Valley and Chapter 11 South Of Fort William.

A hill walking advice leaflet is available from the Scottish Sports Council (address in sports section). A number of people die every year walking in the Scottish hills and mountains. Standard advice is to make sure you are properly equipped, have advised someone when you plan to return and are very clear of where you are going and that you have the ability to make the walk. Never under-estimate the Scottish hills and mountains — prepared trails are rare, and it is usually cross-country. It is also standard practice to leave details of your proposed route in your car so that if things do go wrong and your car is left over night, local people will have an idea of where you have gone. These details can then be passed to mountain rescue groups operated by local volunteers and the armed services.

Two major points to bear in mind are: that there are sheep pretty well everywhere and dogs must be kept under control and that deer stalking and other forms of hunting take place in the summer months. It is wise therefore to check that you are not crossing land where you may be in danger of being accidentally shot.

TRAVEL

For Highland and islands services, a timetable book called *Getting around the Highlands & Islands* is published annually by FHG Publications. This gives details of all services by land, air and sea.

AIR SERVICE

British Airways
☎ 0345 222111

British Airways Express
Local Offices

	Information	Reservations
Barra	☎ 08715 283	
Benbecula	☎ 0870 602290	☎ 0851 703067
Edinburgh	☎ 031 333 1000	☎ 031 333 3338
Glasgow	☎ 041 887 1111	
Inverness	☎ 0463 232471	☎ 0667 4623332
Islay	☎ 0496 2022	
Kirkwall	☎ 0856 872420	☎ 0856 872494 (Internal)
		☎ 0856 873457 (Mainland)
Lerwick	☎ 0595 84246	
Stornoway	☎ 0851 703067	
Tiree	☎ 087 92309	
Unst	☎ 0595 84246	
Wick	☎ 0955 2294	

AIRPORTS

Aberdeen	☎ 0224 722331
Barra	☎ 08715 283
Benbecula	☎ 0870 2051
Campbeltown	☎ 0586 53021
Dundee	☎ 0382 643242
Edinburgh	☎ 031 333 1000
Glasgow	☎ 041 887 1111
	☎ 0292 79822 (Prestwick)
Inverness	☎ 0463 232471
Islay	☎ 0496 22361
Kirkwall	☎ 0856 2421
Lerwick	☎ 0950 60654 (Sumburgh)
	☎ 0595 84306 (Tingwall)
Stornoway	☎ 0851 702256
Tiree	☎ 08792 456
Wick	☎ 0955 2215

AIRPORT CAR-PARKING
Airpark (Glasgow) Limited (Secure Car Park)
Burnbrae Drive
Linwood
Paisley PA3 3BJ
☎ 0505 329000
Fax: 0505 329008

BUS SERVICES
Since deregulation of bus services in the 1980s the services have tended to become irregular and expensive, particularly in areas within a 20 mile (32km) radius of large towns. While services in remote areas and on islands tend to be more stable, it would be unwise to predict here who will be in business and what services they will be operating 6 months from now.

The main national bus companies for inter-town services are:

Citylink
Buchanan Bus Station
Glasgow G2 3NP
Glasgow ☎ 041 332 9191
Edinburgh ☎ 031 557 5717
London ☎ 071 636 9373

Caledonian Express/National
  Express/Stagecoach
Walnut Grove
Perth PH2 7LP
Perth ☎ 0738 33481
Glasgow ☎ 041 332 4100
Edinburgh ☎ 031 452 8777
London ☎ 071 730 0202

Royal Mail Post Buses link rural areas, timetables should be available from post offfices.

FERRY SERVICES
Caledonian MacBrayne Ltd
The Ferry Terminal
Gourock PA19 1QP
☎ 0475 650000 (Reservations, Monday to Saturday 8.30am-5pm).
Fax: 0475 637607

General Enquiries ☎ 0475 650100
Fax: 0475 637607

Caledonian MacBrayne Ltd operate to twenty-three islands on the west coast of Scotland. Local Port Offices are:

Ardrossan	☎ 0294 463470	Fax: 0294 601063
Armadale (Skye)	☎ 04714 248	Fax: 04714 212
Brodick (Arran)	☎ 0770 302166	Fax: 0770 302618
Castlebay (Barra)	☎ 08714 306	Fax: 08714 627
Colintraive	☎ 070084 235	
Coll	☎ 08793 347	
Colonsay	☎ 09512 308	
Craignure (Mull)	☎ 06802 343	
Kennacraig	☎ 088073 253	Fax: 088073 202
Kyleakin	☎ 0599 4482	Fax: 0599 4133
Kyle of Lochalsh	☎ 0599 4218	
Largs	☎ 0475 674134	
Lochboisdale (S Uist)	☎ 0878 700288	Fax: 0878 700635
Lochmaddy (N Uist)	☎ 0876 500337	Fax: 0876 500412
Mallaig	☎ 0687 2403	Fax: 0687 2281
Oban	☎ 0631 62285	Fax: 0631 66588
Port Ellen (Islay)	☎ 0496 2209	Fax: 0496 2557
Portree (Skye)	☎ 0478 612075	Fax: 0478 613090
Rothesay (Bute)	☎ 0700 502707	Fax: 0700 502853
Stornoway (Lewis)	☎ 0851 702361	Fax: 0851 705523
Tarbert (Harris)	☎ 0859 502444	Fax 0859 502017
Tiree	☎ 08792 337	
Tobermory (Mull)	☎ 0688 2017	Fax: 0688 2660
Uig (Skye)	☎ 047042 219	Fax: 047042 387
Ullapool	☎ 0854 2358	Fax: 0854 612433
Wemyss Bay	☎ 0475 520521	
Foula Ferry	☎ 03933 3232	

Other useful addresses are:
Orkney Islands Shipping Company Limited
4 Ayre Road
Kirkwall
Orkney KW15 1QX
☎ 0856 2044

P&O Scottish Ferries
PO Box 5
Terminal Building
Jamieson's Quay
Aberdeen AB9 8DL
☎ 0224 572615

Shetland Isles Council (Ferries)
☎ 0595 2024

RAIL SERVICES
British Rail/Scotrail
58 Port Dundas Road
Glasgow G4 0HG

Aberdeen Station	☎ 0224 594222	(Sleepers ☎ 0224 582005)
Dundee Station	☎ 0382 28046	(Sleepers ☎ 0382 28776)
Edinburgh Station	☎ 031 556 2451	(Sleepers ☎ 031 5556 5633)
Fort William Station	☎ 0397 703791	(Sleepers ☎ 0397 703791)
Glasgow Station	☎ 041 204 2844	(Sleepers Central ☎ 041 221 23055 Queen St ☎ 041 332 9811)
Inverness Station	☎ 0463 238924	(Sleepers ☎ 04463 242124)
Perth Station	☎ 0738 37117	(Sleepers ☎ 0738 37228)
Stirling Station	☎ 0786 64754	(Sleepers ☎ 0786 733812)

Scottish Travelpass gives unlimited travel on Scotland's rail network, most Caledonian MacBrayne ferries and a third off P&O crossings to the Northern Isles.

WHISKY

Distilling seems to have begun in Scotland in the 1400s following earlier development in Ireland. There are two key types of whisky. 'Single malts', from one brew at one distillery, are similar to a vintage wine. The usual age at time of sale is 10 or 12 years, though younger and much older malts are sold. Ageing takes place in the cask not the proximity to the saltiness of the sea, altitude, type and quality of the water source. Distilleries are found from Scotland's south-west corner to Orkney, but the greatest concentration is in Speyside.

'Blends', generally cheaper and better known brand names (Teachers, Bells, J&B etc) are created from often numerous whiskies blended together by experts to create a unique blended identity, often to a recipe held for generations.

Whisky is made by a process of malting, which involves germinating barley seeds so that it can release fementable sugars, then drying the grain over heat; then mashing, fermenting, distilling (twice) and maturing the malt for a legal minimum of 3 years.

WILDLIFE & ENVIRONMENT

DEER

Deer farming has been encouraged in Scotland for some decades but despite the high quality of venison, it has not really caught on as hoped as yet. Numbers of deer are increasing and there are often annual 'culls'. In northern Scotland in particular deer can be a major road hazard,these are extremely mobile animals (unlike most sheep) that can shoot in to the road like a cat, but unlike a cat, can easily write-off a car and seriously damage the occupants.

FORESTS

For information on forest walks etc contact:

Public Information Division
Forestry Commission Headquarters
231 Corstorphine Road
Edinburgh EH12 7AT
☎ 031 334 0303

GARDENS

Scotland has many of the United Kingdom's best gardens. On the west coast in particular a wide variety of plants can be grown from all over the world because the Gulf Stream reaches the United Kingdom coast here. Palm trees are not an uncommon sight in some places. A guide to 400 private and public Scottish gardens is published by:

The General Organiser
Scotland's Gardens Scheme
31 Castle Terrace
Edinburgh EH1 2EL
☎ 031 229 1870

MIDGES

The famous Scottish midge can totally ruin an outdoor holiday, so campers beware. The midges often appear in May and last in to the late summer. They are generally worst and sometimes 'omnipresent' on the west coast but can appear anywhere. Although tiny creatures they swarm in thousands, probably millions, and can get absolutely everywhere, giving you small bites. The creatures are particularly prevalent in sheltered areas on a warm day after rain. Insect repellents do work to some extent. If you are bothered by these creatures it is therefore often worth packing lightweight (cotton) clothes that cover a lot of your body for use on a warm but 'midgey' summer day. It is normally campers that suffer the most, they do not usually invade buildings.

Other useful addresses are:

RSPB (Royal Society for the
    Protection of Birds)
17 Regent Terrace
Edinburgh
EH7 5BN
☎ 031 556 5624
Own or run numerous Reserves
across Scotland

Association for the Protection of
    Rural Scotland
14a Napier Road
Edinburgh EH10 5AY
☎ 031 229 11081

Scottish Countryside Activities
    Council
39 Clepington Road
Dundee DD4 7EL
☎ 0382 41095

Scottish Inland Waterways
    Association
139 Old Dalkeith Road
Edinburgh EH16 4SZ
☎ 031 664 1070

Scottish National Heritage
Caspian House
Mariner Court
Clydebank Business Park
Clydebank G81 2NR

The Scottish Wildlife Trust
25 Johnstone Terrace
Edinburgh EH1 2NH
☎ 031 226 4602

Accommodation and Eating Out

✳✳✳ Expensive
✳✳ Moderate
✳ Inexpensive

Chapter 1 •
The Borders

Accommodation

Galashiels
The Scottish College of
Textiles ✳
Netherdale
TD1 3HF
☎ 0896 3474
Fax: 0896 58965

Innerleithen
Traquair Arms Hotel ✳✳
EH44 6PD
☎ 0896 830229
Fax: 0896 830260

Jedburgh
Froylehurst Guest House ✳
Friars
TD8 6BN
☎ 0835 62477
Fax: 0835 62477

Kelso
Cross Keys Hotel ✳✳
36 The Square
TD5 7HL
☎ 0573 23303
Fax: 0573 25792

Peebles
Venlaw Castle Hotel ✳✳✳
EH45 80G
☎ 0721 20153

West Linton
Dolphinton House
Hotel ✳✳✳
EH46 7AB
☎ 0968 82286

Eating Out

Coldstream
Candy's Kitchen ✳
51 High Street
☎ 0890 882882

Dolphinton
The Old Mill Inn ✳✳
Blyth Bridge
Tweeddale
☎ 0721 52220

St Boswells
The Buccleuch Arms ✳✳✳
Roxburghshire
☎ 0385 22243
Fax: 0385 23965

Chapter 2 •
The South-West

Accommodation

Auchencairn
Balcary Bay Hotel &
Restaurant ✳✳✳
Near Castle Douglas
☎ 055664 217/311

Portpatrick
Broomknowe Guest House ✳
School Brae
☎ 077681 365

Wigtownshire
The Old Place of Monreith ✳✳
Nr Portwilliam
Dumfries & Galloway
☎ (The Landmark Trust)
0628 825925
Fax: 0628 825417

Eating Out

Castle Douglas
Bothy Tearoom ✳
Kelton Mains
☎ 0556 2120

Dumfries
Sawney Beans Bar & Grill ✳✳
Cairndale Hotel &
Leisure Club
English Street
DG1 2DF
☎ 0387 54111

Newton Stewart
Creebridge House Hotel ✳✳✳
☎ 0671 2121

Chapter 3 •
The Clyde Valley

Accommodation

Biggar
Shieldhill Hotel ✳✳✳
Quothquan
ML12 6NA
☎ 0899 20035

Walston Mansion ✳
Mrs M Kirby
Walston
By Carnwath
Biggar ML11 8NF
☎ 08981 338

Symington
Tinto Hotel ✳✳
By Biggar ML12 6PQ
☎ 08993 454

Eating Out

Bothwell
The Grape Vine ✳✳
27 Main Street
G71 8RN
☎ 0698 852014

Hamilton
Equi's Family Restaurant
and Ice Cream Parlour ✳
Peacock Cross
☎ 0698 282494

Lanark
Ristorante La Vigna ✳✳✳
40 Wellgate
ML11 9DT
☎ 0555 664320

Chapter 4 •
Dundee & Angus

Accommodation

Edzell
The Gorse ✳
Dunlappie Road
DD9 7UB
☎ 0356 63448207

Forfar
Royal Hotel ✳✳
Castle Street
Forfar DD8 3AE
Tel/Fax: 0307 62691

Kinclaven
Ballathie House Hotel ✳✳✳
Kinclaven
By Stanley PH1 4QN
☎ 02250 883268
Fax: 0250 883396

Eating Out

Dundee
*Rachel's Coffee House/Bar
and Restaurant* ✳
The Shaftsbury Hotel
1 Hyndford Street
DD2 1HQ
☎ 0382 641598

Forfar
Queen's Hotel ✳✳
The Cross
DD8 1BX
☎ 0307 62533

Wormit
*The Sandford Country
House Hotel* ✳✳✳
Newton Hill
Near Dundee
Fife DD6 8RG
☎ 0382 72594
Fax: 0334 78703

Chapter 5 •
Royal Deeside

Accommodation

Aboyne
Hazklehurst Lodge ✳
Ballater Road
SB34 5HY
☎ 03398 86921

Ballater
Balgonie Country House ✳✳✳
Aberdeenshire
AB35 5RQ
☎ 03397 55482
Fax: 03397 55482

Kincardine O'Neil
Gordon Arms Hotel ✳✳
Aberdeenshire
AB34 5AA
☎ 03398 84236

Eating Out

Ballater
The Coach House Hotel ✳✳
Netherley Place
Aberdeenshire
AB35 5QE
☎ 0561 377677

Blairs
Ardoe House Hotel ✳✳✳
Deeside Road
Aberdeen
☎ 0224 867355
Fax: 0224 867355

Stonehaven
George A Robertson ✳
68-72 Allardice Street
Open: Monday to
Saturday to 4.45pm

Chapter 6 •
The Spey Valley

Accommodation

Aviemore
Mercury Hotel ✳✳
Aviemore Mountain
Resort
PH22 1PF
☎ 0479 810781
Fax: 0479 811167

Carrbridge
An-Airidh Lodge ✳
Station Road
Inverness-shire
☎ 0479 841211

Elgin
Mansion House Hotel ✳✳✳
The Haugh
Grampian IV30 1AW
☎ 0343 548811

Eating Out

Aberlour
Craigellachie Hotel ✳✳
Craigellachie
Banffshire

Fochabers
Spey Restaurant ✳
Baxters of Speyside
Fochabers IV32 7LD
☎ 0343 820393

Rothes
Rothes Glen House ✳✳✳
Moray IV33 7AH
☎ 0340 831254
Fax: 0340 831566

Chapter 7 •
The Black Isle &
Beauly Firth

Accommodation

Contin
Coul House Hotel ✳✳✳
By Strathpeffer
Ross-shire IV14 9EY
☎ 0997 421487

Kiltarlity
Catherine Hayward ✳
Tigh Bea
Kiltarlity
Inverness-shire IV4 7JH
☎ 0463 741425

Kirkhill
Inchmore Hotel ✳✳
Kirkhill
Inverness IV5 7PX

Eating Out

Kiltarlity
Brockies Lodge Hotel ❋
☎ 0463 741257

Beauly
Priory Hotel ❋❋
The Square
☎ 0463 782309

Bunchrew
Bunchrew House Hotel &
Restaurant ❋❋❋
Inverness
☎ 0463 234917

Chapter 8 •
The North-East
Highland Coast

Accommodation

Dornoch
The Royal Golf Hotel ❋❋
Grange Road
Sutherland
IV25 3LG
☎ 0862 810283

Lairg
Aultnagar Lodge ❋❋❋
Near Lairg
IV27 4EX
☎ 054982 245 or 221
Fax: 054982 301

Tain
Carringtons ❋
Morangie Road
Ross-shire
IV19 1PY
☎ 0862 892635

Eating Out

Ardgay
The Station House ❋
☎ 08632 352

Dornoch
Dornoch Castle Hotel ❋❋❋
Castle Street
☎ 0862 810216
Fax: 0862 810981

Spinningdale
Old Mill Inn ❋❋
☎ 086288 322

Chapter 9 •
The North Coast

Accommodation

Bettyhill
Farr Bay Inn ❋❋
Sutherland KW14 7SP
☎ 06412 352

Caithness
Dunnet Head House Bed &
Breakfast ❋
Dunnet Head
Caithness KW14 8XS
☎ 084785 617 or 382

John O'Groats
John O'Groats House
Hotel ❋❋❋
Caithness KW1 4YR
☎ 095581 203

Mey
Castle Arms Hotel ❋❋
Caithness KW14 8XH

Eating Out

Castletown
Greenland House ❋❋
Main Street
Caithness KW14 8TU
☎ 0847 82215

Dunnet
Dunnet Head Tea Room ❋
Dunnet KW14 8YE
☎ 084785 774

Wick
Ackergill Tower ❋❋❋
Ackergill
Wick KW1 4RG
☎ 0955 3556

Chapter 10 •
The North-West
Highlands

Accommodation

Kinlochbervie
Old School ❋
Inshegra
Sutherland
☎ 097182 383

Lochinver
Inver Lodge Hotel ❋❋
Sutherland
IV27 4LU
☎ 05714 496
Fax: 05714 395

Torridon
Loch Torridon Hotel ❋❋❋
Achnasheen
Ross-shire
IV22 2EY
☎ 0445 791242
Fax: 0445 791296

Eating Out

Ullapool
Ceilidh Place ❋
14 West Argyle Street
☎ 0854 612103
Open: all year 8am-10pm

Kinlochbervie
Kinlochbervie Hotel ❋❋
IV27 4RP
☎ 0971 521275

Near Ullapool
Altnaharrie Hotel ❋❋❋
☎ 085483 230
Open: March to October.
Widely regarded as one
of United Kingdom's best
restaurants, if not
world's! Has won many
independent awards to
underline the
personal tributes. Dinner
is at 7.30pm prompt only,
access normally by boat
from Ullapool, guests
often stay the night.

Chapter 11 •
South of Fort William

Accommodation

Appin
*Appin House Apartments &
   Lodge* ✳
Argyll
PA38 4BN
☎ 063193 207
Fax: 063173 567

Ballachulish
Ballachulish Hotel ✳✳✳
Argyll
PA39 4JY
☎ 08552 606
Fax: 08552 629

Duror
The Stewart Hotel ✳✳
PA38 4PW
☎ 063174 268 or 2220
Fax: 063174 328
Open: April to October.

Eating Out

Kilmelford
Cuilfail Hotel ✳✳✳
By Oban
Argyll
☎ 08522 274

Lerags
Barn Bar ✳
Cologi
By Oban
Argyll
☎ 0631 64501

Tobermory
Back Brae Restaurant ✳✳
Isle of Mull
☎ 068022 471

Chapter 12 •
The Western Isles

Accommodation

Bornish
Mrs Shona MacIntyre ✳
(Benbecula/Uists)
6 North Locheynort

South Uist
PA81 5SN
☎ 0878 710320

Stornoway
Royal Hotel ✳
(Harris/Lewis)
Cromwell Street
Isle of Lewis
PA87 2DG
☎ 0851 702109

Castlebay
Isle of Barra Hotel ✳✳
(Barra)
Tangusdale Beach
Isle of Barra
PA80 5XW
☎ 0871 810383
Fax: 0871 810385

Daliburgh
Borrodale Hotel ✳✳
(Benbecula/Uists)
Isle of South Uist
☎ 0878 700444
Fax: 0878 700611

Stornoway
Seaforth Hotel ✳✳
(Harris/Lewis)
James Street
Isle of Lewis
PA87 2QN
☎ 0851 702740
Fax: 0851 702109

Castlebay
Castlebay Hotel ✳✳✳
(Barra)
Isle of Barra
☎ 0871 810223
Fax: 0871 810385

Liniclate
Dark Island Hotel ✳✳✳
(Benbecula/Uists)
Isle of Benbecula
☎ 0870 603030
Fax: 0870 602347

Stornoway
Cabarfeidh Hotel ✳✳✳
(Harris/Lewis)
Manor Park
Isle of Lewis
☎ 0851 702604
Fax: 0851 705572

Eating Out

Lewis
Fear an Eich Tearoom ✳
Coll Pottery
☎ 0851 82219

Stornoway
*Cafe Royale/Princes
   Restaurant* ✳✳
Cromwell Street
Lewis
☎ 0851 702109

North Uist
Westford Inn ✳✳
Claddach Kirkibost
☎ 0876 560653

Ardvourlie
Ardvourlie Castle ✳✳✳
Harris
☎ 0859 502307

Chapter 13 •
Orkney Isles

Accommodation

Longhope Hoy
Glebelands ✳
☎ Hoy 245

Papa Westray
Guest House and Hostel ✳
Baltane House
Orkney KW17 KBU
☎ 08574 251 or 267

Shapinsay
Girnigoe ✳
☎ 0856 71 256

Copinsay
*Lighthouse Keepers
   Accommodation* ✳✳
4 Pool Cottages
Burston
Stafford ST18 0DR
☎ 08897 551 or 0831 098425

North Ronaldsay
Garso Guest House ✳✳
Also self-catering cottage
☎ 08573 244

St Mary's
Commodore Motel ✳✳
Holm KW17 2RU
☎ 0856 78 319
Fax: 0856 78 219

Shapinsay
Balfour Castle ✳✳✳
☎ 0856 71 282

Eating Out

Kirkwall
The Atholl ✳
Albert Street
☎ Kirkwall 872385

St Ola Hotel ✳✳
Harbour Street
☎ 0856 875090
Stronsay
Stronsay Hotel ✳✳
☎ Stronsay 213

South Ronaldsay
The Creel ✳✳✳
Front Road
St Margaret's Hope
☎ 0856 83 311

Chapter 14 •
Shetland

Accommodation

Foula
Ristie Chalet & Hostel ✳
Freyers
Shetland ZE2 9PN
☎ 03933 3233

Lerwick
Glen Orchy House ✳✳
20 Knab Road
Shetland ZE1 0AX
☎ 0595 2031

Shetland Hotel ✳✳✳
Holmsgart Road
Lerwick ZE1 0PW
☎ 0595 5515
Fax: 0595 5828

Eating Out

Hillswick
St Magnus Bay Hotel ✳✳
☎ 080623 371 or 372
Fax: 080623 373

Lerwick
Hasvly Centre Cafe ✳
9 Charlotte Street
Open: Tuesday to
Saturday, 10.30am-5pm
and Thursday evening
7.30-10.30pm including
Christian programme
with music and singing.

Walls
Burrastow House Hotel &
Restaurant ✳✳✳
☎ 059571 307
Open: from late March,
lunch 12noon-2.30pm,
dinner 7.30-9pm by prior
booking only.

Index

Page numbers in **bold** type indicate maps

311

A Note To The Reader

The accommodation and eating out lists in this book are based upon the authors' own experiences and therefore may contain an element of subjective opinion. The contents of this book are believed correct at the time of publication but details given may change. We welcome any information to ensure accuracy in this guide book and to help keep it up-to-date.

Please write to The Editor, Moorland Publishing Co Ltd, Moor Farm Road, Airfield Estate, Ashbourne, Derbyshire, DE6 1HD, England.

American and Canadian readers please write to The Editor, The Globe Pequot Press, 6 Business Park Road, PO Box 833, Old Saybrook, Connecticut 06475-0833, USA.

MPC

The Globe Pequot press

Discover a New World
with
Off The Beaten Track Travel Guides

Austria
Explore the quiet valleys of Bregenzerwald in the west to Carinthia and Burgenland in the east. From picturesque villages in the Tannheimertal to the castles north of Klagenfurt, including Burg Hochosterwitz. This dramatic castle with its many gates stands on a 450ft high limestone cliff and was built to withstand the Turkish army by the man who brought the original Spanish horses to Austria.

Britain
Yes, there are places off the beaten track in even the more populated areas of Britain. Even in the heavily visited national parks there are beautiful places you could easily miss — areas well known to locals but not visitors. This book guides you to such regions to make your visit memorable.

Greece
Brimming with suggested excursions that range from climbing Mitikas, the highest peak of Mount Olympus, the abode of Zeus, to Monemvassia, a fortified medieval town with extensive ruins of a former castle. This book enables you to mix a restful holiday in the sun with the fascinating culture and countryside or rural Greece.

Italy
Beyond the artistic wealth of Rome or Florence and the hill towns of Tuscany lie many fascinating areas of this ancient country just waiting to be discovered. From medieval towns such as Ceriana in the Armea valley to quiet and spectacular areas of the Italian Lakes and the Dolomites further to the east. At the southern end of the country, the book explores Calabria, the 'toe' of Italy as well as Sicily, opening up a whole 'new' area.

Germany

Visit the little market town of Windorf on the north bank of the Danube (with its nature reserve) or the picturesque upper Danube Valley, which even most German's never visit! Or go further north to the Taubertal. Downstream of famous Rothenburg with its medieval castle walls are red sandstone-built villages to explore with such gems as the carved altar in Creglingen church, the finest work by Tilman Riemenschneider — the Master Carver of the Middle Ages. This book includes five areas in the former East Germany.

Portugal

Most visitors to Portugal head to the Algarve and its famous beaches, but even the eastern Algarve is relatively quiet compared to the more popular western area. However, the book also covers the attractive areas of northern Portugal where only the more discerning independent travellers may be found enjoying the delights of this lovely country.

Scandinavia

Covers Norway, Denmark, Sweden and Finland. There is so much to see in these countries that it is all too easy to concentrate on the main tourist areas. That would mean missing so many memorable places that are well worth visiting. For instance, there are still about sixty Viking churches that survive in Norway. Alternatively many private castles and even palaces in Denmark open their gardens to visitors. Here is your guide to ensure that you enjoy the Scandinavian experience to the full.

Spain

From the unique landscape of the Ebrodelta in Catalonia to the majestic Picos d'Europa in the north, the reader is presented with numerous things to see and exciting things to do. With the mix of cultures and climates, there are many possibilities for an endearing holiday for the independent traveller.

Switzerland

Switzerland offers much more than the high mountains and deep valleys with which it is traditionally associated. This book covers lesser known areas of the high mountains — with suggested walks in some cases. It also covers Ticino, the Swiss Lakeland area near to the Italian Lakes and tours over the border into the latter. In the north, the book covers the lesser known areas between Zurich and the Rhine Falls, plus the Lake Constance area, with its lovely little towns like Rorschach, on the edge of the lake.

Northern France

From the sandy inlets of Brittany and the well-watered pastures of Normandy, the hugh flower festival of La Tranche, the eagle reserve at Kintzheim in Alsace et Lorraine, to France's loveliest wine route in Alsace. See the France that most visitor's miss, this book is your key to going Off The Beaten Track in Northern France.

Southern France

From the windy beaches and huge sand dunes of Aquitaine, the grandeur of the Pyrénées, the medieval villages of early English Kings, the spectacular chasm of the Verdon Gorges to the quiet areas of the Camargue. This book will take you to fourteen different areas of Southern France and show you the lesser known sights that reflect this country's true identity.

Scotland

Heather-clad mountains, baronial castles and magnificent coastal scenery, all combined with a rich historical heritage, combine to make this an ideal 'Off The Beaten Track' destination.

Ireland

Ireland not only has a dramatic coastline, quiet fishing harbours and unspoilt rural villages, but also the natural friendliness of its easy-going people. *Off the Beaten Track Ireland* will lead you to a memorable holiday in a country where the pace of life is more relaxing and definitely not hectic.

TRAVEL GUIDE LIST

Airline/Ferry details   ....
....
....
....
....

Telephone No.   ....

Tickets arrived   ☐

Travel insurance ordered   ☐

Car hire details   ....
....
....

Visas arrived   ☐

Passport   ☐

Currency   ☐

Travellers cheques   ☐

Eurocheques   ☐

Accommodation address   ....
....
....
....

Telephone No.   ....

Booking confirmed   ☐

Maps required   ....
....
....